PYTHAGORAS

PYTHAGORAS

His Life, Teaching, and Influence

CHRISTOPH RIEDWEG

Translated by Steven Rendall
in collaboration with Christoph Riedweg and Andreas Schatzmann

Cornell University Press
Ithaca and London

This is a licensed English translation of Christoph Riedweg,
Pythagoras: Leben, Lehre, Nachwirkung. Eine Einführung, published by
C. H. Beck in 2002.

© Verlag C. H. Beck oHG, München 2002

Cornell University Press gratefully acknowledges receipt of a subvention from the Zürcher Universitätsverein, which aided in the publication of this book.

First published 2005 by Cornell University Press
First printing, Cornell Paperbacks, 2008

Printed in the United States of America

Library of Congress Cataloging-in-Publication Data
Riedweg, Christoph.
   Pythagoras : his life, teaching, and influence / Christoph Riedweg ;
translated by Steven Rendall in collaboration with Christoph Riedweg
and Andreas Schatzmann.
      p. cm.
   Includes bibliographical references and index.
   ISBN 13: 978-0-8014-7452-1 (pbk. : alk. paper)
   1. Pythagoras. I. Title.
   B243.R54 2005
   182′.2–dc22

                                        2004023906

Cloth printing   10 9 8 7 6 5 4 3 2
Paperback printing   10 9 8 7 6 5 4 3 2 1

For Walter Burkert

CONTENTS

PREFACE

The importance of an individual thinker owes something to
chance. For it depends upon the fate of his ideas in the minds
of his successors. In this respect Pythagoras was fortunate. His
philosophical speculations reach us through the mind of Plato.

ALFRED NORTH WHITEHEAD, *Science and the Modern World*
(1926, 36)

A peculiar kind of splendor surrounds the name of Pythagoras of Samos—a
splendor probably due in no small measure to the fact that in his person enlightened modern science seems happily fused with ancient wisdom teachings and insights into the mysterious interconnections of the world. The first
is represented by the Pythagorean Theorem that we all learn in school, $a^2 +
b^2 = c^2$, as well as by Pythagoras's recognition of the mathematical character
of the basic musical concords. The transfer of these musical proportions to
the cosmos (the "harmony of the spheres") and the use of music for therapeutic ends, the doctrine of the unity of all animate beings, vegetarianism,
and the transmigration of souls are key terms for the second aspect. Pythagoras has a guaranteed place not only in musicology, mathematics, and the history of science but also in the history of philosophy and religion; in addition,
he has proved attractive to esoteric movements down to the present day.

Who was this wise man from Samos? This question is not easy to answer
because of the problematic state of transmission of the relevant documents. Very little of our information about him dates from his own lifetime—roughly, from 570 to 480 B.C.E. The farther on in time we move, the
richer the documentation becomes for us (in antiquity, the situation was
still somewhat different). The only coherent descriptions of Pythagoras'
life and teaching that have come down to us from antiquity we owe to
authors of the third and fourth centuries C.E.: the biographer of philoso-

phers Diogenes Laertius and the Neoplatonists Porphyry of Tyre and
Iamblichus of Chalcis. Their information is very uneven in quality. Among
the most valuable clues are those they derived from sources (now lost) dating from the fourth and third centuries b.c.e.—including Aristotle and his
pupils as well as the historian Timaeus of Tauromenium. However, since
by the fourth century b.c.e. various groups were already claiming the idealized philosopher Pythagoras as one of their own, considerable caution is
needed in dealing with these witnesses (who contradict one another on
many points). Particularly momentous was the introduction of a strongly
Platonic interpretation of Pythagoras in the Old Academy. Over time, this
led to the ancient Pythagorean tradition being overwritten by Platonic doctrine, to the point it became unrecognizable. This development turned out
not to harm Pythagoras as a philosophical model; on the contrary, his astonishing influence down the centuries would hardly be conceivable without this overlay of Platonic philosophy, which has decisively shaped the
image of Pythagoras up to present times.

Moreover, part of the problem related to Pythagoras tradition originates
from the sociology of the school itself. Pythagoras, who probably left his
home island Samos for good around 530 b.c.e. and emigrated to Croton in
southern Italy, seems to have considered a secret politico-religious community as the appropriate organizational form for imparting his *sophía* (wisdom). In this respect, all the ancient sources for once agree in saying that,
like the mystery cults, he did not immediately communicate his doctrines
to anyone interested in them, but required his adepts—including women
(not a matter of course in the ancient world)—to undergo an initiation-
like preparation and adopt a way of life shaped by ritual regulations. This
aristocratic society, which from a modern point of view had the characteristics of a sect, put particular emphasis on the duty to observe secrecy.
Therefore it is likely that at least down to the anti-Pythagorean rebellions
around the middle of the fifth century b.c.e. (or somewhat later), which
led to the breakup of the Pythagorean communities and almost complete
expulsion of their adherents from southern Italy, only a little information
about the master's teaching leaked out and became known to the outside
world. This vacuum (which due to the rule of secrecy was only ever par-
tially filled) led all the more easily to speculation and personal additions
to the tradition in the form of pseudo-epigraphic writings. These were produced with increasing frequency at least from the Hellenistic age onward
and are interspersed, for the most part, with elements of Platonic and Aristotelian philosophy.

If we now wish to recover as far as possible the original "text" of this repeatedly overwritten and retouched philosophical palimpsest, it is advis-
able to begin with the traditional stories about Pythagoras, and first of all

to inventory the literary tradition, oscillating between fiction and truth in all its contradictory diversity (chapter 1). Next, we approach the historical Pythagoras from the outside, as it were, by briefly sketching the cultural and intellectual context in which he lived and worked. Then we must analyze with special care the oldest testimony, some of which goes back to Pythagoras' own lifetime. It is in this way, if at all, that we are likely to acquire a reasonably authentic idea of this fascinating figure, who clearly combined the characteristics of a guru with those of a scholar, and whose charisma gained him considerable political influence in southern Italy. A separate section is reserved for the question whether the word *philosophy*, without which Western intellectual history is hard to imagine, may have been invented by Pythagoras (the foregoing points are addressed in chapter 2). Other parts of this book are devoted to the nature and organization of the community founded by Pythagoras and the history of his school, to which in the fifth and fourth centuries B.C.E. belonged such significant thinkers as Philolaus of Croton and Plato's friend Archytas of Tarentum (see chapter 3). The final chapter pursues the marks left by the sage of Samos on European thought, beginning with the later pre-Socratics and passing through Plato and the Old Academy, the (highly Platonic) neo-Pythagorean school, and the Latin Middle Ages down to the rise of natural science in the early modern period (Copernicus and Kepler), and the so-called Harmonic Pythagoreanism of the twentieth century (chapter 4).

This introduction to Pythagoras was written at the suggestion of the editor of the Beck series "Thinkers," Otfried Höffe of Tübingen. It could not have been realized without the active support I received in Mainz from Andrea Wiegand-Michelsen and Sabine Föllinger (now at Bamberg), among others, and later in Zurich in particular from Franziska Egli and Andreas Schatzmann. I express here my heartfelt gratitude to all of them. I am also very grateful to Steven Rendall for translating the German version, which has been slightly revised and updated, into English. The translation was funded in part by the Zürcher Universitätsverein. The English version is again dedicated to Walter Burkert, καθ' ὃν (. . .) μεμαθήκασι πάντες not only *in Pythagoricis*.

CHRISTOPH RIEDWEG

Zurich, Switzerland

PYTHAGORAS

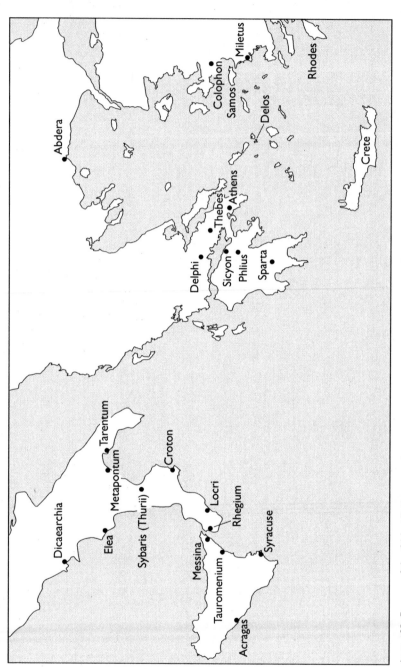

Area of Influence of the Oldest Pythagoreanism

1. FICTION AND TRUTH
Ancient Stories about Pythagoras

Ancient reports about Pythagoras suggest a multifaceted man. Many aspects of this picture are familiar: Pythagoras the mathematician, the discoverer of certain basic principles of acoustics, the natural philosopher, and perhaps also Pythagoras the adherent to vegetarianism and to the doctrine of the transmigration of souls. Other aspects strike us as alien and may make us wonder whether Pythagoras can be considered a "thinker" in the narrow sense at all. With the word *thinker* we usually associate the idea of a philosophically reflective person who strives, by using reason in a methodical way, to achieve clarity regarding things and the foundations of our being. Many a part of the ancient tradition concerning Pythagoras is scarcely compatible with this idea and makes him seem closer to holy men and mystics of the Eastern and Western traditions. He is represented as a politico-religious adviser and leader, a guru with supernatural powers, a seer, a miracle worker, a healer, and a psychiatrist—or as a fraud and a charlatan. Depending on the witness's standpoint, diametrically opposed rhetorical strategies can be seen at work in the texts: Whereas adepts or at least admirers of his teaching tend toward a hagiographic idealization (which may have been promoted already by Pythagoras himself), skeptics and critics react with irony, sarcasm, and defamation, and try to belittle Pythagoras as a person as much as they can. We will see that this kind of reaction is not uncommon in the case of charismatics (in the sociological sense defined by Max Weber). But before we attempt to cautiously approach the historical personality, let us listen to the ancient sources in all their variety. For the moment, we will largely refrain from a critical evaluation. It is important first of all to mark out the field and assemble the diverse notions that were associated in antiquity with Pythagoras' life and teaching.

PYTHAGORAS' APPEARANCE

The Strangely Sublime Man

To begin with outward appearance, Pythagoras is described as making an extremely striking impression. According to Dicaearchus (born c. 375 B.C.E.?), one of the pupils of Aristotle originating from modern-day Messina, he was very tall and of noble stature, and his voice, character, and every other aspect were marked by an exceptional degree of charm and embellishment.[1] His natural aura was still further increased by an unusual way of presenting himself: He dressed in a white robe, wore trousers (which was untypical for Greeks, and makes us think rather of the Thracian Orpheus, with whom Pythagoras is sometimes compared),[2] and crowned his head with a golden wreath,[3] probably as a sign of his elevated status. Under his clothes, too, there was hiding something unique: the famous, hard-to-interpret golden thigh with which Pythagoras was supposed to have been fitted. Only once, it is said, on the occasion of the Olympic festival, was the latter briefly glimpsed as he was rising. Pythagoras also identified himself by means of this golden thigh as the "Hyperborean Apollo" when he met Abaris, the priest of the Hyperboreans, a mythical-paradisiacal people who lived at the northern fringes of the world.[4]

Parapsychology: The Miracle Worker

Pythagoras is surrounded by many fabulous tales of this kind. The stories about his ability to enter into contact with nature are reminiscent of St. Francis of Assisi:[5]

(23) If one is to believe the ancient and noteworthy writers [an allusion amongst others to Aristotle?], his admonitions did reach even irrational animals. The Daunian [i.e., North Apulian] bear, who had committed extensive depredations in the neighborhood, he seized; and after having patted her for a while, and given her barley and fruits, he made her swear never again to touch a living creature, and then released her. She immediately took herself into the woods and the hills, and from that time on never attacked any irrational animal.

(24) At Tarentum, in a mixed pasture, seeing an ox cropping beans, he went to the herdsman, and advised him to tell the ox to abstain from beans. The countryman mocked him, proclaiming his ignorance of the ox-language. So Pythagoras himself went and whispered in the ox's ear. Not only did the bovine at once desist from his diet of beans, but would never touch any thenceforward, though he sur-

vived many years near Hera's temple at Tarentum, until very old, being called the sacred ox, and feeding on what the visitors to the temple offered him.

(25) While he happened to converse with his disciples at the Olympic Games about bird omens, secret signs, and omens from the sky, saying that they were special messages and voices from the gods to those human beings truly dear to them, he is said to have drawn down an eagle which flew overhead, and after stroking it, he released it again. (Porph. VPyth. 23–5 ≈ Iambl. VPyth. 60–62; transl. after K. S. Guthrie; Dillon and Hershbell)

It is obvious that in this version, which goes back to the neo-Pythagorean Nicomachus of Gerasa (second century C.E.),[6] each of the miracle stories is intended to illustrate a Pythagorean rule of conduct: (1) vegetarianism (not eating any creature endowed with a soul); (2) the taboo on beans; (3) the practice of divination. The text goes on to offer an example of Pythagoras' prophetic abilities that again brings to the fore his almost Buddhist concern with respect to the animate creature:

Meeting with some fishermen who were drawing in their nets heavily laden with fishes from the deep, he predicted the exact number of fish they had caught. The fishermen said that if his estimate was accurate they would do whatever he commanded. He then bade them to return the fish alive into the sea after having counted them accurately; and, what is more wonderful, not one of them died, although they had been out of the water a considerable time. (Porph. VPyth. 25 ≈ Iambl. VPyth. 36; transl. after K. S. Guthrie)

This passage may remind readers familiar with the New Testament that in Luke the beginning of Jesus' teaching is associated with an exceptional catch of fish: Jesus tells Simon to cast his nets, though he has caught nothing during the whole of the preceding night, and, behold, Simon catches so many that two boats almost sink under the weight of the fish.[7] This similarity, which ultimately remains rather superficial—crucial elements of the Pythagorean story such as the prediction of the number or saving the lives of the fish are missing[8]—must have struck the Neoplatonic philosopher Iamblichus (c. 240–c. 325 C.E.) when in his treatise *On the Pythagorean Life*, which sometimes assumes characteristics of a pagan alternative to the Gospels, he situates the fishermen episode at the beginning of Pythagoras' career.[9]

To judge by various other anecdotes that in their essence seem to go back as far as to the fourth century B.C.E. (to Aristotle and a certain Andron of Ephesus), parapsychological phenomena appear to have accompanied Pythagoras throughout his life. Once, when he felt thirsty in Metapontum and drank water drawn from a well, he predicted that three days hence an earthquake would occur.[10] He also demonstrated his prophetic ability, for example, by predicting the sinking of a boat, the conquest of the city of Sybaris, and the fraternal feuding among Pythagoreans.[11] And once, when, with several comrades, he was crossing the river Casuentus (Gr. Kasas) near Metapontum, the river is supposed to have said to him, loudly enough for all to hear, "Greetings, Pythagoras!"[12] (It should be noted that in antiquity, rivers were divinities, and therefore the episode contains primarily a religious statement: Even the divine communicates with this exceptional human being.) According to the reports, Pythagoras shares with yogis, shamans, and Christian mystics the gift of being in two places at the same time (bilocation):

> Almost unanimous is the report that on one and the same day he was present at both Metapontum in Italy and at Tauromenium in Sicily, in each place conversing with his friends, though the places are separated by many miles, both at sea and land, demanding a journey of great many days. (Porph. VPyth 27 ≈ Iambl. VPyth. 134; transl. after K. S. Guthrie)

Another similarity between Eastern teachers of wisdom and Pythagoras' was the supernatural "perfect ability" (called *siddhi-* in Sanskrit) to diagnose earlier existences. He is reported to have reminded Myllias of Croton of his rebirth as the Phrygian king Midas.[13] "But himself he proved, by means of indubitable signs, to be Euphorbus, the son of Panthos."[14] In the sixteenth and seventeenth books of Homer's *Iliad,* this "Dardanian" who fought the Greeks at Troy plays a rather significant role in connection with Patroclus' death: Like Paris later on in relation to Achilles' death, Euphorbus acts on the human level as the helper of the god Apollo, who brings about Patroclus' death.[15] The collaboration with Apollo makes it clear why Pythagoras—whom the people of Croton called the "Hyperborean Apollo"—singled out precisely this Trojan warrior as his earlier reincarnation. Etymology may also have played a role in his choice: The name *Euphorbus* means "he who has a good pasture or good food," and this seems highly appropriate for the founder of a way of life characterized by numerous dietary rules.[16] By the way, Homer praises Euphorbus not only for his military and athletic superiority, but also for his beauty, and especially his extremely charming locks of hair, "interlaced" with gold and silver—they are described as "like the Graces."[17] Did Pythagoras, who wore a golden wreath in his hair, feel attracted to Euphorbus in this respect as well? In any event, among the "indubitable signs" by means of which he identified himself with Euphorbus the episode stands out in which, as he was in the shrine of the Argive Hera and saw the booty the victorious Greeks had brought home from Troy and dedicated to the goddess, he recognized Euphorbus' bronze shield: This one, he said, he was carrying when he was killed by Menelaus.[18]

Various other reincarnations are mentioned in the sources—in India as well "one biography is not enough; the lives of saints and saviors are provided with preludes—infinitely expansible—of earlier saintly existences," until the hero, after rising step by step, "at last arrives at that supreme state of embodied spirituality which distinguished his actual, historical biography."[19] The lists of Pythagoras' rebirths differ somewhat depending on the sources. It can easily be seen why Aethalides, the son of Hermes, was included in the series: According to legend, he had received from his divine father the gift not only of remembering everything in his life but even retaining his memory after death. This gift was transmitted to all his subsequent reincarnations,[20] and it is especially characteristic of Pythagoras, whose unique mental and mnemonic abilities are emphasized early on. We shall return later to this subject and to the doctrine of reincarnation (see 36f., 48f. and 52–57, 62f. below).

"Countless other, still more marvelous and divine things were said about this man in the same way and agreeing with each other," the Platonist Porphyry of Tyre (234–c. 305/310 C.E.) noted in concluding his account of the miracle stories. Porphyry also summarily refers to Pythagoras' power of disposing over the forces of nature, which he used to the benefit of his companions, as when he put an end to an epidemic of plague, stopped wind and hail storms, and when necessary calmed the waves,[21] or overcame a poisonous snake—allegedly by biting it back.[22]

BIOGRAPHICAL INFORMATION

Birth

According to the testimony of ancient sources then, this Pythagoras of Samos was a wholly exceptional person. Therefore it is hardly surprising that his early biography also includes astonishing things. A man so far above the average cannot have an ordinary career—so much is required, independent of any question of fact, merely by the literary rules of hagiographic narratives. Over time, even a divine origin was attributed to him. The well-known importance of Apollo for Pythagoras—his name, too, was associated with the Pythian oracle: "He was called Pythagoras because he spoke the truth no less than the Pythian oracle"[23]—suggests the Delphic divinity. His mother, whom Apollonius[24] is able to call by name, is also embedded in this context: Her name is supposed to have been Pythaïs. A writer from Samos—Apollonius goes on in Porphyry VPyth. 2—expressed this divine origin in the following distich:

> and Pythagoras, dear to Zeus, whom Pythaïs has born to Apollo,
> who was the most beautiful amongst the Samian women
>
>   (FGrHist 1064 F1; transl. Radicke)

Here again, relationships with the Christian tradition were noted long ago. Iamblichus examined them in detail in his *On the Pythagorean Life*, and explained, not without a certain malicious undertone, the origin of this interpretation by a story that reminds us of Mary and Joseph: The Samian Mnemarchos—this is Iamblichus' variation on the father's name Mnesarchos given elsewhere (was the variant intended to emphasize the importance of memory [*mnéme*] for Pythagoras?)—as a traveling salesman, was in Delphi with his wife, "whose pregnancy had not yet been noticed," and he asked the oracle about his voyage to Syria. The Pythia prophesied him a highly enjoyable and profitable trip and also told him that his wife was pregnant and would give birth to a child that would surpass humans of all times in beauty and wisdom and would be of the greatest benefit to the human race with regard to the whole of life. Mnemarchos recognized the importance of this prophecy and immediately renamed his wife, previously called Parthenis ("Virginal"), Pythaïs, an unmistakable jibe against the Christian *parthénos* Mary. Iamblichus' implicit polemic later becomes more explicit when he expressly rejects the view (traced back to Epimenides, Eudoxus, and Xenocrates) that Apollo at that time lay with Parthenis and had her pregnancy announced by the prophetess.[25]

However, most accounts of Pythagoras' birth appear to be more sober. From the earliest times, Mnesarchos was named as his father "by common agreement," as Porphyry maintained.[26] Concerning Mnesarchos' origin, the sources differ. Samos, the Levant (Tyre in Syria), and the Tyrrhenian island of Lemnos are mentioned,[27] exceptionally Phlius in the Peloponnesus is also referred to[28]—probably because after the Pythagoreans were driven out of southern Italy they established a new headquarter there. Some of the sources say that Pythagoras' father was a gem engraver,[29] others make him a trader who sold the Samians grain during a famine and was rewarded by being honored with citizenship.[30]

Years of Travel in the Orient

According to tradition, Pythagoras was educated chiefly in the Near East, from which—as modern research has made increasingly clear—the Greeks of the Archaic period actually received crucial cultural stimuli.[31] This fact seems to have been already recognized in ancient times. For example, Herodotus traces countless Greek customs back to Egyptian high culture, whose antiquity is stressed by Plato in his dialogue *Timaeus* (in comparison to the Egyptians, the Greeks remain "always children").[32] The tendency to derive important aspects of Greek culture from the older wisdom of "barbarians" became even stronger in the Hellenistic period, when through Alexander the Great's conquests entirely new geographical realms opened up to the Greeks. At least from that time on, it belongs to the commonplaces of an intellectual biography to explain the outstanding qualities of a thinker by noting that he had made one or several trips to the Orient. A travel to Egypt is mentioned in this context with special frequency. Like Orpheus and Musaeus, Homer, Solon, and Lycurgus, Democritus, Plato, Eudoxus, and others "famous for their insight and learning," Pythagoras of Samos, too, was said to have visited Egypt, in order to be initiated by the priests there into the local customs and cultural achievements.[33] In the biographies of Pythagoras this element is embellished with anecdotes. In his (lost) work *On the Life of Persons of Outstanding Virtue*, a certain Antiphon (Hellenistic period?), about whom we know nothing else, goes particularly far in this respect. In accord with the title of his work, he organizes the narrative so that Pythagoras becomes a model for the virtue of steadfastness (*kartería*): In order to share the Egyptian priests' mode of life, he is supposed to have asked the tyrant Polycrates for a letter of recommendation to the latter's host, the Egyptian king Amasis (who is known for his pro-Greek policies). From Amasis Pythagoras, who is also said to have learned Egyptian,[34] received a letter to the priests. But in Heliopolis he was sent on to Memphis, on the pretext that there the local priests were older, and from Memphis he was sent, on the same pretext, to the priests in Diospolis. The latter did not dare to invent any further grounds for refusing him, but they hoped to dissuade him from his plan by means of very severe rules of conduct that were fundamentally different from the Greek way of life. But Pythagoras eagerly and steadfastly observed all their rules, and this won him such great admiration that he, as the only ever foreigner, was also granted the privilege of sacrificing to the Egyptian gods and taking part in their worship.[35] The meaning of this anecdote, which was clearly influenced by Herodotus' book about Egypt, wherein (erroneously) also the doctrine of rebirth is derived from Egypt (see 55ff., below), is obvious: Pythagoras, it suggests, imported from Egypt many of the ritual rules that sometimes struck Greek ears as alien. Other reporters refer to Persian magicians or even Zarathustra himself as the source for these and other doctrines.[36]

Pythagoras was also said to have acquired from the Egyptians his competence in geometry, while the Phoenicians supposedly taught him arithmetic and the Chaldeans astronomy.[37] As early as the third century B.C.E. the Jews were also mentioned as being among his teachers.[38] According to the novel writer Antonius Diogenes (second century C.E.?), Pythagoras learned from them the art of interpreting dreams.[39] Philostratus mentions, in addition to the Egyptians, Indian sages,[40] and in Iamblichus the list is enlarged to include even the Celts and the Iberians.[41]

Teachers in the Immediate Environment

In the course of extended travels among foreign peoples then, Pythagoras "acquired most of his wisdom."[42] In the same way, we hear of instruction received by Pythagoras in his immediate environment. Hermodamas of Samos, Thales, and Anaximander of Miletus are mentioned, along with the mythical bard Orpheus of Thrace and Pherecydes of Syros. These names stand for certain areas of importance in Pythagoras' thought: Homeric poetry (Hermodamas, whose father was Creophylos, who was, according to legend, Homer's host or rival and probably stands for an indigenous Samian rhapsodic tradition),[43] Ionian natural philosophy (Thales and Anaximander), piety and (mystery) cult (Orpheus as the founder of Greek mystic rites) as well as cosmogonic-cosmological speculation (Pherecydes). Stories about the latter two occupy the most space. The Neoplatonists knew of a "sacred discourse" (*hieròs lógos*) on the gods by Pythagoras, in which a theology of numbers is being developed in Dorian language: Pythagoras, it is said, had received this speech as Orpheus' teaching from the priest of the mysteries Aglaophamus on the occasion of his initiation in Leibethra (a city at the foot of Mt. Olympus):

> This <discourse> is what I Pythagoras, son of Mnemarchus, learned on initiation in the Thracian L<e>ibethra, from Aglaophamus the initiator, who communicated to me that Orpheus, son of Calliope, taught by his mother on Mt. Pangaeon, said: "The eternal being of number is a most provident principle of the whole heaven, earth, and of the intermediate nature; moreover it is a source of permanence for divine [men] and gods and daemons." (Iambl. VPyth. 146 = Pythag. Hier. log. dor. fr. 1, p. 164 Thesleff; transl. Dillon and Hershbell)

In Iamblichus VPyth. 151, Orpheus is mentioned as the model for Pythagoras' way of speaking, spiritual attitude, and of worshiping the gods, and the Pythagorean philosophy of religion is described as a synthesis of all he had learned not least from the followers of Orpheus, moreover also from the Egyptian priests and all other peoples and religions (including the Eleusinian mysteries). As fanciful as the relationship between Orpheus and Pythagoras in the later sources may be, in the fifth century B.C.E. the Samian sage was connected with the mythical Thracian bard and founder of initiation rites (this connection is explored in greater detail below at 49, 52, 62–70).

Ideal typical traits characterize the image the sources give of Pythagoras' contacts with his teacher Pherecydes of Syros (around the middle of the sixth century B.C.E.). Incidentally, similar miracle stories are told about Pherecydes as about Pythagoras: Among other things, he is supposed to have predicted a shipwreck and the conquest of a city (in his case, Messana), and also to have prophesied an earthquake after drinking from a well.[44] Attempting to explain the different aspects of Pythagoras biographically—initially he would have concerned himself with mathematics and numbers, but later on he would not have refrained from Pherecydes' ability to work miracles, either—the paradoxographer Apollonius (second century B.C.E.?) traces Pythagoras' thaumaturgy back to Pherecydes' influence.[45] In general, however, no more is said than that Pherecydes was Pythagoras' teacher.[46] When Pherecydes in his old age had succumbed to the disease recorded as *morbus pedicularis* on Apollo's island of Delos (which is near Syros), Pythagoras went there, in order to care for him and to pay him his last respects. "And he remained with him until the end, and fulfilled the holy duty to his master. So dear to him was care for the teacher."[47] In this moving form, the story may go back to the neo-Pythagorean Nicomachus of Gerasa.[48] Whereas the latter associated this with the first rebellion within the Pythagorean community, which supposedly took place in Pythagoras' absence,[49] Dicaearchus seems to situate Pherecydes' death, regarding which there were various other versions independent of Pythagoras in circulation[50] in before Pythagoras left Samos.[51] In a burst of local patriotic enthusiasm, the Peripatetic and Samian autocrat Duris (c. 340–c. 260 B.C.E.) mentions an epigram on Pherecydes' grave in which the deceased placed Pythagoras' wisdom even higher than his own.[52]

Even if the stories are embellished by legends, in the fifth century B.C.E. it was established that there were contacts (both biographical and substantial) between the two men, and this fact may well have a historical foundation.[53] At least with regard to the doctrine of the soul the two seem to have had very similar views, and Pherecydes' peculiar "theo-cosmology" moves on the borders between mythology and natural philosophy in a way that we find again in Pythagorean oral sayings.[54]

Back to Samos

Most of the sources have Pythagoras returning to Samos after his years of travel and study.[55] Sporadically, they mention that he began teaching on his own island:

> Returning to Ionia [Antiphon reports], he opened in his own country a school which is even now called "Pythagoras' Semicircle,"[56] and in which the Samians meet to deliberate about matters of common interest. Outside the city he adapted a cave to the study of his philosophy, in which he lived day and night, discoursing with a few of his associates. (Porph. VPyth. 9, following Antiphon)[57]

In this context, Iamblichus adds that by adopting arithmetic and geometric proofs, Pythagoras raised astronomy to its highest perfection. The best minds in all Greece, he says, came to Samos because of him, in order to take part in his instruction.[58] It may not be completely out of the question that he taught on Samos.[59] But the account just given with its reference to a building still in use sounds as if it were motivated by local patriotism. It is easy to understand that the Samians would not have wanted to allow southern Italy to lay exclusive claim to their increasingly famous native son.

While he was on Samos, Pythagoras is also supposed to have acted very successfully as a sports instructor:

> As he was spending some time there, he coached the Samian athlete Eurymenes, who—although he was small in body—was able, through Pythagoras' wisdom, to defeat many larger [opponents] and won in Olympia. For whereas the other athletes continued to feed on cheese and figs, in accord with the ancient custom, Eurymenes was the first to eat, on Pythagoras' advice, a certain amount of meat every day, thereby strengthening his body. (Porph. VPyth. 15)[60]

A curious story, especially for a person who is usually thought to have prohibited the consumption of any meat at all. However, on this subject as on so many others, the sources are not at all consistent. Moreover, one of the most famous athletes of antiquity, the exceptionally powerful wrestler Milon of Croton, who is supposed to have eaten nearly twenty pounds of meat a day,[61] was said to be one of Pythagoras' pupils.[62] It was in his house, we are told, that the Pythagoreans had gathered when the rebellion against them began.[63] The tension between Pythagoras the coach and Pythagoras the vegetarian was partly dissolved by assuming that the trainer in question was someone else who bore the same name.[64]

From Samos to Southern Italy

In the sources favorable to Pythagoras, the latter's emigration to Croton is attributed to his political uneasiness regarding the rule of the famous tyrant Polycrates, who reigned on Samos from 538 to 522 B.C.E.:

> When he turned forty, Aristoxenus reports, and saw that the tyranny of Polycrates was a despotic regime too oppressive for a free man to endure, he decided under the circumstances to go away to Italy. (Porph. VPyth. 9 = Aristox. fr. 16 Wehrli)[65]

This fits with the neo-Pythagorean Nicomachus' emphasis on Pythagoras' love of freedom. Conversely, his opponents attributed to him a tendency to tyranny.

Porphyry connects the move with two further odd bits of information. In Delphi Pythagoras is supposed to have put up on Apollo's grave an elegiac distich, in which he announced that Apollo was the son of Silenus, was killed by Pytho, and was buried in the so-called tripod (*trípous*). The tripod had acquired this name because three of Triopas' daughters had mourned Apollo there.[66] This is a very strange story, in which the usual myth—Apollo kills the dreadful dragon and takes possession of the oracle—is turned upside down. The reinterpretation, which perhaps recapitulates Dionysus' fate,[67] may mean something like "Apollo is dead, long live the new Apollo," that is, Pythagoras! Among the Pythagoreans, moreover, the tripod, for whose name a mythical etymology is given here, and the Delphic oracle were the object of speculations in the areas of religion and natural philosophy. It is perhaps also worth noting in this connection that according to part of the tradition, Pythagoras is supposed to have acquired most of his ethical doctrine from a Delphic priestess called Themistocleia ("she who is famed for divine decrees").[68]

According to Porphyry,[69] Pythagoras left behind another epigram—and this again tells of a god's death—on Crete, where he is first purified by the local initiatory priests—the so-called Dactyls ("finger-mannekins") of Mt. Ida, from whom already Orpheus was supposed to have learned his religious craft[70]—with the "thunderstone" in a peculiar ceremony ("early in the morning, stretched out headfirst by the sea, but at night by the river, wreathed in the wool of a black ram"). The purification is followed by a stay of three times nine days down in the Ida cavern, where Pythagoras, once again clothed in black wool, sacrifices to Zeus, sees the throne annually set up here for Zeus, and puts up the epigram: "Here lies the dead Zan, whom they call Zeus." This strange story probably reflects a certain Cretan ritual. Especially striking is the black wool: As the "color of death,"[71] black symbolizes the underworld dimension of this cathartic and initiatory ceremony—whereas when the Pythagoreans sacrificed to the gods, they were obliged to wear brilliant white robes.[72] Moreover, the use of wool stands in striking contrast to the Orphic-Pythagorean taboo on burying the dead in woolen clothing.

Whereas Porphyry situates this episode during the trip from Samos to southern Italy, Diogenes Laertius (middle of the third century c.e.?) locates it in the general context of the travels which Pythagoras as a young man undertook for eagerness to learn and which imparted his special religious knowledge to him.[73]

Arrival in Croton, Moral Instruction, and Political Activities

According to various sources, the effect Pythagoras' charismatic appearance produced in Italy was simply overpowering. After he had through "many fine discussions" won over the Senate in Croton to his cause, this council of the old men entrusted to him the instruction not only of the children and young people but also of the women:

> He made addresses suitable for their age in turn to the young, when bidden by the councillors, and after this to the children gathered in groups from the schools, then to women, when an assembly of women was created for him. (19) When these things happened, fame grew great around him and he won over many followers from this city, not only men but also women, one of whom, Theano at least, made a famous name for herself, and also many from the neighbouring non-Greek territory, both kings and rulers. (Porph. VPyth. 18s. = Dicaearch. fr. 40 Mirhady; transl. Mirhady)

By the inhabitants of the surrounding "non-Greek" countries one has to understand the Italian tribes of the Lucani, Messapi, and Peucetii, and the Romans.[74] As to the "kings and rulers" mentioned at the end of the passage quoted above, they may well refer in particular to Numa Pompilius, the second king of Rome. According to legend, he was a pupil of Pythagoras and reshaped Roman religious institutions and sacred laws to conform to Pythagorean doctrine, which is one reason why Pythagoreanism enjoyed considerable popularity in Rome.

It was thus moral encouragement (*parainéseis*) that Pythagoras addressed to the inhabitants of Croton, both male and female. However, he did not say the same thing to everyone, but instead adapted the content of his admonitions to the specific group targeted. Antisthenes (c. 445–c.365 b.c.e.), a pupil of Socrates, praises him for his rhetorical (and pedagogical) skill. "For being able to find the kind of wisdom digestible by each individual is a sign of wisdom. But it is a sign of stupidity to make use of one single kind of speech when addressing an audience composed of different sorts of people."[75] It is well-known that Plato also assigns greatest importance to the adaptation of each speech (and therefore also of the philosophical transfer of knowledge) to the interlocutor addressed.[76] Could it be that here we glimpse a Socratic doctrine, and that perhaps for Socrates Pythagoras' performance in Croton had in this respect a paradigmatic character? It would then hardly be mere accident that in his comedy *The Clouds* Aristophanes (around the middle of the fifth century-after 388 B.C.E.) lent the "Thinkery" of Socrates (caricatured there as a sophist) certain Orphic-Pythagorean traits.

However that may be, the later tradition is even able to report the content of Pythagoras' speeches.[77] According to Iamblichus, whose description in VPyth. 37–57 could go back to the historian Timaeus (c. 350–c. 260 B.C.E.) from Sicilian Tauromenium (modern Taormina), in an initial speech in the local gymnasium Pythagoras encouraged the young people to respect age and especially their parents. He also entrusted to them the virtue of temperance (*sophrosýne*) and the striving for education (*paideía*) that distinguishes men from animals, Hellenes from barbarians, freemen from slaves, and also philosophers from ordinary people.[78]

In contrast to Dicaearchus' account, in Iamblichus the political authorities start acting only after this discussion with the young people, after their fathers are told what was said. The Council of the Thousand calls Pythagoras to appear before it, praises him for the remarks he addressed to the youths, and urges him, "if he has something useful to say to the people of Croton," he should "let the representatives of the state know."[79] This speech, which Iamblichus then goes on to paraphrase, begins with the suggestion that a shrine to the Muses be established, since the Muses, as a "harmonious" group composed of equals, realize perfect harmony among themselves. The importance of the (musical) doctrine of numbers for the Pythagorean explanation of the world is also discernible when it is said that Pythagoras demonstrated that the power of the Muses extends not only to the "most beautiful objects of contemplation"—an allusion to the heavenly bodies that revolve in accord with musical numerical relationships?—but also to the accord and harmony of existing things. Various sources suggest that the Muses in fact played a significant role in the Pythagoreans' religious and cosmological thought. According to Aristotle (384–322 B.C.E.), Pythagoras called the constellation Pleiades "the lyre of the muses."[80] As Porphyry writes, he believed that the sound of the nine heavenly bodies (seven planets, the sphere of the fixed stars, and the Counter-Earth) was identical with the nine Muses. While he compared the usual sensual pleasures with the "man-killing song of the Sirens," he is said to have equated "pleasure in the good and the just and what is necessary for life with the harmony of the Muses."[81] The Muses also appear in legends about Pythagoras' death: He is said to have taken refuge in their shrine in Metapontum at the beginning of the riots and to have died there as well.[82] The little street in which his house stood was made by the inhabitants of Metapontum into a shrine to the Muses (the house itself was consecrated as a temple to Demeter).[83] In this connection, it is worth noting that Plato later set up a shrine to the Muses in his Academy— whether because he sought to continue the Pythagorean tradition, or because the tradition regarding Pythagoras was modeled on Plato.[84]

So much for the first point. Among the noteworthy counsels Iamblichus' Pythagoras gave the elite at Croton are the following:[85]

—To regard the state as a common pledge, which the leaders have received from the mass of the citizens;
—To be like one's fellow citizens in every way, and to be superior to them only in justice;
—Not to abuse any of the gods by swearing oaths by them, but rather to speak in such a way that what is said is credible without oaths;
—To manage one's own household in an exemplary way, so that it is possible to draw conclusions from this regarding one's political attitude;[86]
—To strive to make children love their parents not because of the blood-bond (which is not in their responsibility) but rather by free choice;
—Not to carry on any extramarital affairs (according to Hieronymus of Rhodes fr. 42 Wehrli, on returning from the Underworld Pythagoras reported that those who did not want to be with their own wives were punished there as well);
—To look upon one's wife as a suppliant whom one has taken to oneself from the hearth in the sight of the gods, making libations;[87]
—To be a model of discipline and temperance for all, and to avoid sluggishness in action (there is nothing more important than the right moment [*kairós*] for each thing);
—Not to tear asunder children and parents (which is the worst injustice);
—To seek honor by emulating the successful runner who does his opponents no harm, but [only] strives to win himself;
—To cling to the truly good repute and be as he wants to appear to others.

These remarks, which in some points are surprising for antiquity (especially those regarding monogamy) and some of which seem not very far removed from Christian ethics (the renunciation of oaths),[88] conclude with a reference to Heracles, who once, when he was driving the giant Geryon's cattle through Italy, had accidentally killed his host Croton and after the latter's solemn funerals promised to found a city named after him.[89] The speech has the desired effect: the shrine to the Muses is built, the men of Croton give up the concubines they had kept in accord with the customs of their country[90] and ask Pythagoras "to speak separately to the children in the shrine of Apollo, and to the women in the shrine of Hera."[91]

In these last two speeches religious matters play a larger role. After urging gentleness (don't begin insulting, and don't defend yourself against those who insult you!), education (*paideía*), a term derived not by chance from the word for children (*paîdes*), and decent conduct (as the foundation for a morally good life), Pythagoras speaks of the special nearness of children to the gods:[92] Because of their purity they are particularly cherished by the gods, and whatever they ask for is granted. It is also for this reason that the most humane of the gods, Apollo and Eros, are represented as children (in the case of the *koûros* Apollo, this holds true only if one assumes with Pythagoras in Diog. Laert. 8,10 that childhood includes the first twenty years of life). A few competitions were arranged for the sake of the children (the Pythian games, for instance, since the snake Python was overcome by a child—Apollo). From Apollo's promise to the leader of the Crotonian colonists, Myscellus, that he would give him progeny,[93] the citizens of Croton were supposed to conclude that Apollo had taken precautions to ensure their birth and that all the gods had taken steps to see to it that they grew up. The speech ends with the request that children should prove themselves worthy of the gods' love, practice listening, and since they stand at the beginning of life's path, they should not contradict adults, who have traveled this path before them.

Pythagoras' conservative ethics for women, finally, revolves around cult practice and women's relationship with their husbands.[94] With respect to successful ritual sacrifice, he urges women to maintain the highest possible upright way of life, since the gods pay attention only to good people and listen to their prayers. Moreover, women should carry sacrifices to the altar with their own hands and without slaves (a sign of humility). As sacrifices, baked goods, honey, and incense are recommended, whereas the sacrifice of meats is—not surprisingly, for Pythagoras—rejected. In the following section, which is devoted to women's relationship to their husbands, Pythagoras deduces, from the premise that even fathers would allow women to love their husbands more than they do their parents, the conclusion that it is right when women completely subordinate themselves to their husbands. Ritually motivated, again, is the following statement—attributed elsewhere to Deino or Theano, both female adherents of Pythagoras:[95] "If a woman comes from her husband, she is allowed on the same day to go to the holy shrines, but if she comes from a man who does not belong to her, never" (according to a traditional notion sexual intercourse invariably causes pollution and therefore always calls for a ritual purification; Pythagoras gives the rule a moral turn by limiting the pollution to adulterous sexual intercourse).[96] He then emphasizes women's good reputation in myth—which ought to be maintained—and finally, once more, the peculiar "disposition" of women to piety: This, he says, can be gathered from the mere fact that each stage of women's life bears the name of a goddess (Kore, Nymphe, Meter, Maia);[97] correspondingly, the oracles in Dodona and Delphi were revealed by women.[98] According to Iamblichus, Pythagoras' praise of piety led to a change of mood amongst the women; henceforth they dressed more simply and took all their many luxurious clothes to the famous shrine of Hera Lacinia in Croton and put them up as votive offerings. This reaction on the part of the women, which is also found in Pompeius Trogus, a Roman historian of the early empire,[99] comes rather as a surprise in Iamblichus, since in his paraphrase of the speech hardly anything is said about this point. Apparently in him as well, the directive handed down by Diodorus is in the background, namely that those performing sacrifices should not appear before the gods in luxurious getups, but rather in brilliant white, clean robes.[100]

These speeches, which were presumably enhanced by legendary ornamentation in Iamblichus' source (Timaeus?), have been discussed in somewhat greater detail because they are, on one hand, among the most interesting continuous texts, and on the other they remind us of another side of the ancient image of Pythagoras that is less familiar today: Pythagoras as a moral authority whose influence stretched not only to his own pupils but as far as the whole society of the city of Croton. He thereby takes the social stratification into account, insofar as he holds up to different age, rank, and gender groups the ethical mirror appropriate to each (as for the social structure, we may find very instructive Timaeus' remark[101] that as a virgin Pythagoras' daughter led—probably during religious and musical events—the virgins of Croton, and as a wife she led the wives). The speeches show Pythagoras' rhetorical skill in cleverly interweaving local tradition (foundation myth) into his remarks. Pythagoras' model no doubt explains the fact that over time certain exoteric treatises (that is, ones addressed to outsiders) on ethical matters were attributed to various Pythagoreans, both male and female (see 120ff. below).

The events following Pythagoras' arrival in Italy are told somewhat differently by the neo-Pythagorean Nicomachus, who focuses his attention on the foundation of the mysterious community:

To such an extent did he [Pythagoras] convert everyone to his cause that, according to Nicomachus, he won over in only one lecture [which he gave after his arrival in Italy] more than two thousand people by his words, so that they did not return home, but together with their wives and children built an immense "common auditorium" (*homakoeîon*) and colonized the region in Italy that is commonly called *Magna Graecia,* and receiving laws and instructions from him as if they were divine orders they strictly abided by them. (FGrHist 1063 F 1 = Porph. VPyth. 20; transl. after Radicke)[102]

Here, as in the preceding case, Pythagoras appears as an exceptionally successful rhetorician.[103] Whether one can therefore regard him as the inventor of rhetoric, as does C. J. de Vogel,[104] may remain a matter of debate. It would be hard to imagine, in any event, how Pythagoras could have gained so much social influence in the cities of southern Italy without persuasive oratorical skill.

Concerning his political attitude, the sources differ considerably in some cases. In the speeches discussed, a kind of hereditary aristocracy seems to be posited as the Pythagorean ideal when rulers are urged to govern in such a way that the citizens' trust is transmitted to their (i.e., the rulers') children.[105] Nicomachus on the other hand describes Pythagoras' political activity in a way that tempts us to see in him virtually a convinced democrat:

And all the cities in Italy and Sicily which, on his journey, he had found—some for many years, some only recently—enslaved by one another he filled with the spirit of freedom and liberated them through the disciples he had in each: Croton, Sybaris, Catane, Rhegium, Himera, Acragas, Tauromenium, and some others. He also gave them laws through Charondas of Catane and Zaleucus of Locris, as a result of which they were envied by their neighbours for a long time. And Simichus, the tyrant of Centoripe, having listened to him resigned his power and divided his property between his sister and his fellow citizens. (FGrHist 1063 F 1 = Porph. VPyth. 21; transl. Radicke)[106]

The famous lawgivers of southern Italy, Charondas (sixth century B.C.E.?) and Zaleucus (c. 650 B.C.E.?), were probably first included in the Pythagorean school by Aristoxenus of Tarentum (c. 370–after 322 B.C.E.),[107] against which the historian Timaeus, among others, objected on good grounds.[108] In addition, Iamblichus also traces, in a tale probably borrowed from Apollonius, the end of the reign of Phalaris (c. 570–c. 549 B.C.E.), a tyrant of Acragas (Lat. Agrigentum) legendary for his cruelty, to the effect of Pythagoras' philosophical admonition.[109]

Pythagoras is also described as freedom-loving or at least as opposed to tyranny by Aristoxenus, according to whom he left Samos because of the tyrannical regime there. Neanthes (late fourth century B.C.E.)[110] attributes the same attitude to the Pythagoreans of the fourth century B.C.E.: Because of their aversion to the autocracy and unlawfulness of the tyrant of Syracuse, Dionysius (II?), they are supposed to have rejected his attempts to win their friendship.[111] But there are also very different voices. They range from a cautious distancing from Pythagoras' politics to the reproach that he or his pupils sought to install a tyranny themselves. As an example of the former we can take an anecdote that Dicaearchus relates (perhaps in a critical debate with Aristoxenus) to suggest that Pythagoreanism achieved no political influence in the southern Italian town of Locri. While fleeing the riots, Dicaearchus writes, Pythagoras came to other towns and also to Locri. A few old men intercepted him at the frontier and politely asked him to go elsewhere: Since they had nothing to complain about in their own laws, they wanted to try to stay with the ones they had.[112] Considered from a historical point of view, this testimony can perhaps be read as an expression of the gap between the existing aristocracies and the new, ideologically freighted Pythagorean aristocracy.[113] In any case, efforts at political and moral reform seem not to have met with the same success everywhere.

At the opposite end of the scale is the general suspicion expressed by the historian Theopompus (378/7– 320 B.C.E.) that Pythagorean philosophy was nothing other than an insidious attempt to establish a tyranny.[114] That the uprisings against the Pythagoreans were ignited by the fear of an imminent tyranny was a view shared by various people according to Diogenes Laertius.[115] In Apollonius' account as well, the rebels make the same accusation against the Pythagoreans and demand that everyone have a share in power.[116] To be sure, this tells us relatively little about Pythagoras' own political views, for in these passages the interest shifts to the anti-Pythagorean rebellions, which were indeed democratically motivated and first broke out only a few decades after Pythagoras' death. In any case, the findings confirm how contradictory the tradition regarding Pythagoras can sometimes be.

Emigration to Metapontum and Death

According to concordant reports, in the long run Pythagoras' political involvement in southern Italy turned out badly. It is true that Aristoxenus praises him for having completely eradicated discord and strife not only among his companions but also among their successors (over several successive generations), and generally in all the cities of Italy and Sicily, both within them and between them; for the avoidance of division, Aristoxenus goes on, is one of the guidelines of Pythagoras' ethics, which he summed up pithily in this frequently repeated utterance:

> We ought to the best of our ability avoid, and even [like a physician] with fire and sword eradicate from the body, sickness; from the soul, ignorance; from the belly, luxury; from a city, sedition; from a family, discord; and from all things, excess. (fr. 17 Wehrli; transl. K. S. Guthrie)

We also read in Porphyry that for a long time Pythagoras himself and the friends living with him were so greatly admired in Italy that the cities even handed over political responsibility to his pupils.[117] But eventually envy and plotting arose, and in the sources, the beginning of this is associated with a name: Cylon, around whom a catching story grew up. This man came from Croton's aristocracy; "by his family, the reputation of his ancestors, and his wealth he was superior to all the other citizens"[118]—and thus at that time he was almost predestined for a career in politics. However, in point of character he was very problematic, "violent and tyrannical," and used his large circle of friends and his money to commit injustices by means of raw power. Full of self-confidence as he was, he believed he, more than anyone else, deserved to take part in Pythagoras' philosophy. Therefore he went to Pythagoras, sang his own praises, and wanted to become his pupil. But Pythagoras, who in antiquity was also considered to be the inventor of physiognomics[119]—"he made no one his friend or acquaintance without first having tested him physiognomically, to see what kind of person he was"[120]—immediately began to make a physiognomical examination in this case, too, and when he saw, on the basis of bodily signs, what Cylon's character was, told him to go away and mind his own business:

> This saddened Cylon not a little, just as if he had been mocked (he was difficult anyway, and was unable to control his anger). (55) So he gathered his friends, slandered Pythagoras and took steps to prepare an attack on him and his companions. (Porph. VPyth. 54s.)

What happened next in the story, which was first recounted by Aristoxenus,[121] is told differently in the various sources. Some of the contradictions can be explained by the fact that Cylon's uprising is usually confused with the (later) anti-Pythagorean rebellions. Sometimes the attack on the com-

munity that had assembled in Milon's house took place in the absence of
Pythagoras, who is said to have gone to Delos to care for his teacher Pherecydes, who was ill. Other sources take Pythagoras as being present at Croton, too, and beginning the flight that according to Dicaearchus brought
him among others to the Locrians, who politely, but firmly turned him
down. The flight ended in Metapontum, where again disturbances are said
to have arisen. Pythagoras took refuge in the shrine of the Muses and died
there, either of natural causes—after enduring forty days without
food[122]—or, in a moving account, by his own hand:

> But others say that his companions, when fire was consuming the
> house in which they had just gathered, threw themselves into the fire
> and made a path for their teacher by using their own bodies to make
> a bridge over the fire. After he had escaped the fire, Pythagoras was
> despondent because he had lost his companions and took his own
> life. (Porph. VPyth. 57)

In another version what Neanthes says about later Pythagoreans[123] is transferred to Pythagoras himself: That as he was fleeing he came to a field full
of beans, and stopped there instantly, in order not to traverse it, and said:
"Better to be captured than to tread on [beans]!" And so, it is said, he was
killed by his pursuers[124] (Hermippus shifts this event to a violent conflict
between Acragas and Syracuse, in which Pythagoras and his companions
are supposed to have fought on the side of the Acragantines).[125] Yet another Pythagorean maxim of conduct, moderation in eating and drinking,[126] is illustrated by the version of Heraclides Lembus (second century
B.C.E.), according to which on his way back from Delos to Italy, Pythagoras
came across an opulent carousal of Cylon's in Croton and emigrated to
Metapontum, where he starved himself to death, since he no longer
wanted to live.[127] So like his birth, Pythagoras' death is recounted with
many variations.

PYTHAGORAS AS A TEACHER

Platonizing Philosophy

What Porphyry writes about Pythagoras' philosophy in his biography
sounds both fascinating, and although from another context, familiar:

> He practiced a philosophy whose goal is to release the mind (*noûs*)'
> that has been granted us from such [i.e., from bodily] cages and
> bonds, and to make it entirely free. Without it no one may be able at

all to either discover or perceive anything reasonable or true, no matter what sense he uses. Because "the mind," for itself, . . .
  sees all and hears all, but everything else is deaf and blind
                                                    (Epicharm. 23 B 12 D.-K.)

When the mind has been purified, then it must be provided with
something useful. He [Pythagoras] did this by devising aids. First
he took it gently to contemplate the eternal, non-corporeal things
related to it, which always remain the same and unchanging, leading onward step by step, so that it [the mind] would not, completely confused by the sudden and massive change, turn away and
give up because of the marked and constant badness of the [pre-
vious] nourishment (*trophē*). (47) Thus through mathematics and
through the [mathematical] objects of contemplation that lie in
the middle between bodies and bodiless things, he prepared [the
mind] in small steps for things that truly are, by turning with ex-
pert guidance the eyes of the soul away from bodily things, which
are never in the same state or remain in the same way in the same
place (even for a very short time), toward the desire for <incorpo-
real> nourishment. Thus he introduced [among humans] the vision of things that truly are and made them blessed. Hence to this
end practice in mathematics was added. (Porph. VPyth. 46s.; cf.
Iambl. VPyth. 228)

This section is shot through with Platonic thought; indeed, it can be regarded as far more a summary of Plato's philosophy than of Pythagoras'.
In Plato's dialog *Phaedo* Socrates speaks explicitly of the "prison" of the
body, from which the soul is to be freed through philosophical purification (*kátharsis*) and a turning away from the senses (the shared concepts
are italicized):

Lovers of knowledge recognize that when *philosophy* takes their soul
in hand, it has been literally bound and glued to the body, and is
forced to view the *things that [really] are* through this [body] as if
through a *cage*, rather than alone by itself; and that it is wallowing in
utter ignorance. Now [philosophy] discerns the cunning of the *prison*,
sees how it is effected through desire, so that the captive himself may
co-operate most of all in his imprisonment. (83a) As I say, then, lovers
of knowledge recognize that their soul is in that state when philosophy takes it in hand, *gently* reassures it and tries to release it, by showing that inquiry through the eyes is full of deceit, and deceitful too is
inquiry through the ears and other *senses;* and by persuading it to

withdraw from these, so far as it need not use them, and by urging it to collect and gather itself together, and to trust none other but itself, (83b) whenever, alone by itself, it thinks of any of the things that are, *alone by itself;* and not to regard as *true* what it observes by other means, and what varies in various things; that kind of thing is sensible and seen, whereas the object of its own vision is *intelligible* and invisible. It is, then, just because it believes it should not oppose this *release* that the soul of the true philosopher abstains from pleasures and desires and pains, so far as it can, etc. (Plat. Phaed. 82e–83b; transl. after Gallop)

In the *Phaedo* Socrates also has something to say about the effects of bad *trophé* (food, care, way of life).[128] Moreover, the fundamental oppositions between mind and sense perception and between what always remains self-identical and the constantly changing (cf., e.g., Tim. 27d–28a), as well as the relationship between mind (as the highest part of the soul) and the incorporeal ideas (cf., e.g., Phaed. 79d) are unmistakably inspired by Plato. Besides the *Phaedo*, it is above all the seventh book of the *Republic* that stands in the background of Porphyry's chapters and exerts a formative influence. In the cave allegory in this book, humans similarly are "in chains," the "change" cannot take place "suddenly" and without preparation, since otherwise there would be a danger of "turning away" and fleeing, but rather the individual must be "freed" in small steps and led to the "vision" of true reality, which leads to a feeling of blessedness.[129] The object of study best suited to turn "the eyes of the soul" toward true light is (in addition to astronomy and music) mathematics, which, when it is rightly practiced (that is, not in a merely commercial and practical way) does not remain with the senses, but leads the soul upward, in that it promotes the use of thought, which seeks to achieve clarity regarding the essence of numbers and geometrical figures. Thus through arithmetic and geometry the soul acquires the necessary lightness in the "turn" from becoming toward truth and being.[130]

One could object that in Pythagorean philosophy as well the doctrine of numbers plays a central role. That is entirely true. But Plato and the Pythagoreans differ here on a fundamental point: According to Aristotle, the "median position" of mathematical objects between the sensible-perceivable and the Ideas—cf. Porph. VPyth. 47 at the beginning of this section—is characteristic of Plato, whereas the Pythagoreans (still) are not aware of the separate status of numbers: For them, numbers fall into the same category as reality perceivable through the senses.[131]

In short, what Porphyry presents as Pythagoras' philosophy turns out on closer inspection to be thoroughly Platonic. And this is not a unique case, even if the relationships are not always that clear. A multiplicity of distinctly Platonic philosophical themes have found their way into most of the accounts of Pythagorean philosophy ever since Hellenistic times, especially into the popular "doxographies"—that is, the ancient handbooks in which the doctrines of various philosophers on a specific range of subjects are collected. A typical example of this is the doctrine of principles. According to the "Pythagorean Records" (probably dating from the third century B.C.E.), which have come down to us by a double refraction—a philologian of the first century B.C.E., Alexander Polyhistor, excerpted the work in his "Successions of the Philosophers," and his excerpt was again summarized by Diogenes Laertius—,[132] the Pythagoreans designated

> the Monad ["unity"] as the origin [principle] of all things; but from the Monad came the unlimited Dyad ["duality"], which as matter is subordinate to the Monad as the cause; from the Monad and the unlimited Dyad came numbers, from numbers points, from the latter lines, from which plane figures emerged, but from planes came solids, and from these bodies that can be perceived by the senses, whose elements are four in number: fire, water, earth, air, etc. (Alex. Polyhist. FGrHist 273 F 93 = Diog. Laert. 8,25)

From Aristotle we know that the Pythagoreans considered numbers the principles of existing things, but that the doctrine paraphrased in this place, with its line Monad-unlimited Dyad-numbers and its series of dimensions point-line-plane-solid, is characteristic of Plato's theory of principles, where according to Aristotle "unlimited duality" (introduced by Plato instead of the Pythagorean unlimited) takes the place of matter.[133] In contrast, the Pythagoreans did not designate the Monad and the Dyad, which Plato conceives as supersensory, as the principles of numbers; the even (= unlimited) and the odd (= limited) are their principles and elements of the universe, that become united in the One, and according to Aristotle it is number (not distinguished by the Pythagoreans from the sensory), that is assigned, so to say, the function of matter in this system.[134] This will be discussed in greater detail in chapter 2 at 84 ff.

To this Platonizing tradition also belongs the appealing explanation for the Pythagoreans' preoccupation with numbers given by the neo-Pythagorean Moderatus of Gades (first century C.E.), the author of an eleven-volume work on the Pythagorean school of thought:[135] Because of the impossibility of clearly and comprehensibly conveying the first "Ideas" (a *vox Platonica*) and principles, in order to illustrate the doctrine didactically they resorted to numbers. In so doing they are said to have followed among others the example of geometry teachers, who also made use of drawings in order to make a supersensory reality (for instance, the idea of a triangle) understandable. In just the same way, Moderatus thinks, numbers in Pythagorean philosophy should be interpreted as symbols of ideal realities—the One, for instance, stands for "unity, sameness, and identity, the cause of the accord and sympathy _(sympátheia)_ of the universe and the preservation of that which remains always self-identical and unchanging," while the Dyad (also a _vox Platonica_) stands for "difference and unlikeness and for everything that is divided, and for what is in change and is sometimes one way, sometimes another."[136]

This passage, too, is imbued with Platonic-Aristotelian concepts. This holds not only once again for the ontological dichotomy between what always remains itself and what is constantly changing and for the individual categories that the first two numbers illustrate, but also for the reference to geometry teachers, whose use of figures Plato describes in the _Republic_ in a very similar way.[137] In addition, Moderatus' hermeneutics finds its exact counterpart in the discussion within the Academy regarding Plato's _Timaeus:_ Just as the neo-Pythagorean wants to see Pythagoras' doctrine of numbers as merely a pedagogical-communicative aid, so Xenocrates and other pupils of Plato argue against the literal interpretation (proposed by Aristotle, among others) of the famous account of the creation in this dialogue; according to them, Plato was speaking instead like teachers of geometry, who drew figures about the origin—not that the world ever would have had an origin, but on didactic grounds [!], so that it can be better recognized, as when one observes the origin of a geometrical figure.[138] The question as to which interpretation of the Platonic account of creation was more appropriate was intensively discussed in the early Roman Empire.[139] Therefore it is hardly surprising to find the same interpretive paradigm in Moderatus. The transfer to Pythagorean philosophy was made even easier because in antiquity the protagonist of Plato's dialog, Timaeus of Locri, was generally thought to be a Pythagorean (see 116ff. below).

Iamblichus' definition of Pythagorean "wisdom" as "knowledge of the truth in the domain of existing things" is purely Platonic:

> Existing things he recognized and declared to be immaterial, eternal, and solely active, that is, things which are incorporeal. Other "existing things" are equivocally so called by sharing in existing things themselves, that is, corporeal and material forms, which are both generable and corruptible, and never truly existing. Wisdom is knowledge of things truly existing, not of those equivocally existing, since corporeal things are neither knowable nor admit of firm knowledge, being devoid of limit and not comprehensible by knowledge. Virtu-

ally non-existent by comparison with the universals, they cannot even be easily defined. (Iambl. VPyth. 159; transl. Dillon and Hershbell)

In this passage, Pythagoras appears to be almost the founder of Western metaphysics, but against the background of Aristotle's account of the Pythagoreans' philosophy of number this cannot be the case (see 88f. below).

Even if since Hellenistic times Pythagorean philosophy has often been aligned with Plato's to the point of becoming unrecognizable, under the Platonic surface older material can at times also be clearly discerned in the reports. Thus, for instance, what Moderatus writes in the subsequent passage regarding the number three—that it refers to everything that has a beginning, a middle, and an end; if something is perfect, then it has this principle and is ordered in accord with it[140]—seems to receive, through the unsuspected testimony of Aristotle, a certain confirmation: He attributes to the Pythagoreans the view that the universe and all things are limited by the number three; for end, middle, and beginning contain the number of the universe, but the latter contains the number three.[141]

Mathematics

In his natural philosophy, "Pythagoras mixed astronomy, geometry, music [and arithmetic]," writes the early Christian author Hippolytus (died 235/6 c.e.) in his doxographic outline of pagan philosophy.[142] Iamblichus also refers to studies in geometry and astronomy and connects them with Pythagoras' travels among the peoples of Egypt and Chaldea, who were generally considered the inventors of both these branches of knowledge:[143]

They say he was particularly concerned with geometry; for among the Egyptians there is much geometrical theorising, ever since ancient times and by way of the gods. Because of the Nile's floodings and recedings, the learned among the Egyptians have been forced to measure out all the land which they inhabit; hence [this science] is named "geo-metry" ["land-measurement"]. But the theory of heavenly bodies was also not cursorily researched by them, and in this study Pythagoras was very well experienced. Indeed, all theorems about lines seem to be derived from there [Egypt]; while theorems about counting and numbers, they say, were discovered by the Phoenicians. Theories about celestial bodies are referred by some to the Egyptians and Chaldeans in common. They say, then, that Pythagoras took over and joined in promoting all these investigations, and so advanced the sciences and explained them clearly and elegantly to his hearers. (Iambl. VPyth. 158s.; transl. Dillon and Hershbell)

Hecataeus of Abdera (c. 360–290 B.C.E.) expresses the view that Pythagoras learned from the Egyptians, in addition to ritual regulations and the doctrine of reincarnation, "the geometric and arithmetic theorems,"[144] and Anticleides, one of the writers of Alexander's history (c. 300 B.C.E.), tells us that he perfected geometry, after (the Egyptian) Moeris had discovered its elementary foundations.[145]

Iamblichus goes into still greater detail in his treatise *On General Mathematical Science*, which is handed down to us separately, but which was originally the third book of his comprehensive work *On the Pythagorean School of Philosophers* (cf. 127f. below). In it he names among those who stimulated Pythagoras, in addition to the Egyptians and Chaldeans, Thales of Miletus, who was, according to Iamblichus, also a pupil of the Egyptians.[146] To what he learned from these sources, Pythagoras is said to have added a great deal of his own, and systematized mathematics to make it a deductive science working with rigorous proofs. The main philosophical utility of mathematics is seen in its ability to purify the soul and to lead to the first (supersensory) principles.[147] The Pythagoreans, Iamblichus says, have connected scientific observation of the world with mathematics and discovered many mathematical regularities, relating, for example, to the movement of the heavenly bodies.[148] Iamblichus also mentions as a peculiarity that Pythagoras considered this mathematics that would lead to intelligible Ideas (!) subject to the school's policy of secrecy. But within the school a powerful flowering of "mathematical philosophy" and scientific geometry is supposed to have taken place, and Pythagoras is described as having laid the foundations for virtually all later improvements.[149] There were various accounts of the way in which mathematical secrets leaked out of the schools' circle. On one hand, this is presented as a matter of betrayal: The Pythagorean Hippasus of Metapontum is supposed to have been the first to betray the secret by drawing the sphere consisting of twelve congruent pentagons (the pentagonal dodecahedron must have been—like the pentagram—an important Pythagorean secret symbol), whereupon he drowned in the sea as a godless blasphemer. On the other hand, it is described as another example of typical Pythagorean solidarity: When a Pythagorean lost his fortune, he was given permission, under such circumstances, to use geometry to make money.[150] Whatever the truth may be, according to Iamblichus Pythagoras' discoveries were widely known and made possible a significant increase in knowledge.[151]

Pythagoras' most famous mathematical achievement was already for the ancients the well-known theorem still named after him, according to which "in a right-angled triangle the square of the hypotenuse is equal to [the sum of] the squares of the other two sides."[152] In his enthusiasm over the discovery of this theorem, which is fundamental for mathematics, and which—as modern research has shown—the Babylonians had been using for centuries, Pythagoras is said to have immediately sacrificed a bull, or even made a hecatomb, that is, sacrificed a hundred bulls. An epigram about this event has also come down to us:

Accomplished by Pythagoras: he discovered that glorious figure
whereupon he carried out a famous sacrifice of oxen

(Apollodorus [of Cyzicus?] FGrHist 1097 F 1c; transl. after Radicke)

This report contrasts conspicuously with the widespread tradition that Pythagoras rejected blood sacrifices. For Cicero (106–43 B.C.E.), that was sufficient reason to doubt the account.[153] Others—"more precise authorities," as Porphyry writes–believed to know "that it was a bull made of dough."[154] A similar substitute sacrifice was offered, according to tradition, by Empedocles on the occasion of his victory in a horse race at Olympia, "since he was a Pythagorean and abstained from eating creatures with souls."[155]

Music and the Harmony of the Spheres

Since antiquity Pythagoras has been famous for another discovery that still ensures him a place in every manual or dictionary of music history: the discovery that music has mathematical foundations, most notably that the perfect intervals of an octave, a fifth, and a fourth can be reduced to simple numerical relations. "Pythagoras discovered that the intervals in music also do not originate without numbers."[156] Often, Pythagoras is considered at the same time also as the discoverer of the monochord. In antiquity, this instrument was usually called a *kanón*, that is, "a straight rod" or "straightedge," on which a string was provided with a moveable bridge, and on which the mathematical relationships of musical intervals could be clearly demonstrated.[157]

In the sources, the "discovery of musicology (*harmonikè epistéme*) and of the musical proportions"[158] is once again embellished with legends. Once when Pythagoras was deep in thought about whether he could invent an aid for hearing similar to the circle, the straight edge, and the scale, the neo-Pythagorean Nicomachus tells us in a story taken over more or less verbatim by Iamblichus, he walked by a forge, where he heard by a divine chance hammers beating iron on an anvil, and making mixed sounds in full harmony with one another, except for one combination. He recognized in these the octave and the fifth and the fourth, and he saw the interval between the fourth and the fifth was dissonant in itself, but was capable of completing the range of greatness between them. Delighted, then, that his project had the backing of the divinity, he rushed into the forge, and with varied tests he found that difference of sounds was produced by the weights [sizes] of the hammers, not by the force of the blows or by the shapes of the hammers or by the position of the iron being struck. When he had noted accurately the weights and the exact balancing of the hammers, he went home.

From a single peg fixed to an angle between two walls, which he chose lest any differentiation should make itself felt on this account, or there should be any variation owing to the difference between particular pegs, he suspended four strings of the same material, of the same number of strands, of equal thickness, and of equal torsion. And from each string he hung one weight by attaching the weight at the bottom and making certain that all the strings had equal lengths. Then, striking groups of two strings alternately, he found the aforementioned concords sounded in the various combinations of strings. He found that the string stretched by the greatest weight sounded together with that stretched by the smallest weight, produced an octave; the former string supported twelve weights and the latter six, so he determined that the octave was in duple proportion, as was shown, indeed, by the weights themselves. And again, he showed that the string with the greatest weight when sounded together with the string with the next to least weight, that is, the string with eight weights, produces the consonance of the fifth; in doing so, he showed this consonance to consist of a proportion of 3:2, the same proportion in which the weights themselves stand in relation to each other; while, in combination with the string second greatest in weight, that consisting of nine weights, a fourth was produced, proportionately with the weights. And he found this string [with 9 weights] in a proportion of 4:3 with the greatest string; yet he found this same string to be in a natural proportion of 3:2 with the smallest string, for 9 stands in such a relationship with 6. In the same way, the second smallest string, that from which 8 weights are suspended, stood in a proportion of 4:3 with that having 6 weights, but in a relationship of 2:3 with that having 12 weights. Therefore, the interval between the fifth and the fourth [that by which the fifth is greater than the fourth], was confirmed to be a proportion of 9:8, etc. (Nicom. Enchir 6 = Iambl.

VPyth 115–8, transl. Dillon and Hershbell; also found in a Latin version in Macrob. Somn. 2,1,9ss. and Boeth. Inst. mus. 1,10)

In the following passage, Nicomachus has Pythagoras not remain content to pursue his experiments solely with the lyre and other instruments, including the monochord—"in all of them he found that the numerical interpretation was confirmed without variation"—but go on to develop the classical Greek tonal system with the tetrachord as the basis and the three scales, diatonic, chromatic, and enharmonic.[159] "In this way, then, he is said to have discovered music, organized it into a system, and presented it to his followers for all noblest purposes."[160] That the experiments don't work in the way described—sound and weight of a metal body are not directly proportional, and in order to get the desired harmonies with strings that are identical but have different degrees of tautness, figures given for the weights ought to be squared[161]—was recognized to some extent in antiquity[162] and repeatedly emphasized from the seventeenth century on. The version, however, that has Hippasus, an important Pythagorean of the fifth century B.C.E., as its protagonist is physically correct. He is said to have carried out the experiment with bronze disks of equal size, but differing thicknesses.[163]

If the series of the first four numbers, the so-called *tetraktýs*, became for the Pythagoreans a kind of secret key to the explanation of the world—in a famous oath, adepts praised their master for having entrusted them with the *tetraktýs*, "which contains in itself the source and root of the ever-flowing nature"[164]—this is surely partly explained by the fact that in this set of numbers the basic harmonies of music are contained (on this subject, see 82 below). According to the sources, Pythagoras not only found this numerical relationship in music but also considered it basic to the construction of the entire cosmos. For instance, in his abridged version of Pythagoras' philosophy Hippolytus writes that Pythagoras maintained that the cosmos sang and was musically composed, "and he was the first to put down the movement of the seven stars to rhythm and melody."[165] This formulation refers to another fascinating idea for which Pythagoras has been famous from antiquity through the Middle Ages and down to our own time: The harmony of the spheres, which was, as it were, grounded in physics by the Pythagoreans (on this subject, see 82–83 below). The master was, as is said, the only mortal able to hear this cosmic music:

He himself used to listen to the harmonious music of the universe, since he perceived the overall harmony of the spheres and of the stars that move within them, which we do not hear because our nature is limited. (Porph. VPyth. 30 = Nicom. FGrHist 1063 F 1)[166]

As for the nine Muses, Porphyry states, following Nicomachus, that Pythagoras considered them the sounds of the seven planets, the sphere of the fixed stars, and the so-called Counter-Earth; "and the mingling and concord and, as it were, connection of all of them, of which each as of an eternal and everlasting being is part and emanation, he called Mnemosyne" (the mother of the Muses).[167] The extremely beneficial effect this cosmic music had on him he sought to transmit as well as he could to his pupils by imitating it with instruments and his own voice.[168]

Pythagorean Way of Life

According to the sources, music played a prominent role in the everyday life of the Pythagoreans. Just as they used medicine for the purification (*kátharsis*) of the body, Aristoxenus tells us, in the same way they used music for the purification of the soul.[169] Quintilian, the Roman rhetorician (first century C.E.), writes:

> On awakening, it was the Pythagoreans' custom to arouse their souls with the sound of the lyre, so that they might be more alert for action, and before going to sleep they soothed their minds by means of this same music in order to calm them down, in case too turbulent thoughts might still inhabit them. (Inst. orat. 9,4,12)

According to Antonius Diogenes, Pythagoras used to put himself in the right mood in the morning by means of the lyre and song, by singing old paeans (ritual healing songs) of Thaletas of Sparta or passages from Homer and Hesiod, which he considered suitable for calming the soul.[170] Paeans are shortly afterward mentioned again in connection with Pythagoras' care for his disciples:

> While they were in good health he always conversed with them; if they were sick, he nursed them; if they were afflicted in mind, he solaced them . . . some by incantations and magic charms, others by music. He had prepared songs for the diseases of the body, by singing which he cured the sick. He had also some that caused forgetfulness of sorrow, mitigation of anger, and destruction of lust. (Antonius Diogenes, in Porph. VPyth. 33; transl. K. S. Guthrie)[171]

Thus music is conceived as psycho-physical therapy, by means of which Pythagoras is also said to have once prevented a group of drunken youths from breaking down the door of a virtuous young lady: He had a solemn song consisting of long syllables sung (spondee), and the youths' "raging willfulness" abated.[172]

Concerning the Pythagorean way of life, the novelist Antonius Diogenes knew to report many other fine anecdotes. In addition to music and poetry, Pythagoras also made therapeutic use of certain dances, which in his opinion promoted the mobility and health of the body. Also on the daily program were walks, which Pythagoras generally took neither alone nor in large groups, but rather "with one or two other persons in shrines or groves, seeking out the most peaceful and most beautiful places."[173] Iamblichus goes into still more detail in describing this eurhythmic lifestyle. He adds to the picture some details that seem almost monastic (this is not entirely surprising, insofar as Iamblichus' *On the Pythagorean Life* can also be read as a pagan alternative to flourishing monasticism and the Christian way of life in general). In his account, Pythagoreans took

> morning walks alone and in such places where there was suitable calmness and stillness, and where there were temples and sacred groves and anything else that gladdened the heart. For they thought it necessary not to meet anyone until they set their own soul in order and were composed in their intellect; and such quietness is agreeable to the composure of the intellect. For to be shoved together in crowds immediately on arising they considered disturbing. Thus all Pythagoreans always selected places most becoming the sacred. And after the morning walk, they associated with one another, especially in temples; but if not, at least in similar places. They used this time for instruction and lessons, and for the improvement of their characters. (97) After such study, they turned to the care of their bodies. Most used oil-rubs and took part in footraces; a lesser number wrestled in gardens and groves: some engaged in long-jumping or in shadow boxing, taking care to choose exercises well-adapted to their bodily strength. (Iambl. VPyth. 96s., transl. Dillon and Hershbell)

In a way not unlike modern "wellness" programs, the *vita Pythagorica* was concerned with a healthy, balanced diet. For breakfast, Pythagoras prescribed, as part of his dietetics, honey and bread,[174] and for supper "bread made from millet or barley, cooked or raw vegetables, and on rare occasions meat from sacrificed animals, and even then not from every part of the animal."[175] This is a reference to old Pythagorean rules that do not absolutely prohibit eating meat, but only the consumption of certain parts of the animal, such as the heart. There is an elaborate recipe for power food that Pythagoras is said to have prepared before undertaking long stays in the innermost part of shrines (*ádyton*):

For the most part, when he was to penetrate the innermost parts of
the gods' temples and wanted to spend some time there, he used
foods that made [him] free from hunger and thirst; the "hunger-
free" one (*á-limos*) he made from poppy seed, sesame seed, and
squill, which were carefully washed until they were cleansed of the
sap that surrounded them, and also of asphodel stems and mallow
leaves, barley flour and chickpeas; all these [ingredients] he cut in
equal parts and moisted them with honey from Mt. Hymettus. The
"thirst-free" (*á-dipsos*) [food he made] of cucumber seeds and plump
raisins, whose seeds he removed, and also from coriander flowers and
likewise from mallow seeds, purslane, and grated cheese, the finest
wheat flour, and milk fat; all of this he mixed with honey from the
islands.
(35) He claimed that Heracles had learnt these [recipes] from
Demeter when he set out for waterless Libya. (Antonius Diogenes in
Porph. VPyth. 34s.)

These could be successfully marketed today in health-food stores or as en-
ergy bars for athletes; in this case, the remarks concluding the section on
dietetics should not be lacking:

For that reason his body always maintained the same form, as if on a
straight line; he was not sometimes well, sometimes ill, and also not
sometimes fattened and sometimes losing weight and getting thin-
ner. (loc. cit.)

Originally, this was probably conceived as a magical diet. In ancient literature, it is also encountered in connection with the legendary Cretan purification priest Epimenides, in whose company Pythagoras is also
supposed to have descended into the cave on Mt. Ida in Crete at that
time.[176] For Epimenides, the "hunger-free" food consists solely of asphodel and mallow[177]—both plants that were put on graves and deposited in
the temple of Apollo on Delos as sacrificial offerings in memory of the first
food eaten by the human race[178] (according to Aelian, Pythagoras described mallow as the "most sacred plant";[179] its cultivation is recommended in a Pythagorean "oral saying," but its consumption is
forbidden).[180] Epimenides, who is said to have spent fifty-seven years
asleep in a grotto, is supposed to have got the magical food from nymphs,
and kept it in an ox's hoof.[181] The magic-ritual context is still dimly discernible in Antonius Diogenes' story about Pythagoras, at least at the beginning. In another account the marvel of complete abstinence takes the

place of the magical food: "He used to stay in sacred precincts, and was never seen drinking or eating."[182]

Pythagorean daily life also included moments of self-reflection in the morning and in the evening:

> Most of all, he recommended two moments for thoughtful reflection: when one goes to sleep and when one wakes up. For in each of these two moments it is fitting to think about what has already been done and what is yet to happen, each person accounting to himself for what has happened, but taking precautions for the future. Thus before sleeping everyone should sing himself these verses:
>
> Also, do not receive sleep on your tender eyes,
> before you have thrice gone through each of the day's deeds:
> Where have I failed myself? What have I done? What duty have I
>   not fulfilled?
>
> But before getting up, [sing] these [verses]:
>
> When you awaken from sleep, the honey to the heart,
> first watch very carefully, what deeds you want to perform this day.

(Porph. VPyth. 40)

The first three hexameters are also found in the Pythagorean "Golden Verses" (40–42)—a collection of ethical maxims that contains much that is worth thinking about. When they took the present form is still debated by specialists; the recently suggested dating to the second half of the fourth century B.C.E.[183] is probably too early. Individual sections of this work, which was to become particularly popular under the Empire, and not least the verses quoted by Porphyry, may nonetheless be quite old. Seneca testifies to the practice of morning and evening self-examination as being also the practice of a Roman philosopher of the Augustan age, Sextius, who was influenced by neo-Pythagoreanism.[184] Even the Christian examination of conscience may have been suggested by this Pythagorean exercise.

Among the Pythagoreans, meditation was probably not aimed solely at ethical perfection, but also served as a form of mental training for the faculty of memory (*mnéme*). In his section on the importance of memory, among other things, Iamblichus reports that no Pythagorean got out of bed before he had recalled the events of the preceding day, trying to repeat mentally the first thing he said or did or ordered his servants, and then the second thing, and then the third, and so on. And again whom he met first when he went out of the house, and whom second, and what words

were first uttered, and which words next, and so on. But if he had enough
time, he would then have tried to repeat in the same way what happened
the day before yesterday—all this in order to exercise the memory, for
nothing was for the Pythagoreans more important for knowledge, experience, and insight than the ability to remember.[185] In addition, memory
may also have had an "eschatological" importance: The soul needed this
spiritual power in the Underworld to remember Pythagoras' advices
"regarding the move from here" and to choose a good life when being
reincarnated.

Piety, Worship, and Ritual

In Iamblichus we find the observations just paraphrased in the chapter on
Pythagorean "wisdom" (*sophía*). His essay "On the Pythagorean Life,"
which is not particularly well organized as a whole or in its details, nonetheless follows in its second half (134–240) a general structure based on the
cardinal virtues, with piety coming first, followed by wisdom, justice, temperance, and courage, as well as friendship.[186] The effort to stylize the
Pythagorean lifestyle as the quintessence of a virtuous existence is obvious.
The chapter on piety begins with a short summary of the various miracles.
Then, in a lapidary formulation, Iamblichus emphasizes the eminent importance in the life of the Pythagoreans of veneration for the gods:

> All such injunctions which define what is to be done or what is not to
> be done are directed at concordance with the divine, and this is a first
> principle, and their whole way of life is arranged for following the
> deity. (Iambl. VPyth. 137; transl. Dillon and Hershbell)[187]

In the following passage, Iamblichus refers to the difficulty of knowing
which actions please the god. He names three possible ways of achieving
this knowledge: (1) from one who has heard a god; (2) directly from a god,
and (3) by means of "divine art." The latter refers to the art of divination
(*mantikê*), which the Pythagoreans—according to Iamblichus, who himself
considered theurgy an indispensable presupposition for the unification of
the soul with the divine, and also according to other witnesses—practiced
intensively.[188] It alone offers the possibility of translating the gods'
thoughts.[189] However, the main source regarding the Pythagoreans' rules
of conduct remains, of course, the master himself, whose miracles legitimate him, in their view, as a teacher:

> On the assumption that these things [the miracles] are agreed upon,
> and that it is impossible that they happened to one who was a human

being, the Pythagoreans now think it clear that it is necessary to accept the things said by him as issuing from a higher power, and not from a mortal. That is also the meaning of the following riddle, which they recite:

"Two-footed is a human being, and a bird, and a third thing as
well,"
for the third thing is Pythagoras. (Iambl. VPyth. 143s.; transl. Dillon and Hershbell)

Other sources, too, show that Pythagoras' followers attributed a superhuman status to him. But of what kind were the numerous counsels regarding conduct that the Pythagoreans were obliged to observe? In the main, they were rules regarding cult and ritual. The following are some of the commands and prohibitions enumerated by Iamblichus in his *Vita Pythagorica*:

—Refrain from blood sacrifices in prophecy (147)
—Forego animal skins as clothing (149)
—Make libations for the gods during a meal (149, cf. 155s)
—Make sacrifices of incense, millet, baked goods, honeycomb, myrrh, and other fragrant stuffs for burning, but no living beings (150)
—It is forbidden to swear oaths in the names of the gods (150; cf. 155)
—Wear white, clean garments when going into the shrine (153)
—When blood is involuntarily shed in the shrine, it must be cleaned up with gold or with sea water (153)
—It is forbidden to give birth in the shrine [with Platonizing justification: it is not pious for the divine aspect of the soul to be bound up with the body in the shrine] (153)
—It is forbidden to cut one's hair or nails during a festival (154)
—Even a louse may not be killed in the shrine (154)
—The gods are to be worshipped with cedar, laurel, cypress, oak, and myrtle; it is forbidden to use these woods in purifying the body (154)
—It is forbidden to roast the boiled (154)
—It is forbidden to burn the dead (154)
—One should pay the dead one's last respects in white robes, coffins made of cypress wood are not to be used (155)[190]
—It is better to suffer an injustice than to kill a man (155; cf. 179)
—It is forbidden to offer up libations with closed eyes (156)
—When it thunders, touch the earth (156)
—One should enter shrines on the right side and leave them on the left (156)

A very peculiar hodgepodge of ritual instructions, which in addition is poorly structured in Iamblichus. The prohibitions at least are for the major part taken from mystery rituals, according to Iamblichus (138). Moreover, the enumeration is in no way exhaustive, as Iamblichus remarks at the end. Other sources, some of them old ones, offer many further rules, from which subsequent interpretations quite often derive ethical demands. We shall examine this interesting subject in greater detail at 63–70 below.

Vegetarianism, the Prohibition of Beans, and the Doctrine of the Soul

Today, Pythagoras is famous above all for two prohibitions: (1) The refraining from blood sacrifices and thus also from eating meat, and (2) the abstention from beans. In both cases, however, the sources contradict each other, and are in some respects even diametrically opposed. Vegetarianism does at first sight make sense against the background of the doctrine of reincarnation documented for Pythagoras from earliest times: If the human soul can also enter into "other kinds of living beings" in the cycle of reincarnations, this logically implies not only "the relatedness of all ensouled creatures,"[191] but also the view that slaughtering any living creature is equivalent to murder. The Roman poet Ovid (43 b.c.e.–17 c.e.) put this in a particularly striking way in the last book of his *Metamorphoses,* where he has Pythagoras, whom he provides with some Empedoclean characteristics, say:

> "Refrain, mortals, from defiling your bodies with unspeakable feasts!
> (. . .)
> Alas, what a great crime it is for guts to be buried in guts
> and for a greedy body to grow fat by stuffing itself with a body
> and for a breathing one to live by the death of another breathing
>   one."
>
> (Ovid Met. 15,75s. and 88–90; transl. Hill)

And in the passage following the main part of his discourse, in which Pythagoras, as Ovid's alter ego, provides, as it were, the philosophical underpinning for the theme of the "Metamorphoses" and points out the permanent transformation of all things as a cosmic principle, he once again refers to the fact that also human beings are continuously transformed in the ongoing process of reincarnation and, in words that remind us of Empedocles,[192] repeats the urgent warning not to kill any creature with a soul:

> "Let us allow bodies, which could have held the spirits
> of our parents or of our brothers, or of those joined to us by some

bond, or of humans at least, to be safe and respected,
and let us not heap up Thyestean banquets in our guts!"

(Ovid Met. 15,459–462; transl. Hill)

Only destructive animals may be killed (but not eaten).[193] Similarly, we
find in Porphyry:

> But he also gave the following advice: Do not harm, neither destroy
> nor hurt, cultivated and fruit-bearing plants or living creatures that
> by their very nature do not harm humankind! (VPyth. 39)

The brilliant mathematician Eudoxus of Cnidos (c. 390–c. 340 B.C.E.) exaggerates still further Pythagoras' desire for ritual purity and his rejection
of bloodshed and those who committed it, to the point of claiming that
Pythagoras not only abstained from eating animate beings, but also avoided
any contact with cooks and hunters.[194] In opposition to this, other witnesses, of almost equal antiquity and no less authority (for instance, Aristotle), attribute to Pythagoras and his followers simply a prohibition on eating
certain parts of animals, such as the womb and the heart, as well as many
kinds of fish. We shall later ask how these contradictions may be explained.

The tradition is also far from being unanimous regarding the prohibition
of beans. It is true that here the testimonies in favor of a rigorous observance
of the taboo in Pythagoreanism are clearly preponderant—as we have seen,
the prohibition is also the subject of various stories about the founder of this
way of life. But alongside this there is also the dissident opinion of Aristoxenus, according to whom Pythagoras preferred beans to any other legumi-
nous plant, and in fact on medicinal grounds, because he prized their
laxative effect.[195] Aristoxenus also firmly explains that Pythagoras did not abstain from eating ensouled creatures;[196] he is said to have forbidden killing
only two animals: the ox for plowing and the ram.[197] The (missing) ground
for this is in the first case easy to supply: As a "collaborator" of humans, the
plow ox deserves protection (accordingly, Ovid's Pythagoras particularly emphasizes the injustice committed in killing field oxen).[198] Aristoxenus, as an
"enlightened" Pythagorean—he is supposed to have been a pupil of the
Pythagorean Xenophilus[199]—obviously tends to rationalize Pythagoras'
rules of conduct and to cleanse them of magic-ritualistic components.

Justice and Other Virtues

After piety and wisdom, Iamblichus discusses justice, temperance, and
courage, before at the end of his catalog of Pythagorean virtues considering the status of friendship in the Pythagorean community. His idealizing

descriptions cannot be discussed in a comprehensive way here. I limit myself to a few points relating to justice and the fanciful stories with which the individual virtues are illustrated. According to Iamblichus, the origin of justice is the feeling of a community and equality of everybody, and further to call the same thing both "mine" and "belonging to another."[200] Pythagoras is said to have laid the foundations for such a view with the establishment of the community of property, and through further ideological and institutional measures he created the ideal framework conditions for the realization of this virtue. He prevented people from committing injustices not solely by connecting the laws with the divine, but also by the doctrine of the "judgment of the soul."[201] After a section on justice in the realm of interpersonal relations, Iamblichus recounts the following anecdote as an example of the Pythagoreans' absolute mutual reliability: Once Lysis, who according to Aristoxenus had escaped along with Archippus the arson attacks on the Pythagoreans,[202] on emerging from a shrine of Hera after prayer, encountered at the door of the temple a fellow Pythagorean, Euryphamus of Syracuse. The latter told him to wait until he had prayed and come out again. Lysis sat down on a stone bench.

> As Euryphamus worshipped, he became absorbed in thought and deep reflection, and having quite forgotten the agreement, he left by another gate. But Lysis, without moving, stayed the rest of the day, the following night, and the greater part of the next day. And perhaps he would have been there longer if Euryphamus had not been in the "common auditorium" [*homakoeîon*] the next day, and remembered Lysis, when hearing that he was missed by his fellow disciples. He then went back and found him still waiting according to the agreement, and led him away, stating the cause of his forgetfulness and adding "one of the gods implanted this forgetfulness in me to be a means of testing your steadfastness about an agreement." (Iambl. VPyth. 185; transl. after Dillon and Hershbell)

This episode could as well be used as an illustration of the Pythagorean cultivation of friendship. Drawing on a creepy story that goes back to Neanthes, Iamblichus next illustrates both the Pythagoreans' temperance and courage.[203] Since the dictator of Syracuse, Dionysius (II?), has not succeeded, despite assiduous efforts, in making friends with one of the Pythagoreans—they rejected his advances on political grounds—he resorts, like a typical tyrant, to military power, telling a certain Eurymenes and his troops to lie in ambush between Tarentum and Metapontum, where in this tale the Pythagoreans are moving for the season ("for they adapted themselves to changes of the seasons, and selected suitable places for such"),[204] and to capture them alive. Since they are vastly outnumbered, the Pythagoreans decide to flee—for they know (as it is put in an allusion to Plato's definition of this virtue) that courage is the knowledge of when one should flee and when one should stand fast. As they are fleeing, however, they come upon a bean field in full bloom. In order not to violate the prohibition on touching beans, they stop where they are, taking up stones and sticks and other objects that happen to be available for their defense, but they are nonetheless all killed by the palace guard. Thereupon Eurymenes and his men find themselves in a difficult situation, since they had been ordered to take the Pythagoreans alive. On the way back, they run into Myllias from Croton and his wife Timycha, originating from Sparta, who had lagged behind the rest of the group because she was ten months pregnant. They take them prisoner and, relieved, bring them before the tyrant. Dionysius is very saddened by what has happened, and offers them, as a compensation, a share in his rule. But they refuse. When Dionysius asks them at least to grant him a single wish and tell him why their companions preferred to die rather than tread upon the bean field, the story moves toward its spine-chilling conclusion. Myllias brusquely replies: "Those people accepted death rather than tread on beans, but I would rather tread on beans than betray to you the reason why." Neanthes' Dionysius thereupon resumes his tyrant's face, has Myllias taken away, and tries to extract the secret from his wife by torture. But Timycha bites off her own tongue and spits it at the tyrant, in order to prevent herself from revealing any of the group's secrets. This bloody story thereby not only makes it clear how "difficult it was to get Pythagoreans to form friendships with outsiders" (Iamblichus), but also lets us perceive the importance of secrecy, which Iamblichus regards, along with maintaining complete silence, as an exercise in temperance: "For mastery of the tongue is the most difficult of all instances of self-temperance."[205]

Cultivation of Friendship

Numerous sources indicate that the Pythagoreans cultivated unconditional friendship with their peers.

> But he loved his friends beyond all measure, and he was the first to formulate the view that among friends everything is held in common (*tà tôn fílon koinâ*) and that a friend is an *alter ego*. (Antonius Diogenes in Porph. VPyth. 33)

The basis for this friendship seems on the one hand to be a strict selection that precedes admission to the group and on the other the economic equalization of all members of the group through community of property. For "friendship [is] equality," says a Greek proverb that was, according to Iamblichus, coined by Pythagoras.[206] The Pythagoreans' legendary fidelity in friendship is also the object of a story whose plot, through Schiller's ballad "Die Bürgschaft" ("The Pledge"), has become part of the collective cultural memory, at least within the German-speaking world, although its Pythagorean provenance may no longer be widely known. For in Schiller's poem there is no hint that the heroes of the ballad belong to the Pythagorean secret society. The same is true for his immediate source, the Latin mythographer Hyginus (second century C.E.?), whom Schiller follows quite closely, especially in the first stanzas.[207] In the rest of the ancient tradition the two protagonists are expressly identified as Pythagoreans. Their names are not usually given, as in Hyginus, as Moerus and Selinuntius, but rather as Phintias and Damon. The main source is Aristoxenus, who himself heard the story, as he says, personally from Dionysius II, who was then living in exile in Corinth.[208]

In Aristoxenus' frame story the cause of the pledge is played down rather circumstantially, so that one is tempted to agree with Wehrli[209] that here we have another deliberately apologetic glossing over on the part of this Pythagorean author.[210] Whereas in Diodorus the Pythagorean Phintias is involved in a genuine conspiracy against Dionysius,[211] Aristoxenus refers to people belonging to the tyrant's entourage, who in his presence had spoken very disparagingly of the Pythagoreans, described them as braggarts, and expressed the opinion that their proud behavior, hypocritical fidelity (to their friends), and detachment would probably come to an end if they were given a good scare. A few others contradicted them, and a dispute resulted. This was the occasion of plotting the following "dramatic action" against Phintias and his friends:

> Dionysius said that he summoned Phintias and told him, in the presence of one of his accusers, that he, Phintias, was obviously involved in a plot against him [Dionysius]. This was confirmed by those present, and [Dionysius] himself showed very plausible displeasure. Phintias was astonished at the speech. And when Dionysius himself said firmly that these things had been investigated carefully, and that he must die, Phintias replied that, if this was his decision, he wanted from him at least the rest of the day to settle both his own affairs and those of Damon. For these men lived together and shared all things, but Phintias, being older, had taken on himself the main management of the household. He requested, then, to be released for this business, and appointed Damon as security. (Aristox. fr. 31 Wehrli = Iambl. VPyth. 235s., transl. Dillon and Hershbell)

In what follows Aristoxenus narrates the story in considerable detail, inserting still another dialogue between the astonished Dionysius and Phintias, who then has Damon brought. The latter, when he has been informed, declares himself ready to serve as a pledge: He will remain at the palace until Phintias has returned. In a further twist, Aristoxenus describes once again the reaction of his informant (that is, Dionysius himself, who is involved in the event narrated and thus "homodiegetic" in Gérard Genette's terminology) and his entourage: He, Dionysius, was immediately shaken by this, but those who had from the outset staged the test mocked Damon, saying that he would be left in the lurch; he would be offered as a deer instead (of Iphigeneia):

> But then, just at sunset, when Phintias came to die, all were astonished and subdued. Dionysius then said that he embraced and kissed the men, and asked to be received as a third into their friendship, but they, although he persisted, were not at all ready to agree to such a proposal. (Aristox. fr. 31 Wehrli = Iambl. VPyth. 236, transl. Dillon and Hershbell)

The anecdote about Myllias and Timycha mentioned above could easily be added here for the sequence of events (*histoire*). Therefore it may very well be that our episode, conceived as a refutation of the proverbial piece of popular wisdom "pledge leads to damages," was originally intended to clarify not only the Pythagoreans' unconditional fidelity in friendship, but also their opposition to tyranny. Aristoxenus does judge the Pythagoreans' political behavior in just this way. But he presumably considered violence against tyrants incompatible with the Pythagorean ideal, as he understood it, and therefore replaced the conspiracy with a test of the Pythagoreans' convictions instigated by court officials.[212] Thus we see once again how each author to some extent writes his own history, blithely adapting the tradition to his own image of Pythagoras.

2. IN SEARCH OF THE HISTORICAL PYTHAGORAS

In the preceding chapter we presented the simultaneously stimulating and confusing multiplicity of ancient reports regarding Pythagoras and his school. Turning now to the historical roots of this figure, we are immediately confronted by a fundamental question: Can we really know anything at all about Pythagoras himself, who probably lived from about 570 B.C.E. to around 480 B.C.E. (the precise dates of his life are uncertain)?[1] Isn't direct access to him entirely foreclosed—and all the more so because like Buddha, Socrates, and Jesus, the sage of Samos is supposed deliberately not to have written anything, so that basically there ought to be no original fragments of his work either? It was this reflection that led Diels and Kranz, for instance, in their edition of the fragments of the pre-Socratics (although published for the first time more than a century ago, as a whole this edition has yet to be superseded) to forgo in the case of Pythagoras, contrary to their usual practice, the sections B (i.e., genuine fragments, followed by dubious and forged ones) and C (i.e., imitations and echoes). Their decision continues to shape our picture of Pythagoras and brands him as a hard-to-grasp exceptional figure among the pre-Socratics of the sixth and early fifth centuries B.C.E.

However, even in the case of a purely oral tradition it would not be impossible that *ipsissima verba* have come down to us. The numerous "oral sayings" (*akoúsmata*), which transmit for instance detailed rules regarding the Pythagoreans' conduct, and whose authenticity is today widely accepted, may stand as an example. Moreover, a thorough examination of the relevant texts shows that the explicit claim that Pythagoras left no written documents is not to be found in antiquity before neo-Pythagoreanism, and probably resulted from an attempt to come to terms with pseudo-Pythagorean writings (which became increasingly numerous since the Hellenistic age). By contrast, the oldest reports seem to take more or less for granted the existence of writings by Pythagoras.[2] There may be several reasons for the fact that hardly any trace of these writings has been preserved. First, in analogy to mystery cults, the Pythagoreans observed the rule of secrecy, so that if there were any writings, they were certainly not in circulation outside the school. Second, the master's teachings were undoubtedly further elaborated by his followers. Over time, their new versions may have partly displaced Pythagoras' explanation of the world, which against the background of important advances in knowledge must have seemed increasingly old-fashioned and obsolete. Finally, it is possible that the disastrous arson attacks on the Pythagoreans mentioned earlier may have led to a decisive break in the tradition.

Be that as it may, we are now faced with the urgent task of recuperating so far as possible the original elements among the sometimes colorful tales that pursue their own narrative strategies and proceed from different periods and sociocultural contexts. This is a difficult undertaking, no doubt. There is a great danger that in setting aside rewritings old variants may also be erased. The delicate issue of the distinction between Pythagorean and Platonic, which is a major problem, requires particular caution. In his history of philosophy, Guthrie aptly described the difficulties involved:

> In general the separation of early Pythagoreanism from the teaching of Plato is one of the historian's most difficult tasks, to which he can scarcely avoid bringing a subjective bias of his own. If later Pythagoreanism was coloured by Platonic influences, it is equally undeniable that Plato himself was deeply affected by earlier Pythagorean beliefs; but in deciding the extent to which each has influenced the other, most people have found it impossible to avoid being guided by the extent of their admiration for Plato and consequent unwillingness to minimize his originality. (Guthrie 1962, 170)

In order to confront the difficulties, it seems best first to historically contextualize Pythagoras and to outline very briefly the general cultural and intellectual environment in which he lived, first on Samos and later in southern Italy. Second, we must inquire into the oldest direct testimonies to see what picture of his personality and teaching they sketch. From this we may be able to derive criteria that will allow us to filter some authentic evidence out of later reports. For dealing with the Pythagorean tradition is fundamentally no different than dealing with manuscripts: Later witnesses are not necessarily worse (*recentiores non deteriores*), and even statements made by informants during the Empire that are heavily colored by Platonism may still contain traces of genuine Pythagorean thought.

THE CULTURAL-HISTORICAL AND INTELLECTUAL ENVIRONMENT

Pythagoras was born into an intellectually exciting time. The sixth century B.C.E. is characterized by important and indeed occasionally sensational advances in the most diverse areas. It can be said without exaggeration that this is the period which in natural philosophy, literature (the earliest writings in prose), art, and architecture, as well as in medicine and technology, laid the foundations for the flowering of Greek culture in the age of Pericles and beyond. The focal point of these developments was less the Greek homeland than Ionia in Asia Minor, of which Pythagoras' native island of Samos was also a part. Between this region and the up and coming colonies in southern Italy and Sicily there was brisk interchange.

Milesian Investigation of the World:
Anaximander, Anaximenes, Hecataeus

Among the most astonishing events was certainly the development of Ionian natural philosophy, which is associated with the name of a quite wealthy coastal city that flourished in the seventh and sixth centuries B.C.E. and was relatively easy to reach from Samos: Miletus. From Miletus came the legendary engineer, geometer, and astronomer Thales, who was—for Aristotle—also the "first philosopher." Thales was said, for example, to have predicted an eclipse of the sun (28 May 585 B.C.E.) and given a naturalistic explanation for earthquakes. Other notable Milesians include Anaximander, Anaximenes, and Hecataeus. With ANAXIMANDER (early sixth century B.C.E.), who is named along with Thales as Pythagoras' teacher[3] and who with Pherecydes of Syros shares the honor of having written the first book in prose, tradition associates the first production of a map and a celestial globe, among other things. He is also supposed to have "invented"—inspired by the Babylonians?[4]—the "pointer" (*gnómon*) on the sundial and discovered important astronomical points of reference. His explanation of the world is not without interest for Pythagorean cosmology: the "construction material" (Aristotle's matter) is a not further specified "unlimited" (*ápeiron*) that comprises the world, without being identified with one of its parts. (Later on, in ANAXIMENES, this "unlimited" will be qualitatively defined as air, which surrounds the world and at the same time constitutes a part of it. Anaximenes is supposed to have flourished between 546 and 525 B.C.E. and can therefore be considered more or less a contemporary of Pythagoras: see also the two fictitious letters of Anaximenes to Pythagoras in Diogenes Laertius.[5]) Turning back to Anaximander, opposites are fundamental for Anaximander just as they are for Pythagorean and pre-Socratic thinking in general: For him, the coming-into-being of the world begins with the separation of what produces hot and cold (cf. the beginning of the Pythagorean cosmogony with its joining together of the One, which unites within itself the opposites "even" and "odd"). According to Eudemus of Rhodes (born before 350 B.C.E.), Anaximander also was the first to determine "the size and distances" of the planets, while the Pythagoreans, he says, were the first to (correctly) establish their arrangement.[6]

Herodotus's predecessor Hecataeus, whose lifetime approximately coincides with that of Pythagoras (c. 560/550–c. 480 B.C.E.) and who traveled around a great deal (he spent a long time in Egypt, for instance) was also Milesian.[7] He was similarly said to have been a pupil of Anaximander's. In any case, he improved the latter's map of the world and wrote, more or less as a commentary on it, a *Description of the World* (*Perihégesis* or *Períhodos gês*) that included information about ethnography and cultural history as well. In another work in prose (*Genealogíai*, also called *Historíai* or *Heroología*), he dealt critically with the myths of heroes and demigods to which noble families traced their ancestry. These myths Hecataeus considered to a great extent "ridiculous"[8] in the form in which they were told by the Greeks, and he confidently sought, by rationalizing them, to uncover their hidden historical core.

Architecture, Arts, and Crafts

Thus the Ionian elite, at least, seems to have been exceptionally open-minded, curious, and urbane. That fits with the fact that at this period architectonic and technological masterpieces were realized on Samos that a century later still aroused Herodotus' unqualified admiration. These included a tunnel dug through the hill with the city wall in order to ensure the town's water supply, a huge jetty in the harbor, and "third, the largest temple we know of, whose first architect was Rhoikos, the son of Phileas, a native of the island."[9] Another architect of the temple was said to be THEODORUS—he, too, from Samos—who dealt with the giant temple of Hera with double peristyl also in a book for specialists.[10] This exceptionally many-faceted and innovative artist, who is supposed to have invented among other things a device for measuring angles, the water-level, and the lathe,[11] was a sculptor, technician, architect, and—like Pythagoras' father, according to part of the tradition—a gem cutter, all rolled into one. He made, for example, the famous ring of Polycrates, the huge silver *krater* that Croesus dedicated to Delphi, and—not to be forgotten because of its connection to Pythagoras, the "Hyperborean Apollo"—the cult image of Apollo Pythius on Samos.

The tunnel dug through the mountain ridge north of the city, which was constructed by the master builder EUPALINUS of Megara to guarantee a long-term water supply, is celebrated to this day as an "unsurpassed feat of engineering."[12] In order to shorten construction time, the bold decision was taken to tackle the tunnel, which measures 1,036 meters, from both sides at the same time. In the middle of the work, an increasing danger that the tunnel might collapse and an influx of water obviously required the plotting of a new line, which demanded significant abilities in designing and calculating on the part of those involved (the detour around the problematic zone was carried out, probably by using a planning model, in the form of a large isosceles triangle). From a practical point of view as well this engineering achievement is astonishing: Almost five thousand cubic meters of rock were hacked out of the mountain using hammers and chisels and carried to daylight, and a further three hundred cubic meters had to be brought in again to finish, with the greatest care, the walls of the tunnel. On the basis of archaeological finds, this structure is today thought to date from about 550 B.C.E., that is, still before the time when Polycrates seized power (c. 535 B.C.E.). Thus its construction falls in Pythagoras' later youth. It is hardly conceivable that he was not familiar with this bold engineering project, which was obviously designed on a drawing board, and which must have taken years to complete.[13]

Ionian Festival Culture

This kind of civilizatory achievement presupposes a high standard of living on the island of Samos in the sixth century B.C.E. The local epic poet Asius (sixth century B.C.E.?) offers an impressive picture of Samian display of splendor in cultic action:

> And they would go like that, when they had combed their locks
> to Hera's precinct, wrapped in fine garments,
> in snowy tunics reaching down to the ground [?];
> there were gold brooches on them, like crickets;
> their hair floated in the wind, bound in gold;
> round their arms there were ornate bracelets.

(Asius fr. 13 Bernabé; transl. West)

May the resemblances to the festive external appearance of Pythagoras be more than an accident? The description of the Ionians' assembly on Delos in the Homeric hymn to Apollo, which probably was performed shortly before Polycrates' violent death (522 B.C.E.), also captures wonderfully the atmosphere of Ionian festal communities:

But it is in Delos, Phoibos, that your heart most delights,
where the Ionians with trailing robes assemble
with their children and wives on your avenue,
and when they have seated the gathering they think of you
and entertain you with boxing, dancing, and singing.
A man might think they were the unaging immortals
if he came along then when the Ionians are all together:
he would take in the beauty of the whole scene, and be delighted
at the spectacle of the men and the fair-girt women,
the swift ships and the people's piles of belonging.

(Hom. h. Apoll. 146–155; transl. West)

Pythagoras was familiar with this thriving festival culture, no doubt, and he may have observed the pageantry not uncritically (cf. the demand mentioned at 36 above that luxurious getups be avoided when making sacrifices; he concurs in this point with his critic Xenophanes).[14]

Cultural Exchange between Asia Minor and Magna Graecia

We are rather well informed about Polycrates' cultural policy. Along with the Athenian tyrant Pisistratus, he was one of the first to collect books and set up a library.[15] He also brought in, for example, ANACREON of Teos, the composer of sympotic songs and erotic poetry who later entered the canon of the nine lyric poets, and appointed him as his son's tutor. We have already mentioned the works the artist Theodorus did for Polycrates. If the modern dating of Eupalinus' tunnel in the middle of the sixth century B.C.E. is correct, Samos was already a prosperous and culturally significant island before Polycrates' reign. This fits with the fact that according to tradition, a famous poet who hailed from southern Italy (as did the somewhat older choral lyric poet, Stesichorus), IBYCUS of Rhegium (modern day Reggio di Calabria), had already come to Samos during the reign of Polycrates' father.

Ibycus is only one example of the many-sided cultural contacts between Magna Graecia[16] and Ionic Asia Minor at this time, the exchange flowing in both directions. The poet, theologian, and natural philosopher Xenophanes (c. 580–c. 475 B.C.E.), who is famous for his moral criticism of Homer, and to whom we owe the earliest extant report regarding Pythagoras, came from the city of Colophon, some forty kilometers northeast of Samos. In connection with a tyrant's dissolution of the aristocracy there, he was exiled around 555 and lived for a while in Ionia before moving around 540, along with the inhabitants of the harbor city Phocaea in Asia

Minor, which had been conquered by the Persians, to Elea (today Castellamare di Veglia), performing his poems in southern Italy and Sicily as an itinerant rhapsode. Whereas Xenophanes—like Pythagoras, who was about the same age—moved from Ionia to southern Italy, the voyage of the physician DEMOCEDES led him from his home town of Croton by way of Aegina and Athens to Samos, where he entered the service of Polycrates, who is said to have paid him the considerable amount of two talents. Whether Pythagoras' and Democedes' paths crossed, we do not know. In any case, Apollonius' account of the anti-Pythagorean rebellions mentions a Democedes who was a follower of Pythagoras.[17] This is compatible with the fact that, according to Herodotus, Democedes, having given after Polycrates' death extremely impressive proofs of his medical skill at the Persian court, over the time riskily got back to Croton, where he married the daughter of the wrestler Milon,[18] whom the sources associate with Pythagoras on various occasions (see 10 above).

Pythagoras' path from Samos to Croton was thus to some extent traced out. According to at least part of the tradition, at about the time when Pythagoras emigrated (c. 530 B.C.E.), Samian compatriots founded the coastal city of Dicaearchia (today Pozzuoli) not far from Naples.[19]

THE OLDEST TESTIMONIES

Xenophanes of Colophon

In view of their importance for approaching the historical Pythagoras, the relatively scanty oldest reports shall be presented in this chapter individually, and sifted with particular care. I will limit myself to the (pre-Platonic) witnesses of the sixth and fifth centuries B.C.E. The direct tradition regarding Pythagoras begins with a very derisive anecdote told by his contemporary Xenophanes of Colophon, who also emigrated, as we have seen, to Italy:

> That he [Pythagoras] was sometimes this person, sometimes that, Xenophanes confirms in the elegy that begins:

> Now I turn to another tale and I shall show the way.

> But what he says about him [Pythagoras] goes like this:

> And once, when he passed by as a puppy was being beaten, they say, he pitied it and said these words:

"Stop, don't beat it, for truly it is the soul of a friend:
I recognized it when I heard it utter sounds."

(Diog. Laert 8,36, within it Xenophanes 21 B 7 D.-K.)

In Diogenes Laertius, the quotation from Xenophanes is surrounded by other mocking verses: In the preceding section Timon of Phlius (c. 320–230 B.C.E.), a skeptical philosopher who was also the author (as a literary successor of Xenophanes) of invective verse, ridicules Pythagoras as a charlatan and con man fond of overblown speech,[20] and in the passage following the quotation from Xenophanes, an Athenian comic poet of the fourth century B.C.E., Cratinus the younger, jokes about the Pythagoreans' habit of using all the rules of rhetorical art to confuse those interested in their doctrines.[21] Xenophanes himself is well known to have poured scorn on other Greek poets and thinkers as well: In sarcastic verses, he attacked Homer's and Hesiod's theology as wholly immoral;[22] he seems to have spoken critically of Thales' prediction of a solar eclipse,[23] indirectly opposed Anaximander's speculations in natural philosophy,[24] attacked Epimenides of Crete,[25] and criticized divination in general.[26] A figure like Pythagoras, whose appearance reflected religious pretensions, must have particularly provoked Xenophanes, since he considered it certain not only that human beings had no precise knowledge regarding the gods, but also that "(sham) opinion" (*dókos*) is stuck to everything.[27]

A small discrepancy between Diogenes Laertius' introduction and the content of the verses quoted is striking. On the basis of the introduction, one would expect a series of reincarnations, such as Porphyry, for example, records ("the first time, I was Euphorbus, the second, Aethalides, the third, Hermotimus, the fourth, Pyrrhus, but now I am Pythagoras").[28] But the mocking verses merely shed light on the general conviction that the human soul (*psyché*) can also be reborn in animals. Did Diogenes Laertius skip a few verses? In any case, the beginning of the quotation—"And once he . . ."—clearly suggests that the poet-philosopher Xenophanes wrote more than the four quoted verses against Pythagoras: At the very least, the name of the person being mocked must already have been given, and other episodes—"another time"—could hardly have been lacking (was the firm rejection of divination also related to Pythagoras?). Furthermore, the insertion "they say" (*phasín*) is important: Xenophanes was not himself present at this little scene, he is simply reporting rumors. Did he have any direct acquaintance with Pythagoras at all?

Heraclitus of Ephesus

In any event, Pythagoras, whether during his own lifetime (until about 480 B.C.E.?) or afterward—Xenophanes' verses perhaps sound more like a posthumous comment—was a subject of conversation in southern Italy. And not only there: In Asia Minor as well his somewhat younger "colleague" Heraclitus of Ephesus (fl. around 503–500 B.C.E.) also referred to Pythagoras in a similar tone:

> Pythagoras, the son of Mnesarchus, practiced inquiry (*historíe*) most of all men; he made a selection of these writings and created his own "wisdom" (*sophíe*)—much learning, artful knavery. (Heraclit. 22 B 129 D.-K.).

A very interesting and informative document. The formal naming of the father, Mnesarchus, suggests that in this passage Heraclitus is speaking of Pythagoras for the first time. His discussion of Pythagoras probably comes in connection with the general dismantling of acknowledged intellectual authorities such as Homer, Hesiod, and others. Pythagoras probably served Heraclitus as an outstanding example of how even "the most respected person knows and harbors only opinions."[29] True, he grants that Mnesarchus' son has carried out extraordinarily intensive research: "Most of all men," he has practiced "inquiry" (*historíe*), that is, the desire to see, hear, and learn from others—the kind of curiosity that characterized the Ionian natural philosophers as well as the first "historians," who acquired their knowledge by traveling and questioning local informants. But in Heraclitus, what may at first seem like praise suddenly turns into mordant criticism: Pythagoras' investigations remained, according to Heraclitus, limited to "writings." From the latter he made a selection and declared the result to be his own "wisdom"—a claim Heraclitus reveals to be merely "much learning" and "artful knavery." Almost every one of these words requires a brief explication.

When Heraclitus speaks of "these writings," he is apparently referring to works mentioned previously. Since the context has been lost, we inevitably have trouble with this piece of source-critical information. Babylonian treatises on mathematics have been mentioned. This fits well with our current image of Pythagoras, but would seem rather surprising in Heraclitus and does not by itself explain the accusation that he had engaged in "artful knavery." In the extant fragments, Heraclitus himself mentions literary authorities such as Homer and Archilochus, who in his opinion ought to be thrown out of the contest and beaten,[30] and also Hesiod, Xenophanes, and Hecataeus, whom Heraclitus accuses, as he does Pythagoras, of "much learning" without having any deeper insight:

> Much learning does not teach understanding, otherwise it would have taught Hesiod and Pythagoras, and also Xenophanes and Hecataeus. (Heraclit. 22 B 40 D.-K.).

It seems rather unlikely that individual works of Pythagoras' two contemporaries Xenophanes and Hecataeus were already in circulation when Pythagoras outlined his doctrine. On the other hand, Hesiod is certainly a possible source, especially if one thinks of the consolatory function the epic poet (active around 700 B.C.E.) attributed to the Muses' art in cases of psychological sorrow[31] (on Pythagoras and Hesiod, see 30 above). How little esteem Heraclitus had for Hesiod is shown by another saying whose rhetorical structure is similar to the one of B 129 D.-K.: An introduction, which can at first be read as positive—"Hesiod is the teacher of most; about him they know that he knows most"—is followed by the annihilating addition, "He, who didn't recognize day and night! For they are one" (alluding to Hes. Theog. 123–125, where "black night" is named as the genealogical mother of day, and especially 748–757, where Hesiod emphasizes the difference between the two, which greet each other only at the "bronze threshold" and are never at home together).[32] In another fragment, Homer, too, who was "wiser than all the Greeks," is unmasked as an ignorant man who allowed himself to be deceived by the riddling speech of boys killing lice ("What we have seen and grasped, we leave behind; but what we have neither seen nor grasped, we carry with us": Heraclit. 22 B 56 D.-K.).[33] To their own disadvantage, Heraclitus says elsewhere, people believe in "folk singers" whose teaching, however, simply reflects the general ignorance.[34] If Pythagoras draws on low-quality sources of this kind, his compilation in Heraclitus' view surely condemns itself.

Although it is not mentioned in the extant fragments of Heraclitus, modern researchers see Orphic poetry as a further possible source of inspiration for Pythagoras. Evidence for this includes not only the relationships between Orphism and Pythagoras that have been established from the fifth century B.C.E. onward but also numerous similarities between the rules of the Pythagorean way of life and ritual taboos of the Orphic-Bacchic mystery cults. It seems entirely conceivable that Pythagoras, inspired by Orphic "sacred discourses" (*hieroì lógoi*) (examined later in this chapter) wrote hexameter verses of this kind for his secret community, and it is quite possible that one or another of the few lines handed down under his name—for instance, "Young people, venerate with silence all these things"[35]—may in fact go back to a didactic religious poem by the master (see 100ff. below).[36] Moreover, since the word used by Heraclitus, *syngraphaí*, denotes chiefly writings in prose, we may also think of Anaximander of Miletus and Pherecydes of Syros, who were alternatively mentioned in antiquity as being the founder of prose literature, and of whom especially Pherecydes was often mentioned as teacher of Pythagoras.

Heraclitus mocks the result of Pythagoras' inquiries, his so-called "wisdom," not merely as mindless "much learning," but also as *kakotechníe* ("artful knavery, foul tricks"). A strong word. In this context, it refers first of all to Pythagoras' passing other people's knowledge off as his own. But apart from this, it reminds us of the unmistakable tendency to lend the doctrine the highest authority through supernatural certifications, such as that provided by Pythagoras' golden thigh or the trip to the Underworld—feigned, according to Hermippus.[37] Heraclitus' threat that

> Dike [that is, personified Justice] will seize the craftsmen of lies and [their] witnesses. (Heraclit. 22 B 28b D.-K.)

has therefore plausibly been connected with Pythagoras and his followers.[38] And all the more so since Timaeus affirms that another phrase was applied to Pythagoras: "Ancestor of swindlers" (Heraclit. 22 B 81 D.-K. = FGrHist 566 F 132). If "swindlers" refers to the Pythagoreans as those who pass on the "shady tricks" of their master, then this fragment is the earliest evidence that Pythagoras founded a school that was famous for its cohesion, news of which obviously got back to his homeland.

The intensity of Heraclitus' dispute with Pythagoras is actually surprising.[39] Apparently, he felt challenged by the appearance of his somewhat older contemporary and by the success (in Heraclitus' opinion, founded on dishonest grounds) of his doctrine. And as so often happens when one deals intensely with a position one dislikes, Heraclitus may not have remained uninfluenced by the Pythagorean body of thought. At least this is suggested by the importance of the "invisible harmony" (*harmonie*, also "fitting together") of opposites which in B 54 D.-K. is contrasted with the measurable and "visible harmony," privileged by the Pythagoreans.[40]

Ion of Chios

The reaction to Heraclitus' violent objections was not long in coming. The many-sided writer Ion of Chios (c. 490–422 B.C.E.), who worked in Athens, seems to be defending Pythagoras in verses that, according to our informant, Diogenes Laertius, were meant for Pherecydes of Syros:

> Thus the one [Pherecydes] who distinguished himself by his manliness and also reverence,
>   has even after his death a delightful life for his soul,
> if Pythagoras is truly sage, he who more than all
>   saw men's mental dispositions and came to know them well.
>
> (Ion of Chios 36 B 4 D.-K., with the emendation
made in line 3 by Sandbach 1958/9)

The second distich conspicuously alludes to Heraclitus' fragment 22 B 129 D.-K.: Compare "wise" with Heraclitus' "wisdom," "more than all" with "most of all men," and the turn of phrase "[he] saw men's mental dispositions and came to know them well"—evidently inspired by *Odyssey* 1,3, "many men's cities he [Odysseus] saw and came to know their minds"— can be related to Pythagoras' practice of *historíe* according to Heraclitus. It is almost as though Ion were deliberately seeking to correct Heraclitus' portrayal.[41]

Because the context has been lost, the sense of the passage as a whole is not easy to grasp. One might, with Walter Kranz, presume that to "the one" (Pherecydes) is opposed in the following passage another person as a negative example, a person who had lived a morally reprehensible life and who would therefore have to suffer accordingly in the Beyond.[42] What precisely is being certified by Pythagoras' authority? Why does Ion invoke this "true sage"? In order to accredit the survival of the soul after death, its immortality in general? Or the consequences in the Beyond produced by the kind of life one has lead? Or the ethical excellence of Pherecydes? Perhaps to confirm all that together, the accent probably falling chiefly on the connection between behavior in this world and one's fate in the Beyond—a connection that was later strongly emphasized in Plato's work and was perhaps already posited in Orphic ideas about the Beyond. There is no mention here of the transmigration of souls, yet the reference to a "delightful life" after death may perhaps remind us of Empedocles, who foresees, for those who have successfully traversed the highest stage of reincarnation, a life at the table of the immortals, free of any human suffering.[43]

The fact that Pherecydes' and Pythagoras' names are associated here is noteworthy against the background of the later tradition that assumes a teacher-pupil relationship between the two. Ion is also the earliest witness to the latter's proximity to the Orphics:

> Ion of Chios says in the 'Triagmoi' [triads] that he [Pythagoras] composed several poems and attributed them to Orpheus. (Diog. Laert. 8,8 = Ion 36 B 2 D.-K.)

That sounds—as does, incidentally, Heraclitus' fragment 22 B 129 D.-K.— like a kind of literary criticism: Ion apparently knew poems attributed to Orpheus whose similarities (in content) to Pythagorean ideas led him to assume that Pythagoras was their author. Or does this perhaps intimate that Pythagoras practiced the Orphic poetic genre of the *hieroì lógoi?* In any case, not the least interesting aspect of all this is the way it is taken for granted that Pythagoras wrote poems. Here there is as yet no trace of the later assumption that he wrote nothing at all.

Empedocles of Acragas

Since antiquity, there has been a tendency to associate with Pythagoras the description of a man endowed with exceptional spiritual powers, which figured in the "Purifications" of Empedocles from Acragas (c. 494–c. 434 B.C.E.). This Sicilian natural philosopher, whose poems, by the way, also betray some unmistakable Orphic influences,[44] does not mention the man's name, so that the relationship with Pythagoras is not entirely certain (in antiquity, Parmenides was also suggested, and in the modern age a guide whom the first-person narrator met in the Underworld).[45] However, there are good grounds for assuming that Empedocles was thinking of Pythagoras, to whom he comes conspicuously close not only in his rejection of killing anything with a soul and in the taboo on beans, but also in the getup and in staging himself as a divine person[46] (this does not exclude differences on specific points such as the Pythagorean assumption of a void in the cosmos).[47] The larger context of the verses is also debated. Usually, they are connected with Empedocles' description of a "Golden Age" that was ruled by the goddess of love Aphrodite and that knew neither war nor blood sacrifices.[48] In this case, however, one would have to think, on chronological grounds, of an earlier incarnation of Pythagoras—unless one posits, with Günther Zuntz, a series of generations inspired by Hesiod, with Pythagoras as the representative of the generation immediately preceding Empedocles.'[49] Against this view, the objection has to be raised, with Rosemary Wright, that Empedocles could hardly have believed in "a distinctive heroic age only fifty years before his own time."[50] In short, the debate over the embedding of the fragment has not yet reached a definitive solution.

> There was however among them a man of outstanding knowledge,
> who indeed had acquired greatest riches in his mental organs,
> most [of all] a ruler over many and diverse wise activities.
> For when he stretched himself with all his mental organs,
> he easily saw every one of all the things that are,
> in ten as well as twenty generations of men.
>
> (Emp. 31 B 129 D.-K.)

The first two verses are—like Ion 36 B 4,3s. D.-K.—the positive counterpart of Heraclitus' sarcastic admission that Pythagoras had made exceptional efforts to acquire knowledge (*historíe*). The key word *wise* also reappears, though what these "many and diverse wise activities" were remains rather obscure—does the reference perhaps include the various miracles? Amongst them after all ranks Pythagoras' ability to remind himself and others of earlier reincarnations. This seems to be alluded to in verses 4–6, as are perhaps, more generally, his divinatory powers and his "X-ray vision" into all things (Porphyry cites the verses as proof of Pythagoras' superior senses, which also allowed him to hear the harmony of the spheres).[51] By making full use of his mental organs he can, not unlike the Homeric gods, "easily" see into everything and strides through vast periods of time, probably including the future.[52] So vividly does Empedocles describe this bodily-mental exertion that one might almost presume that he himself had experienced the master. In any case, these verses are the enthusiastic praise, if not of a follower and pupil of Pythagoras, then at least of a sympathizer.[53]

Herodotus of Halicarnassus

Whereas Empedocles' fragment, as it were, offers an inside view, Herodotus (c. 485–424 B.C.E.), the "father of history" (as Cicero calls him), provides the outside view of the phenomenon, which is no less informative, of course. From the scattered reports we can with due caution extract two points that are constitutive for his image of Pythagoras: (1) The dependency of Pythagoras on Egyptian teachings; (2) his proximity to religious charlatanry. However, both points are merely hinted at. In a famous passage of his book on Egypt, Herodotus mentions one of the Egyptians' religious taboos: Whereas in everyday life they wore white woolen garments over linen skirts with fringes around their legs, they were forbidden to bring woolen things into shrines or to put them into tombs.

> This custom agrees with the ritual prescriptions known as Orphic and Bacchic which are actually Egyptian and Pythagorean; for anyone initiated into these rites is similarly debarred from burial in a garment of wool. They have a "sacred discourse" [*hieròs lógos*] which explains the reason for this. (2,81,2, the first sentence in what is presumably the original longer version; transl. after Selincourt/Burn)

We have mentioned the importance of ritualistic rules in Pythagoreanism. Herodotus' description of Orphic-Bacchic taboos as rather actually Pythagorean reminds us of Ion of Chios. What is new here is the addition of the Egyptian element, which for Herodotus is obviously very closely connected with the Pythagorean. This is also indicated by his discussion of the immortality of the soul and its various rebirths in other living creatures, which after passing through all creatures of the land, water, and air ends up being reincarnated again in a human body.[54] According to Herodotus, the Egyptians were the first to propose this view, which the Greeks then adopted:

This theory has been adopted by certain Greek writers, some earlier, some later, who have put it forward as their own. Their names are known to me, but I refrain from mentioning them. (Hdt. 2,123,3; transl. Selincourt/Burn)

Even if Herodotus does not give us the names, there is hardly any doubt that he was thinking not only of Pherecydes, the Orphics, and Empedocles, but not the least also of Pythagoras. This emerges particularly from the association of "Egyptian" and "Pythagorean" in the passage just discussed, 2,81,2. In essence, Herodotus' statement is incorrect: Current knowledge indicates that the Egyptians were not familiar with the doctrine of rebirth. Perhaps we may conclude that Herodotus adopted this view partly because he was aware of the tradition that Pythagoras went to Egypt for the sake of (especially religious) *historíe*. He would therefore be the earliest witness to such a journey, which may well have a historical foundation.[55] If this interpretation is correct, then we find in Herodotus as well the objection already raised by Heraclitus: Pythagoras presents the insights of others as his own "wisdom."

So much for the first point. In the case of the second—Pythagoras' proximity to religious charlatanry—we are again dealing with subtle hints. It is as if Herodotus could not or would not clearly and distinctly express his skepticism with regard to Pythagoras (perhaps out of consideration for the numerous Pythagoreans around his new home in southern Italy, Thurii [today Sibari], where he moved along with other colonists in 444/3 B.C.E.?). The characterization of Pythagoras as "not the feeblest clever man (*sophistés*) among the Greeks,"[56] which taken by itself is laudatory, comes in the context of an ethnographic excursus on the Getae that indirectly also puts Pythagoras in a rather dubious light. Herodotus reports on the beliefs about immortality among this north Thracian people, who assume that deceased people do not die, but rather go to the *daimon* Salmoxis (every four years, the Getae also sent him a messenger, who was supposed to transmit all their wishes; the brutal way in which they killed this messenger is described in detail). The historian claims to have inquired into the subject among the Greeks living nearby. According to their (euhemeristic) reports, Salmoxis was a human being and, on Samos, he was the slave of Mnesarchus' son Pythagoras. Having gained his freedom, he acquired a great deal of money, and then returned home. The backwardness of his native people with respect to civilization and intellectual achievements, on one hand, and the fact that Salmoxis knew "the Ionian way of life and its mores, which were more deeply grounded than those in Thrace"—which was only to be expected of someone who "had consorted with the Greeks and with one who was not the feeblest clever man among them, Pythagoras"—is given as the reason why Salmoxis was able to succeed in carrying out the following religious fraud:

> He built himself a banqueting-hall in which he used to entertain the leading men of the country with much liberality, and endeavor to teach them that neither he nor his fellow-drinkers nor any of their descendents, would ever die, but would go to a place where they would live in perpetual enjoyment of every blessing. (Hdt. 4,95,3; transl. after Selincourt/Burns)

This sounds like a satire on Orphic concepts of the Beyond, with the "sacred meadows and groves of Persephone"[57] and the "symposium of the pious."[58] We may also recall the "delightful life" Ion attributes, referring to Pythagoras, to the soul of Pherecydes. Let us keep in mind that this promise is made only to the "leading men of the country"—an aristocratic touch that not only is generally characteristic of the doctrine of rebirth, but may also make us think of the aristocratic Pythagorean community. According to Herodotus' rationalist explanation, to lend credence to his teaching Salmoxis had an underground chamber built, into which he withdrew for three years, missed and mourned by the (north) Thracians as if he had died:

> Then in the fourth year he reappeared, and in this way persuaded the Thracians that the doctrine he had taught was true. (Hdt. 4,95,5; trans. Selincourt/Burn)[59]

So much for the report of the Greeks living near the Hellespont and Pontus, who clearly had a concept of Pythagoras in the fifth century B.C.E. In the following passage, Herodotus takes care to distance himself from this report: He wants neither to disbelieve nor again to wholly believe this explanation, and puts forward the view that Salmoxis lived many years before Pythagoras (Hdt. 4,96,1). Despite the distancing, however, Herodotus' narrative casts at least an indirect shadow on Salmoxis' earlier master, from whom he might have learned in particular the "trick" with the underground chamber, behind which may have originally stood a ritual *katábasis*.[60] It is true that the corresponding story about Pythagoras is first explicitly recounted in the third century B.C.E. only.[61] But it seems presupposed in verses from Sophocles' *Electra*, which the scholiast has good grounds for relating to Pythagoras, and in which are again mentioned "wise men" who "according to their word idly die," only to be all the "more respected" when they return.[62] The similarities are so striking that one is tempted to suggest that in Herodotus' story of Salmoxis the story of his teacher Pythagoras is also being told.

Democritus of Abdera

On the other hand, Pythagoras seems to have enjoyed a certain popularity in the Thracian coastal city of Abdera (northeast of the island of Thasos). One thing that suggests this is that the list of works by the Abderite philosopher of nature and leading representative of ancient atomism, Democritus (born c. 460 B.C.E.?), includes, among his writings on ethics, a work entitled *Pythagoras*, concerning whose content we can at most speculate on the basis of the immediately following headings, "On the Attitude of the Wise" and "On Things in Hades."[63] His contemporary Glaucus of Rhegium identifies him as a pupil "of a Pythagorean."[64] To what extent Democritus' philosophy was in fact inspired by the Pythagoreans cannot be decided on the basis of what we now know, even if similarities in the ways the world is explained (the common assumption of a void) and in ethics (the importance of moderation, which is in any case fundamental for Greek ethics in general) are conspicuous.

Iconographic Testimonies

From Abdera also comes the earliest iconographic evidence regarding Pythagoras. This is constituted by two silver coins (*tetradrachms*) from the period between 430 and 425 B.C.E., which bear on the obverse an image of a griffin as the symbol of Abdera's mother city of Teos, and on the reverse a bearded man in a square frame, around which the name *Pythagóres* is written as it was pronounced in Ionia. The image must refer to the master coiner, as usual. Since these officials were not allowed to put their own portraits on coins, each chose a symbol referring to his name—a master coiner named Apollus, for instance, choose a statue of Apollo, one named Python the Pythian tripod, one named Nicostratus (the "victor over armies") an attacking warrior, and so on. The director of the municipal coinage in question seems to have proceeded in the same way and chosen his namesake Pythagoras as a significant symbol. As realistic as the head on the coin preserved in Lisbon may seem, it is probably based on an idealized statue only made a few decades after Pythagoras' death (c. 440 B.C.E.?), and thus it shows "what the fifth century thought of his personality and activity."[65]

The type of the bearded man with middle-length hair—in Iamblichus, Pythagoras is called "long-haired" (*komêtes*), perhaps alluding to the secondary sense "comet"[66]—recurs on a Spartan devotional relief, where he sits holding scrolls in his hands opposite a beardless youth sitting, with a *kithara* on his thigh and surrounded by various animals, on a stone block. On grounds worth considering, the archeologist Strocka interprets this relief, which probably dates from the late fourth century B.C.E., as depicting

Pythagoras being instructed by Orpheus.[67] The placement of an eagle over the head of this Pythagoras mythified by his followers (and therefore also represented as larger) can be connected with the miracle related by Porphyry, according to whom in Olympia Pythagoras, as has already been mentioned, brought an eagle down from the skies and stroked it. Still later pictorial representations of Pythagoras include the famous bronze bust from the Villa dei Papiri in Herculaneum and the second-century C.E. bronze coins from Samos, for which I refer the reader to Schefold's study.[68]

Pythagoras in the Literature of the Early Fourth Century B.C.E.

In the literary heritage around the beginning of the fourth century B.C.E. a positive attitude toward Pythagoras and his doctrines seems predominant. We have discussed the laudatory reference to Pythagoras' rhetorical abilities made by Socrates' pupil Antisthenes. Aristippus (c. 430–355 B.C.E.), another pupil of Socrates, explained the name "Pyth-agoras" by saying that "he spoke the truth no less than did the Pythian." In a book entitled *Tripod*, which deals with the Seven Sages, a certain Andron of Ephesus, whose dates are uncertain—a clue may be provided by Porphyry's hint that Theopompus plagiarized him[69]—reported Pythagoras' prediction of an earthquake and other miracles. The younger Anaximander of Miletus (probably c. 400 B.C.E.?) wrote an *Interpretation of the Pythagorean Sýmbola,* something of which may have made its way into later sources, even if his name hardly ever appears in them.

Hand in hand with the Platonic Academy's increasing monopolization of Pythagoras, the documents relating to Pythagoras become steadily more numerous in the course of the fourth century B.C.E. We shall examine them later at 118 below. Here let us simply mention the interesting observations made by Isocrates (436–338 B.C.E.) in his eulogy of Busiris. In this speech Pythagoras is presented as the perfect example of the many wondrous elements of Egyptian piety: He is said to have been in Egypt, where he became the pupil of the inhabitants; he is supposed to have been the first to bring philosophy to the Greeks and also the first to have concerned himself, in a more visible way than others, with sacrifices and ritual acts in shrines. With a distinctly ironic undertone, Isocrates attributes to Pythagoras, as his motivation for this concern, the assumption

> that even if he thereby gained from the gods no advantage for himself, he would at least enjoy greatest respect from people on the basis of these things. (29) Which did in fact happen to him. For he surpassed the others so much in grand repute that all the young people asked to become his pupils, and their elders preferred to see their chil-

dren with him than taking care of their own effects. And one cannot refuse to believe these things. For people still admire those who claim to be his pupils on account of their silence more than they admire those who have greatest fame for their speech.[70] (Isocr. Or. 11,28s.)

Thus the voyage to Egypt and the central importance of sacrifice and ritual are not the only traits that are taken more or less for granted as components of the image of Pythagoras between 380 and 375 B.C.E.—the period when the eulogy was written. The success of his activities in southern Italy, too, seems presupposed in § 29, and the last sentence may allude to the duty to keep silence, for which the Pythagoreans were also famous later on.

GURU AND SCHOLAR

The Charismatic

One fact at least may have clearly resulted from our examination of the oldest reports: Pythagoras exercised on his contemporaries a strongly polarizing influence. Either people made fun of him (Xenophanes) and rejected his doctrine wholesale as plagiarism and shameless fraud (Heraclitus), or else they enthusiastically praised his superior, unique knowledge and power of thought, which they deemed capable of overcoming the limits of time and space (Empedocles). There was obviously no room for indifference toward him: Anyone who came in contact with him had to be either for him or against him. No doubt, this Pythagoras of Samos, who on the evidence quickly acquired widespread prominence, cannot have been a "normal" man, an average Ionian of the Late Archaic Age. From a sociological point of view, the reaction of those around him points instead to the type of a charismatic as defined by Max Weber, for whom it is characteristic that his followers attribute to him special abilities (*Gnadengaben*) different from "everyday" ones, whereas outsiders usually reject him more or less brusquely ("facing a leader whose charisma we do not recognize, we are not indifferent, but tend to adopt a hostile or scornful attitude: For us he is a deceiver or a madman").[71] There is no lack of examples, either in the past or the present, in either the religious or the political realms, and also the phenomenon of Pythagoras can most appropriately be understood sociologically through the category of the charismatic structure of power.[72]

Political Advisor and Educator

In this connection, even though the reports regarding Pythagoras' exceptionally successful political and educational effect on southern Italy may have been transfigured by legend, it is difficult to deny them a certain core of authenticity—and all the more so because the direct testimonies begin in the early fourth century B.C.E. at the latest (Antisthenes and Isocrates; on Heraclitus' allusion to the founding of a school [cf. 52 above]). It is plausible that when the charismatic Pythagoras—who had traveled extensively and, according to Heraclitus, was exceptionally well-read and equipped with wide-ranging knowledge—arrived in Croton, probably around 530 B.C.E.,[73] he made a strong impression, rather quickly won the trust of the local elite, and acquired considerable influence over the education and way of life of the city's people.[74] Concerning the kind of social changes he initiated we can do little more than speculate. A more demanding ethics on all levels—in the family, in the state, in dealing with the gods—was, as has been mentioned, most likely part of the reform. It is said that Pythagoras used his authority to make the inhabitants of Croton give up the (aristocratic) obsession with grandeur, luxury, and dissipation, and led them back to a moderate way of life.[75]

A leading idea of his political activity may have been *harmonía* (underpinned by number philosophy and cosmology?) among the various social groups, which was supposed to ensure social cohesion. This is suggested, for instance, by the advice given political officials to erect a shrine to the Muses.[76] The politically active Pythagorean Archytas of Tarentum also later said that the right standard puts an end to disputes and increases harmony and at the same time bridges the gap between rich and poor. Croton's political and military superiority in those years—might the proverb "All other cities are worthless in comparison to Croton"[77] go back to this time?—is commonly attributed to Pythagoras' influence. This may actually be true for the victory over the neighboring city of Sybaris in the year 510 B.C.E., in which Milon, the star athlete associated with Pythagoras in certain texts, is also supposed to have played a decisive part.[78] Relatively soon afterward, however, tensions with individual representatives of the local aristocracy seem to have arisen and led Pythagoras to move—around the turn of the century?—to Metapontum.

It is unclear whether Pythagoras' followers continued at least to help shape Croton's fate (around 494 a tyrant named Cleinias seems to have seized power for a short time).[79] Until the middle of the fifth century B.C.E. the city exercised a certain hegemony over southern Italy. This can be gathered from alliance coins, one side of which bears the tripod as the emblem of Croton and initials of the state, whereas the other side carries the emblems and the initials of one of the other cities.[80] The temptation is strong to see in this flowering a long-term effect of Pythagorean reforms in Croton. But this remains speculation, because of the lack of clear evidence. In this same period the Pythagoreans probably spread out over the most important cities in the region, including not only Metapontum but also Locri, Rhegium, and Tarentum. We know almost nothing about the influence of the secret society on local politics.[81] (Aristoxenus speaks in a very general way about the cities' desire to hand over the political leadership to the Pythagoreans;[82] since Pythagoras' followers were often aristocrats, one might be inclined to assume with Apollonius[83] that at least a few of them did assume political leadership responsibilities.) Regarding Pythagoras himself, it may be recorded that his political influence outside the community he founded probably went hardly beyond advice and spiritual leadership in ethical-social and religious questions.[84]

Doctrine of Reincarnation, Relatedness of All Ensouled Creatures, Return of Things, Eschatology

On another point, the doctrine of the soul, we are on far firmer ground. The reports leave no doubt that Pythagoras—presumably taking up concepts developed by Orphics (?)[85] and Pherecydes of Syros[86]—paid special attention to the soul (*psyché*) and its survival after death. This idea was also known outside the school from the earliest times. In the oldest document, the anecdote handed down by Xenophanes, the outlines of his doctrine of the soul are easily discerned, despite all the mockery: According to Pythagoras, the human soul lives on after death and can—in the framework of reincarnations—even enter animals (in Heraclides Ponticus plants are added).[87] As it appears, individual characteristics are retained during this process (this is at least part of the joke: Pythagoras recognizes the voice of a friend in the yelp of the dog being beaten). Xenophanes' verses therefore essentially confirm Dicaearchus' representation of the part of the theory known outside the Pythagorean secret society:

> What he said to those with him, however, it is not possible for anyone
> to say exactly, for there was no ordinary silence among them. How-
> ever, it was especially well-known by all, first, that he said that the soul
> is immortal, then, that it transmigrates into other kinds of animals,
> and in addition that what happens happens again at some time ac-
> cording to certain cycles, that, in short, there is nothing new, and that
> it is necessary to believe that all ensouled beings are of the same kind.
> For it appears that Pythagoras was the first to bring these teachings
> into Greece. (Dicaearch. fr. 40 Mirhady = Porph. VPyth. 19; transl.
> Mirhady)

The last-mentioned relatedness of all creatures with souls is basically nothing else than the logical consequence of metempsychosis: If the human soul also enters into other kinds of creatures, then what animates the latter cannot be essentially different from the human soul. Dicaearchus' account suggests that Pythagoras also taught that all things periodically return. That sounds like a cosmic generalization of the idea of reincarnation and recalls above all the assumption of a great world-year, which we know chiefly from Plato, and concerning which the Pythagorean Philolaus of Croton (c. 470 [?]–after 399 B.C.E.) seems to have made calculations.[88] Another pupil of Aristotle, Eudemus of Rhodes (born before 350 B.C.E.), also testifies to speculations by the Pythagoreans regarding the periodic return of the same state of the world, the identity being based on number.[89]

An additional facet of the Pythagorean doctrine of the soul can be recovered from Ion's fragment B 4 in combination with Herodotus 4,95,3 (both discussed above at 52 and 55): Obviously, Pythagoras promised his followers a good lot in the Beyond—Ion speaks of a "delightful life," and Herodotus of the place where one will have "every blessing." On this point Pythagoras' "doctrine of salvation" resembles the Orphic-Bacchic as well as the Eleusinian mysteries. Famous are the lines taken from the Homeric hymn to Demeter where those of the mortals who have "looked upon" the Eleusinian mysteries are blessed;[90] in the Beyond, only they are "to live," whereas for the rest "everything is bad," as Sophocles has it.[91] Similarly, the Orphic mystery priests promised prospective initiates that by carrying out the initiation rites, which were accompanied by "sacrifices and pleasurable delights," they would free themselves from the misery in the Beyond that awaited others.[92] Pythagoras is also an "Orphic" insofar as in his doctrine this promise was certainly connected with observing rituals and regulations in everyday life that were quite drastic and in many respects remarkably divergent from the usual Greek way of life. However, the stress on *ethical* excellence (Ion), points beyond the Orphic; in a Pythagorean context it obviously amounts to a guarantee of happiness in the Beyond. The Orphics, on the other hand, if one believes Plato's account (which is, however, polemically overdrawn), proclaimed that even terrible criminals would be "absolved" and "purified," if only they had themselves initiated.[93] In comparison with this purely ritualistic attitude it is perhaps not so wrong to describe Pythagoras as has been done occasionally in the past as a kind of Reformer of Orphic beliefs who also made elevated ethical demands on his followers.[94]

Ritual Way of Life

But that does not mean that for Pythagoras ritual played no role, on the contrary. In Herodotus we have encountered both the Orphic-Bacchic and also—following the corresponding Egyptian prohibitions—the Pythagorean taboo on burying the dead in woolen garments, and as we have seen, Pythagoras' special concern with rituals of sacrifice and worship is documented no later than Isocrates. These two reports are richly confirmed in the tradition. Particularly informative in this respect is a long section from Iamblichus' *On the Pythagorean Way of Life*, which in all likelihood goes back to Aristotle's *On the Pythagoreans*.[95] According to this text, among the many "oral sayings" (*akoúsmata*) that regulated "what one should or shouldn't do," the most detailed were devoted to the following topics:

1. "sacrificial offerings, how one should perform them at each particular point in time"
2. "the remaining <honors for the gods>"
3. "moving from here"
4. "tombs, how one should be buried" (85)

For the fourth topic—documented by Herodotus—no example is given in the preceding enumeration of short rules.[96] To the third topic can perhaps be related the enigmatic instruction that one should not "break the bread, since it is not advantageous for judgment in Hades."[97] However, this was only one of various explanations. Another—"because in earlier times the friends gathered around *a single* loaf of bread, as barbarians still do"—with its reference to the circle of friends so important for the Pythagoreans' self-conception, sounds no less ancient.[98] In any case, the fact that there were obviously detailed rules for correct behavior during the "move" into the Beyond is particularly instructive. This is another point on which the Orphics and the Pythagoreans are very close. We have only to recall the increasing number of Orphic-Bacchic Gold Leaves that have come to light over the past decades, on which detailed instructions addressed to the initiates regarding travel to the Underworld are engraved.[99]

By far the most frequent in Iamblichus' excerpt are rules related to the first and second topics. Among them are, for instance:[100]

—"Pour libations to the gods from a drinking cup's handle [the 'ear'], for the sake of the [good] omen, and lest you drink from the same part" (84); from the second explanation we can conclude that it is a matter of maintaining a strict separation between the divine and the human; cf. Diog. Laert.: "[Do] not touch fish that are sacred; for it is not acceptable that gods and humans should be served the same, any more than free men and slaves."[101]

—"One should sacrifice and enter temples without shoes."

—"One ought not turn aside into a temple; for the god must not be made secondary" (85; cf. Iambl: "On your way to the shrine to pray, neither say nor do anything else in between that belongs to everyday life").[102]

—"[Do] not [sacrifice] a white cock, for he is a suppliant and sacred to the Moon (*Mên*), which is why they indicate the time of day" (84).

—"Only into those animals which it is lawful to sacrifice does there not enter a human soul; for this reason those who are allowed to eat [meat] should eat only animals that can be sacrificed, but no other living being" (85)

Basically, we can discern a strong effort to avoid any kind of defilement. From this "obsession with ritual purity" (as Giangiulio aptly puts it)[103] obviously also springs an instruction like the following one:

—"[Do] not wear a god's image as signet on a ring, so that it may not be polluted" (which would be inevitable if it were worn in everyday life); "for it is an image, which ought to be set up in the house" (84)

On the human level, the pronounced striving for purity is expressed in admonitions such as to avoid "roads traveled by the public," "vessels for lustral water (at sacrifices)," and (public) "bathing houses," for in the case of all these things, "it is unclear whether those using them are pure" (83).

In general, a very extensive sacralization of all areas of life seems typical of the *vita Pythagorica*. The boundaries between profane-moralizing and religious-ritual admonitions therefore sometimes become fluid:

—"One should produce children; for one must leave behind at his place other *worshippers of god*" (83).

—"Do not join in putting a burden down (for one should not become *a cause* of someone's not working), but join in taking it up" (84); cf. 85: "Labors are good, but pleasures are bad in every way; for having come [to Earth] for *punishment*—an interesting idea for the doctrine of reincarnation!—"one must be punished."

—"One ought not drive out" [or rather "abuse"?[104]] "one's own wife, for she is a *suppliant;* hence, we also lead her from the hearth, and take her by the right hand" (allusion to the wedding ceremony, in which the woman was led from the new domestic hearth into the marriage chamber) (84).[105]

—"And to advise nothing short of the best for one asking advice; for counsel is *sacred.*" (85)

Often there is no explanation at all. As a result, not a few "oral sayings" remain obscure for us, no matter how suggestive they may sound. Around 400 B.C.E. Anaximander the younger, in his *Interpretation of the Pythagorean Symbola*, undertook an attempt to shed light on this obscurity.[106] His example was followed by the Pythagoreans Androcydes[107] and Hippome-don,[108] who remain even more shadowy for us, and in the first century B.C.E., by Alexander Polyhistor.[109] Iamblichus (or rather Aristotle) may be thinking primarily of Anaximander the younger when he writes:

> And in the case of some [rules], a reason why is added. . . . But for other [instructions], no reason is added. And some of the reasons given seem to have been attached from the beginning and others later. . . . The probable reasons given about such matters are not Pythagorean, but were devised by *some outside the school* trying to give a likely reason. (Iambl. VPyth. 86; transl. Dillon and Hershbell)

In a few cases later ethical-philosophical explanations may in fact be quite clearly distinguished from the original ritualistic ones. For example, compare the following explanations in the account given by Porphyry with the ones quoted above:

"Do not take roads traveled by the public": with this [*symbolon*] he forbade following the opinions of the masses, yet [he bade] to follow the ones of the few and the educated.	Fear of being defiled by the impure
"and [do] not wear images of the gods on rings": that is, one should not have the teaching and knowledge of the gods quickly at hand and visible [for everyone], nor communicate them to the masses.	Fear of defiling them by wearing them
"and pour libations for the gods from a drinking cup's handle [the 'ear']": thereby he enigmatically hints that the gods should be honored and praised with music; for it goes through the ears	Efforts to keep the divine and the human strictly separate
(Porph. VPyth. 42)	(Aristotle-Iamblichus)

The differences are striking. Obviously, over time individual Pythagoreans strove to give to maxims that proceeded chiefly from the religious-ritualis-tic thought and that seemed increasingly old-fashioned a more intellectual meaning that corresponded to contemporary philosophical discussion. For the reconstruction of what Pythagoras himself might have taught, these explanations are not of much help. Taboos such as "Do not exceed the yoke" (or "beam of a balance," in the sense of "the measure"?), "Do not poke the fire with a [long] knife," "Do not tear the wreath to bits," "Do not sit on the grain measure," or "Nor do take swallows into the house"[110] remain largely mysterious, even if parallels can sometimes be found in Homer and especially in Hesiod, in popular beliefs, and in other cults and cultures.[111]

The rules given here and others may not all be equally old. Yet one thing is clear: The life of the Pythagoreans was thoroughly ritualized by means of countless prohibitions and obligations. Even everyday details such as putting on one's shoes were scrupulously regulated (in accord with the Pythagoreans' general privileging of the right side, one had to begin with the right foot). In antiquity, a comparable density of rules is found actually only for cult priests, whose way of life, especially during the period preceding rituals they were to carry out, was partly subject to significant restrictions (as priests, at such moments they had to meet particularly high standards of purity). Could the Pythagoreans have seen themselves as a kind of priests, and their whole lives as a continual practice of worship, ordered down to its smallest details by rituals?[112] In any case, their hopes of receiving a better lot in the Beyond and in the cycle of reincarnation were based not least on their observance of ritual rules and the superior "purity" it produced.

Dietary Rules

It may seem surprising that in examining the "oral sayings" we have not yet encountered a general prohibition on killing and eating creatures with souls. Such a prohibition is in fact not entirely lacking in the relevant tradition—in Iamblichus' enumeration of the *sýmbola* in his *Protrepticus* we find at the end the command "Abstain from creatures with souls!"[113] Far more numerous, however, are the rules that forbid sacrificing or eating only certain species of animals. Once again religious viewpoints seem to be in the foreground. Prohibited are:

—white cocks, since they are sacred to the moon (according to other sources, also to the sun; the white color corresponds to the bright light of the moon and sun);
—fish, so far as they are sacred to the gods;[114] red mullet, black-tail—"Abstain from black-tail, for it belongs to the chthonian gods"—,[115] sea barbel, and sea anemone are specified;[116]

—in general, animals that may not be sacrificed, since only these are entered by human souls.[117]

In addition, the Pythagoreans are forbidden to consume certain parts of animals' bodies:

—the womb and the heart;[118]
—the brain.[119]

Behind this probably stands an insight into the central importance of these organs for the origin and thriving of living things. Accordingly, in Porphyry loins, testicles, and the sex organs in general are taboo:

> Do not eat what is not allowed: origin, growth, beginning, end, and also that from which the first foundation of all things comes into being. (Porph. VPyth. 43) He said that one should abstain from the loins, testicles, sex organs, bone marrow, feet, and heads of sacrificed [animals]. For he called the loins "basis," because living creatures build on them as on a foundation; but he called the testicles and the sex organs "coming into being," for without their effects no living creature comes into being; "growth" he called the bone marrow, which is for all living creatures the cause of growth; however, he called the feet the "beginning," the head the "end"; the latter have the greatest control over the body. (Porph. VPyth. 42s.)

Basic biological-medical concepts seem here to be connected with religious awe before the elementary forces of nature.

These taboos, which also partly applied to initiations into the mysteries,[120] stand in a remarkable contrast to the fundamental vegetarianism, which is well documented outside the tradition of the *akoúsmata* for Pythagoras and his followers (Eudoxus and Dicaearchus presuppose it; vegetarianism is moreover a further point on which Pythagoreanism and Orphic doctrine agree).[121] The strict renunciation of eating meat follows almost as inevitably from the doctrine of the transmigration of souls as it can be derived from the oldest reports about Pythagoras. If the soul can enter into the bodies of animals, then the taboo on killing humans must be extended to them. Otherwise there would be a danger of killing not only another member of one's own species, but also possibly even a close relative, as Empedocles drastically puts it.[122]

Both positions—the fundamental vegetarianism as well as the specific taboos—are in all likelihood old. This makes it all the more urgent to seek an explanation of the contradiction between them. A solution begins to emerge from the *ákousma* cited, according to which the only animals into which the soul does not enter are those that may be sacrificed.[123] The conflict between the doctrine of the transmigration of souls and the ritual sacrifice is thereby defused and a justification for the practice of sacrifice, without which Greek religion is virtually unthinkable, is suggested. A small addition to this text is worth our attention:

> For that reason those *who are allowed to eat [meat]* should eat only animals that can be sacrificed. (Porph. VPyth. 42s.)

It looks as if two different groups were distinguished: If this information is correct, there were Pythagoreans who were not obliged to entirely abstain from eating meat. This is not surprising in view of the fundamental social significance the Greek *polis* attributed to the sacrifice of animals. Sacrifices were usually public occasions, sometimes accompanied by festive processions and subsequent community banquets. Anyone who refused to take part in the animal sacrifices isolated himself from society in a way that politically active people in particular could hardly afford to do. Therefore it is immediately plausible that in Pythagoreanism the general prohibition of eating "creatures with souls" did not hold for everyone to the same degree or under all circumstances. Strict vegetarianism was probably limited to the inner circle of the Pythagorean community,[124] where the "criteria of social normality"[125] were repealed amongst other things by joint property. Incidentally, another "oral saying," in which to the question "what is the most just?" the lapidary answer is given: "sacrifice,"[126] remains remarkably ambivalent. Does this perhaps refer specifically to sacrifices that do not involve bloodshed, such as have been recorded for Pythagoras and which were, according to Orphic and Empedoclean interpretations, common in a happier earlier age?[127]

The rules regarding food are complemented by the famous prohibition on eating beans (which does not refer to our ordinary sort of garden beans that originated in the Americas, but rather to broad or fava beans, *vicia faba*):

> But about beans, Aristotle says in his work "On the Pythagoreans" that he [Pythagoras] warned people to abstain from beans, either because they resembled the genitals, or the gates of Hades (for it is the only [plant] without joints), or because [the plant] is harmful or because it resembles the nature of the universe or because it is <not> oligarchical (they were used to draw lots [for offices] [a custom particularly widespread in democracies]). (Aristot. fr. 157 Gigon)

A variegated bunch of explanations. The first one is connected with the prohibition on consuming organs important in procreation and the maintenance of life. Wherein the resemblance to human sexual organs consists can be gathered from Porphyry's comments, which at the same time explain the cosmic relationship also mentioned by Aristotle.[128] Porphyry speaks of a disordered original beginning of the universe, in which many things were combined in the earth—"sown together and decaying together"—before a general differentiation came about in which animals and plants emerged together. "At that time," according to Porphyry, "human beings and beans sprouted from the same putrified material." For this macrocosmic event, which has a parallel in Anaxagoras' and Democritus' accounts of the creation of the world, Pythagoras is supposed to have provided "clear proofs" in the form of the following experiment:

> If one chews up a bean and crushes it with his teeth, and then puts it for a short time in the warmth of the sun's rays: [If] he then goes away and returns a short time later, he will probably discover that it smells like human semen. But if the beans are in bloom and one takes a bit of the blooms that turn black and puts it in an earthenware vessel, seals it with a lid, and buries it in the earth, and keeps an eye on what has been buried for ninety days: When he afterward digs it up again and takes off the lid, he will be able to discover that where the beans were the head of a child or the sexual organs of a woman have formed. (Porph. VPyth. 44)[129]

The first experiment seems in itself correct: If one treats fava beans in the way described, they in fact smell "something like sperm."[130] As for the associations evoked by the germinating plants, there is of course no limit to the imagination. The head and sexual organs, of which they reminded the Pythagoreans, are considered by the latter as taboo in the case of sacrificial animals, so that the prohibition on beans also seems logical on the basis of this resemblance, which strikes one as totemistic. The assumption of a primeval relationship between human beings and beans suggests the hypothesis that the Pythagoreans may have considered beans also as being "ensouled" (according to Pliny, they believed that the souls of the dead were in them).[131] Everyday experience may have confirmed their opinion: Fava beans are hard to digest and known for causing "wind"—this was certainly among the reasons why in Greece, as well as in India, seers, priests, and those making sacrifices had to abstain from eating beans (which were considered "impure") for a certain period before the ceremonies[132] ("wind" can easily be associated with the soul; after all, in Greek the latter is actually called "[life] breath" [*psyché*]). On the pragmatic level, the allergy to fava beans (the so called "favism") that is still widespread in Mediterranean countries and can indeed be dangerous may also have played a role.[133]

In any case, for the Pythagoreans as well as for the Orphics and Empedocles, the taboo on beans seems very closely related to the doctrine of the reincarnation of souls. To Orpheus is attributed the following verse which Heraclides Ponticus, however, cites with respect to Pythagoras:

Eating beans and eating the heads of one's parents amounts to the
    same thing

(OF 291 = Heracl. Pont. fr. 41 Wehrli)

Similarly, Empedocles shouts to his audience:

Wretched, most wretched, keep your hands off beans!

(31 B 141 D.-K.)

In connection with Pythagoras, another reason given for the taboo on beans is that souls return to earth through bean blossoms when they "climb up out of the houses of Hades."[134] That fits with Aristotle's attribution to the Pythagoreans of the view that beans resemble "the gates of Hades."[135]

Such arguments sound extremely alien to us. Superstitious ingredients seem mixed with semiscientific observations in a peculiar way. Yet we have to admit at least that the numerous ritual rules were not followed more or less mindlessly, simply as a traditional body of regulations. Rather a network of cleverly devised reasons, with the doctrine of the transmigration of souls at its center, held the whole system together and made the individual rules seem sensible. In this aspect as well, the sociocultural classification of Pythagoras as a charismatic is confirmed, since "interwovenness of meaning(s)" (*Sinnverflochtenheit*) can be regarded as an outstanding mark of charisma ("charisma makes it possible to illuminate existence in various directions").[136] Because of the unfavorable state of transmission, this "ideological superstructure" often remains unrecognizable to us but for its first signs.

The Superhuman Master and Apollo

A further "oral saying" handed down under Pythagoras' name goes like this:

With respect to the gods, receive nothing miraculous with mistrust, and also nothing that has to do with the divine teachings. (Iambl. Protr. 21, no. 25)

According to Iamblichus, the "divine teachings" are those the spiritual master himself handed down.[137] "Miraculous things" that from the earliest times outsiders met with great skepticism, surround Pythagoras in manifold ways—and this too is a characteristic of the charismatic, who, according to Max Weber's investigations into the sociology of religion and of domination, appears "supernatural," "superhuman," or at least "outside the ordinary or everyday."[138] Here we shall not return to Pythagoras' self-staging and numerous miracles. On the part of his followers, they find their answer in the doctrine, which according to Aristotle was handed on in secrecy, that Pythagoras occupied a position intermediate between humans and gods:

In his work on Pythagorean philosophy, also Aristotle reports that such a difference was kept entirely secret by the men: Of the rational living creatures, one is God, a second is man, and the third is like Pythagoras. (Aristot. fr. 156 Gigon.)[139]

Pythagoras' particularly close connection with Apollo is frequently stressed. A reference to the Pythian god could be discovered in his name. The fact that Pythagoras chose Euphorbus as his earlier incarnation is certainly explained in part by this Trojan warrior's collaboration with Apollo in causing the death of Patroclus. Apollo's island of Delos and the Delphic oracle of Apollo play a prominent role in Pythagoras' biography. On Delos, he is said to have cared for his sick teacher Pherecydes; only at the local altar "of Apollo the begetter" is he supposed to have performed prayers, because on this altar only bloodless sacrifices such as wheat, barley, and baked offerings were offered[140] (according to Iamblichus, Pythagoras thereby caused quite a sensation).[141] On Delphi again, it is said, he put up a distich that announced Apollo's death (mentioned above at 11)—and thus opened the way for Pythagoras as the "Hyperborean Apollo"? According to the tradition, following this event Pythagoras went to the city of Croton, where in addition to Hera Lacinia, Apollo was an especially important divinity. Even before Pythagoras' arrival, there seems to have been a temple of the Pythian Apollo. The foundation narrative reports that Croton was founded c. 710 B.C.E. by the Achaean colonist Myscellus in accord with instructions from Delphi. Since the beginning of municipal coinage around 530, the tripod, which clearly represents the Pythian oracle, was accordingly taken as the city's emblem. In Croton, and also in Metapontum, the way then was paved for the Apollonian charismatic.[142]

Natural Philosophical Oral Sayings I: Exegesis of Orphic Poetry?

To the oracle in Delphi is also devoted a Pythagorean maxim that may lead us to our next point and allow us to see that the "interwovenness of meaning(s)" in Pythagoreanism extended beyond the realm of religious-ritualistic rules of life to nature and the cosmos as a whole. The modern period, for which *mýthos* and *lógos*, (superstitious) belief and (natural) science have represented insuperable oppositions ever since the rationalistic positivism of the nineteenth century, often finds it difficult to bring together the two aspects of Pythagoras, the charismatic guru and the natural philosopher. *Lore and Science* (*Weisheit und Wissenschaft*) is the main title of Walter Burkert's influential book, in which the accent, however, clearly falls on "lore." Burkert sees Pythagoras as a "shaman," and denies him—in contrast to Philolaus and especially Archytas—any scientific side.[143] On the other hand, there have been—incidentally, since antiquity, as in the case of Aristoxenus—repeated attempts to cleanse the image of Pythagoras of ritualistic elements considered crude. The most recent example of this is Leonid Zhmud, according to whose somewhat apodictically presented thesis the taboos included in the *sýmbola* "were not taken seriously" by the Pythagoreans.[144] Little justification can be provided for either emphasis.[145] No matter how extraordinary the charismatic Pythagoras may have been in many respects, there is still no lack of indications that the man from Samos must also be viewed as part of the flourishing culture of the later sixth and early fifth centuries B.C.E. and that he actually deserves a place among the so-called pre-Socratic philosophers. In any case, by using a concept of knowledge all too narrowly based on mathematics and the natural sciences one can not do justice to the thinking and "exploration of nature" (*perì phýseos historía*)[146] practiced by these philosophers who are so important to European intellectual history and yet very different from each other individually.

Here again, the state of the transmission of relevant documents poses a major problem. On one hand, there are some further "oral sayings" (*akoúsmata* or *sýmbola*) attested with some certainty for Pythagoras, which in contrast to those previously mentioned give no instructions for the conduct of life ("What must be done, what must be refrained from?"), but rather, in accord with a systematics probably going back to Aristotle, either inquire into the true nature of a thing ("What is x?") or into the highest form of a specific quality—"What is most y?"[147] The first case ("What is x?") usually concerns mythical-religious items, for which an explanation is given. For example, the following *akoúsmata* have come down to us:

—What are the Islands of the Blessed? Sun and moon.
—What is the oracle in Delphi? "Fourthness" (*tetraktýs*); this is the "harmony" in which the Sirens [sing]. (Iambl. VPyth. 82, following Aristotle)

Under the same type of *akoúsmata* also fall a few of the identifications handed down by Aristotle:

> But he also said certain things in a mysterious way symbolically, which Aristotle has recorded in greater detail. For instance, he called the sea "the tears <of Kronos>," but [the constellations] Ursae [Major and Minor] he called "the hands of Rhea," the Pleiades "the Muses' lyre," and the planets "Persephone's dogs." (Aristot. fr. 159 Gigon = Porph. VPyth. 41)

These latter examples can easily be translated into the question-answer mode found above: "What are the tears of Kronos? The sea. What are Rhea's hands? Ursae Major and Minor," and so on. In this form, the "oral sayings" look like early examples of allegories: They decode the true, real meaning in a (figurative) mythical mode of expression. If this kind of decoding remained limited to members of the secret association, as it probably did, then the variations in the tradition seem only natural: To those outside the group, Pythagoras spoke in a "mystical-symbolic" mode—that is, in the language of traditional myths—of Kronos' tears, Rhea's hands, etc. But within the group, he explained the meaning of such remarks and explained the mythological elements "rationally," in terms of his philosophy of nature. We know of corresponding procedures in the ancient ceremonies of initiation into the mysteries, which—and this is often overlooked—also all had a didactic part, in which the initiates were introduced to the relevant cultic myth and its correct interpretation. Various ancient witnesses indicate how much it was taken for granted that in the Eleusinian myth of Hades' rape of Persephone and Demeter's search for her lost daughter, Demeter stood for "Mother Earth" and Persephone for grain. In the Orphic-Bacchic mysteries the myth of Dionysus' dismemberment by the Titans was "made to correspond step by step to the production of wine," and this kind of natural allegory is also well documented for other mystery cults.[148]

Did Pythagoras perhaps develop his theory of nature chiefly through the interpretation of theogonic and other "sacred" poetry by "Orpheus"?[149] If we make this assumption, many details in the tradition become easier to understand—not only why Orpheus is frequently named as Pythagoras' teacher and why Orphic and Pythagorean doctrines relating to the soul, its luck in the Beyond, and rules regarding ritual and diet often coincide, but also, for instance, why the ancient Pythagorean account of the origin of numbers (arithmogony) strikingly resembles an Orphic cosmogony (this last assertion is explored in greater detail below). Since in antiquity there was in general hardly anything corresponding to copyright and especially since the corpus of writings that circulated under Orpheus' name was at that time still not in any way fixed, it would also not be surprising if Pythagoras and his disciples not only interpreted Orphic texts but also further elaborated on them, as was assumed by Ion and another writer of the early fourth century about whom we know virtually nothing else, Epigenes.[150] In any case, among the writings mentioned by Heraclitus from which Pythagoras cobbled together his own "wisdom" some may have also been Orphic.

If it is true that Pythagorean cosmology did grow out of a naturalistic reading of Orphic poetry, then Pythagoras might be considered a forerunner of the author of the Derveni papyrus (toward the end of the fifth century B.C.E.), who in a bold allegorical interpretation read into Orpheus' theogony the natural philosophy of Anaxagoras (c. 500–428 B.C.E.) and Diogenes of Apollonia (fl. 440/430 B.C.E.).[151] To be sure, Pythagoras' rationalizing of myth is still less far-reaching, and the boundaries between mythical narrative and naturalistic explanation remain fluid. Also natural events could therefore conversely be explained in mythical terms. Pythagoras is thus reported to have interpreted earthquakes as a result of "a gathering of the dead," and considered the "sounds which often intrude upon the ears" (tinnitus) as "the voices of higher powers," that is, probably as divinatory signs.[152] The sound produced by mineral ore when it is struck he explained (again according to Aristotle) as the "voice of a *daímon* that is imprisoned in the ore."[153] His explanation of Zeus' thunderbolts—"a threat to the inhabitants of Tartarus, to frighten them"[154]—also belongs to this context, whereas the explanation of the rainbow as "the radiance of the sun" again betrays stronger cosmological interests.[155]

It is difficult to imagine that all these maxims represented isolated units without any relation to each other. An overarching fabric of meaning can at least be divined. On *mythical* levels we can glimpse intimations of the succession myth, also adopted in Orpheus' theogony, according to which Kronos and Rhea were the ruling couple of the ancestors of the gods preceding Zeus and Hera. Does Kronos weep because he has been dispossessed of power? Do "Rhea's hands" refer to the trick by means of which she prevented Kronos from swallowing up Zeus along with the rest of his siblings ("With her hands she took him and hid him in the deepest cave" on Crete, as we read in Hesiod, and gave his father instead a large stone wrapped in swaddling clothes)?[156] In any case, since being overthrown by Zeus, Kronos and his siblings the Titans have been "inhabitants of Tartarus," whom Zeus keeps threatening with his thunderbolts.[157] And Iris (the Greek name for the rainbow), Zeus' favorite messenger, is mentioned by Hesiod primarily in connection with the description of Tartarus and its inhabitants.[158] Furthermore, a (possibly Orphic?) poem about the fate of the souls on Earth and in the Beyond might have been among the texts that Pythagoras interpreted. This is suggested by the "Island of the Blessed," where, according to Hesiod, the "divine race of heroes" enjoys a carefree life after death,[159] by the "gathering of the dead" in the Underworld (as a cause of earthquakes), and by the Pythagorean saying that human beings have come (to Earth) for punishment and should therefore in fact be punished.[160] Perhaps even the *daímon* imprisoned in mineral ore should be seen in this context—Empedocles calls souls *daímones*[161]—and Pythagoras' explanation recalls Thales, who similarly attributed, Aristotle tells us, a "soul" to the lodestone, "because it moves iron."[162] As to "Persephone's dogs" finally, we can presume that they had the task of keeping certain souls from gaining access to Hades, so that the latter roam the Earth and their voices may be heard as a ringing in the ears.[163]

So far as the *doctrine of nature* (developed by interpreting such poems) is concerned, we cannot deny the scattered "oral sayings" a certain coherence either. The sun and moon, Ursae Major and Minor, the Pleiades (as fixed stars), and planets, and also the rainbow, thunder, earthquakes, and the sea —all these imply that Pythagoras developed a relatively systematic explanation of the world such as we find, even if detached from mythical narratives, in the Milesians Anaximander and Anaximenes. In particular, there are similarities with Anaximander's model of the world,[164] and Pythagoras' contemporary Anaximenes seems to have explained rainbows in a very similar way as "radiances of the sun" that occur when the sun's rays strike thick, solid, moist air.[165]

Natural Philosophical "Oral Sayings" II: Numbers, Names, Medicine, Harmony

The second group of "oral sayings"—which according to Aristotle (in Iamblichus) takes up an old form of pieces of wisdom as attested for Thales, the Seven Sages, and others, and which examine certain qualities in order to inquire into their highest realizations ("What is most y?")—is equally of interest for the oldest Pythagorean philosophy of nature. In addition to examples like the one already mentioned—"What is most just? To sacrifice" or "What is best? To have a good *daímon* [i.e., luck and blessedness]," the following *akoúsmata* have also been preserved:

—What is the wisest? Number; but secondly, what gives things names.
—What is the wisest thing in the human realm? The art of medicine.
—What is most beautiful? "Harmony."
—What is strongest? Insight.

(Iambl. VPyth. 82, following Aristotle)

In their brevity these sayings are simultaneously enigmatic and suggestive. Did the unique "strength" of (true) "insight" perhaps explain the miracles performed by the master, whose superior wisdom Empedocles praises? Moreover, isn't Pythagoras described in the sources as a healer—"he also did not neglect the art of medicine"[166]—and isn't the prominent physician Democedes presented as being part of his milieu in Croton? The distinction between what is wisest in the human and (as is probably to be supplemented in the first saying) divine realms makes us prick up our ears: Wasn't Pythagoras celebrated by his followers as a superhuman being? Again, "number" (as being the "wisest element") can hardly stand for an "objective" magnitude, but must designate here something like the key to the world that has to be discovered. Wasn't the recognition of the numerical nature of the world (perceivable by the senses) described, at least as early as Aristotle, as the quintessence of Pythagorean philosophy (more on this in a moment)? And wasn't the wisest (superhuman) thing (in other passages mostly understood to be a person) "that gave names to things," apart from the divine giver of language and names,[167] taken primarily to be Pythagoras, whose word-creating power is emphasized in the sources more than once? According to the tradition, he invented such important terms as *philosophy* and *cosmos*—"order, ornament, artful work"—as a designation for the well-ordered universe,[168] moreover for instance also the *tetraktýs* ("fourthness") and the coinage of the proverb "Friendship [is] equality," which in Greek involves a paronomastic play on words (*par-onomasía*): *philótes isótes*.[169]

In short, the "oral sayings" just mentioned awaken a multitude of associations and once again suggest that Pythagoras was more than simply a guru and a charismatic.

Aristotle on the Pythagoreans

More detailed information regarding the Pythagorean philosophy of nature is provided above all by Aristotle, who wrote two lost works *Against the Pythagoreans* and *On the Pythagoreans* (or *On the Pythagoreans' Opinions; the* title is handed down in different forms) and who also in his extant works repeatedly deals with Pythagorean philosophy and doctrine of nature, with special intensity in his *Metaphysics*. Scholarly opinion differs as to whether Aristotle's explanations shed light on Pythagoras' own teaching, too, or simply reflect the views of Pythagoreans of the fifth century B.C.E., and particularly those of Philolaus of Croton. Since relatively reliable witnesses regarding Pythagoras are very scanty, and since his thinking in natural philosophy can be reconstructed from them at most in outline, answering this question is of considerable importance.

Skepticism is fed essentially by the fact that in connection with views on the philosophy of nature, Aristotle speaks exclusively of "the Pythagoreans" or—in a somewhat distanced but not (in contrast to our expression "so-called") derogative way[170]—of "those who are called Pythagoreans," whereas he seems to refer to Pythagoras himself by name only when it is a question of miracles and ritual taboos. On the basis of this observation, Walter Burkert, for example, critically following Eduard Zeller, concluded that Pythagoras' original teaching was still free of any kind of "exact science"[171] and that Aristotle's description of the Pythagoreans' number philosophy and cosmology was based mainly on the Pythagorean Philolaus of Croton (whom Aristotle nonetheless never mentions by name in connection with philosophy of nature), who was, according to the tradition, the "first Pythagorean to publish a book 'On Nature' "[172] (various fragments of this work have come down to us).

The fact that on Pythagoras' philosophy of nature Aristotle had no authentic work at hand and had to rely on one or several writings—complemented by oral tradition?—by more recent Pythagoreans might in fact be an important reason why in this context he uses only the group designation "Pythagoreans" or even the place name "Italians" (in his doxographical survey of philosophical opinions, Aristotle usually bases himself on writings; he also sometimes succeeds in defining the Pythagoreans' positions so distinctly and precisely that we have fundamentally to assume that he was working from written documents). This does, however, not necessarily mean that Pythagoras himself still had no real natural philosophy of his own, and that Philolaus was the first to have attempted to transpose the "completely pre-scientific" lore, as the "shaman" Pythagoras practiced it, into the language of a "recently founded" philosophy of nature.[173] For one thing, pre-Socratic investigation of nature had begun long before in immediate proximity to Pythagoras' home island of Samos, and the attitude of curious inquiry and desire to know things (*historíe*) characteristic of the earliest Ionian thinkers was unambiguously attributed by Heraclitus to Pythagoras, even if in his opinion it led in the case of Mnesarchus' son only to "much learning" and alleged wisdom.[174] In Croton, again, Pythagoras may have found an existing medical school,[175] and dialogues between Pythagoreans and Italian natural philosophers, such as is attested for Alcmaeon of Croton (early fifth century B.C.E.), could hardly have begun only after Pythagoras' death (around 480 B.C.E.?). Moreover, against the view just outlined there is also the fact that in the lost works, Aristotle discusses both aspects, the gurulike and the natural philosophical, together, and that even in connection with the "oral sayings" he sometimes refers to "the Pythagoreans" in place of Pythagoras.[176] (Incidentally, in referring to Plato and the early Academy he also sometimes uses collective constructions such as "those who hold the ideas").

It may be added, that neither the reports regarding Philolaus nor the extant fragments present this Pythagorean, whom we find so much easier to grasp, as an "innovator."[177] Instead, key concepts and ideas we encountered in the "oral sayings" obviously still occupy an important place in his philosophy: We may mention the "fourthness,"[178] *harmonía*, and the general esteem of "number," and perhaps also the interpretation of reincarnation as punishment (however, the authenticity of the relevant fragment[179] is debated). Like Pythagoras, who is said to have described the sea as "the tears of Kronos" and Ursae Major and Minor as "Rhea's hands," Philolaus also uses mythical names for astronomical phenomena: He calls the central fire "Zeus' house"—Aristotle's "Pythagoreans" speak of "Zeus' tower" or "guard"[180]—or "the mother of the gods" or the "hearth."[181] In short, it certainly looks as though Philolaus continued down the paths laid out by Pythagoras. That does not exclude the possibility, to be sure, that he further elaborated Pythagoras' teachings and added elements of his own to them.[182] Yet the continuity was probably greater than modern accounts[183] suggest: "His [Pythagoras'] successors deviated little from his thinking," as Hippolytus put it.[184] For a sectlike movement as was the Pythagorean secret society, in a certain sense this goes without saying. The words of the (charismatic) foundress or founder always enjoy the highest authority in a sect. Any member who develops his own ideas seeks to connect them as much as possible with the master's teaching. Group identity prevails over individuality. Outsiders therefore perceive members of the sect as a unit, and tend to use collective terms to describe them.

In Aristotle it is much the same. Occasionally he may distinguish between various representatives of this philosophical school[185]—which clearly shows that for him "the Pythagoreans" could not be simply identified with Philolaus, and that he also had other sources, among them probably oral ones, at his disposal. But on the whole in his discussions the Pythagoreans appear as a quite homogeneous group, whose activity partly falls into the age of the atomists Leucippus and Democritus (born c. 460 B.C.E.?), partly still "earlier"—that is, probably in the first half of the fifth century B.C.E., and thus also before Philolaus as well.[186] So far as their natural philosophy can be related to the "oral sayings," Aristotle's information may therefore be used—with appropriate caution—to illuminate the context of the earliest testimonies regarding Pythagoras.

Pythagorean Number Philosophy

These Aristotelian Pythagoreans could easily have agreed that "number [is] the wisest." According to Aristotle, they considered the whole of reality as numerical in its nature. Of numbers not only all bodily things consist,[187] but also the (melodious) musical "fitting together" (*harmonía*) and the "whole heaven" along with the stars that move "in harmony."[188] Also concepts which we would consider as abstract, such as "insight," the "whole," or "justice," and even the gods they equated with certain numbers. We can agree with Aristotle when he connects this privileging of number in Pythagoreanism with the pre-Socratic inquiry into the "origin" (*archê*) of all things that exist *realiter*[189]—an inquiry that is always characterized by "violant generalizations."[190] What Anaximander called the "unlimited" (materially conceived), Anaximenes "air," Xenophanes "water and earth," and Heraclitus "fire" is for the Pythagoreans—and with them presumably also for Pythagoras himself—"number": the original material out of which everything was created and of which it still consists.

How did they arrive at this view? According to Aristotle, they discovered "resemblances"—one could also say: structural analogies—between all things on one hand, and numbers, as well as what "happens to them" (in simple mathematical operations)—their "changes in condition" or "modifications" (*páthe*)—on the other:

> In numbers they seemed to see many resemblances to the things that exist and come into being—more than in fire and earth and water (such and such a modification [*páthos*] of numbers being "justice," another being "soul" and "reason," another being "opportunity"— and similarly almost all other things being numerically expressible); since, again, they saw that the modifications and the ratios of the musical scales were expressible in numbers;—since, then, all other things seemed in their whole nature to be modeled on numbers, and numbers seemed to be the first things in the whole of nature, they supposed (986a1) the elements of numbers to be the elements of all things, and the whole heaven to be a musical scale and a number. And all the properties of numbers and scales which they could show to agree with the attributes and parts and the whole arrangement of

the heavens [*diakósmesis*], they collected and fitted into their scheme.[191] (Arist. Metaph. 985b27–986a6; transl. Ross)

An extremely dense text, in which almost every element calls for explanation. The interpretation of "ideal" items by means of numbers seems particularly enigmatic. Here a commentator on Aristotle of the Imperial Period, Alexander of Aphrodisias (c. 200 C.E.), can help us. He still had access to Aristotle's treatise on the Pythagorean philosophy, which has since been lost, and in his explications of the *Metaphysics* he paraphrases the corresponding passages from it.[192] Evidently the Pythagoreans determined the essence of justice, for example, as strict reciprocity—in terms of criminal law, this means that an offender must "suffer in return" (*antipáschein*) exactly what he has done to the other person.[193] In the domain of numbers, this *lex talionis* finds its structural counterpart in "the same times the same." For that reason, according to what Aristotle tells us, the Pythagoreans defined either the number four (2×2) or the number nine (3×3) as "justice."[194] Again, they considered the number seven as the "opportunity" or the "right point in time" (*kairós*), since natural processes of growth were completed in units of seven (e.g., seven-month children, the growth of teeth after seven months, puberty at about age fourteen [$= 2 \times 7$], and seven was also central in cosmology: in the Pythagorean model of the heavens, the sun, as the author of the "right points in time" for prosperity, occupies the seventh position counting from the periphery). Since furthermore the number seven is in a certain sense a "virgin" prime number—"it produces none of the first ten numbers, nor is it produced by one of them" (by being added to itself or multiplied by itself)—they equated it with the "motherless" and "ever-virginal" goddess Athena, who sprang from the forehead of Zeus. It should be noted how closely mythology and mathematical thought are connected here. We also owe to Alexander's excerpt from Aristotle the following identifications:

—They called the number five "wedding," since a wedding is a coming together of male and female, but in their view [the Pythagoreans'], male is odd, while female is even; but this is the first number that originates from two, as the first even number, and three, as the first odd number.
—They called the number one "insight" (*noûs*) and "essence" (*ousía*).... Because of its constancy, its equality in every respect, and its ruling quality, they called insight unity [*monás*] and the number one, but also essentiality, because the First is the essentiality.

—They called the number two "opinion," since it can change in both directions; but they also called it "movement" and "attack." (Aristot. fr. 162, p. 412b,23–413a,12 Gigon)

Drawing on other writings by Aristotle we can add two further correspondences:

—three = number of the "whole," since "end, middle and beginning contain the number of the whole, whereas the latter [encloses] the number of the triad." (Aristot. De cael. 268a10–13)
—ten = "perfect number," since it "seems to comprise the whole nature of numbers." (Aristot. Metaph. 986a8s.)[195]

Tetraktýs, Cosmic Harmony, and the Numerical Relationships of Harmonic Intervals

"Fourthness" (*tetraktýs*) was, as it seems, of central importance for the Pythagoreans, and they used to swear by its discoverer—their master Pythagoras, who according to Iamblichus also coined the word.[196] "Fourthness" means the series of the first four numbers.[197] It is extolled in the oath almost hymnically: It is said to comprehend within itself "the source and root of the ever-flowing nature." This fits with the previously mentioned "oral saying" in which the Delphic oracle—considered at least since the early classical period as "navel of the world"—is equated with "fourthness." Obviously the Apollonian charismatic and his followers saw in the *tetraktýs* no less than the secret key to the understanding of nature and the cosmos. It may be that the word also has a ritual connotation—Burkert points to the analogously constructed word *triktýs*, which denoted among other things a sacrificial offering consisting of three animals, as well as to Pythagorean speculations that revolved around the Delphic tripod.[198] However, the "oral saying" continues in a way that points in another direction: The "fourthness" is given a musical interpretation and equated with the "harmony of the Sirens." Here it is hard not to think of the famous cosmic harmony, again said by Aristotle and others to have been a belief of the Pythagoreans. In the concluding myth—inspired by Pythagoreanism—of Plato's *Republic* the individual stars are each assigned a Siren that revolves with them, and each "can be heard to emit a single voice, a single tone; but out of all eight voices there results a single harmony" (the diatonic scale), and the three Fates sing to the "harmony of the Sirens" the past, present, and future[199] (according to the *Cratylus*, the god Apollo governs the cosmic harmony).[200]

In the background of the Pythagorean mystification of the *tetraktýs* and its application to the heavens—"the whole heaven is harmony and number"[201]—in all likelihood stands the recognition that in the first four numbers are contained the consonant intervals of the octave, the fifth, and the fourth (moreover the sum of the *tetraktýs* is equivalent to the "perfect" number ten and can be represented as a "perfect" triangle):

> However, since they also saw that the consonant intervals are composed in accord with a certain number, they said that numbers are also their principles. For the octave consists in the ratio 2:1, the fifth 3:2, the fourth 4:3. (Aristot. fr. 162, p. 413a,17–21 Gigon)[202]

To be sure, the later tradition embellished with legends the reports about how Pythagoras is supposed to have arrived at this discovery, and they contain physically impossible experiments. It may, however, hardly be doubted that the insight into the numerical nature of the basic concords was an essential reason for the enormous fascination that, according to the "oral sayings," numbers had for Pythagoras. "But to number everything is equivalent," says an oft-cited hemistich,[203] whose age cannot be determined with certainty, but which coincides in the essence with Aristotle's and Aristoxenus' statements:[204] "He equated all things with numbers," as Aristoxenus put it.[205] Where reality seemed to fall short of this maxim, the Pythagoreans apparently wouldn't shrink back from bold constructs.

Model of the Universe

As an example of this kind of construct, Aristotle mentions the "Counter-Earth": Since the number ten seems to be perfect and to include the entire nature of numbers, the Pythagoreans are said to have maintained that the celestial bodies were ten in number as well. But since only nine of them were visible, they therefore created the Counter-Earth as the tenth.[206] We find more details regarding this astronomical model in other works of Aristotle, where we note in passing that with regard to this point, the "Pythagoreans" are once again presented as a completely homogeneous group. According to the Pythagorean conception, at the center of the universe is not the Earth, but rather a fire. The Earth is only one of the heavenly bodies that revolve around this fire: starting from the center, the first is the (invisible) Counter-Earth, then the Earth, the moon, the sun, the five planets (Mercury, Venus, Mars, Jupiter, Saturn), and furthest out, the sphere of the fixed stars.[207] In modern times, this model has attracted a lot of attention chiefly because it no longer puts Earth in the central position—according to his own declaration, it was one of the influences that led Nicholas Copernicus ultimately to abandon the geocentric model of the universe. However, the Pythagoreans did not arrive at their conclusion, which from a modern point of view seems nothing less than revolutionary, on the basis of empirical observations. Instead, what was crucial for them, to judge on the basis of Aristotle's remarks, was fundamental reflection on the value of the individual things, their "hierarchy" in the order of the universe:[208] The center is considered the "most precious" place; it is assigned to fire, because in comparison to earth fire is thought to be "of higher value," and since the most important place most deserves to be guarded, they called the cosmic central fire "the guard of Zeus," the highest Olympian god.[209] We get the impression that here we glimpse the comparison, particularly common later among the Stoics, between the world as macrocosm and the city-state as microcosm. Just as in a well-ordered polis the hearth-fire in the prytaneum is the symbolic center, so fire occupies this well-guarded position in the Pythagoreans' great order of the heavens and the world. Accordingly, Philolaus is said to have called this fire the "hearth" (*hestía*).[210] Questions of rank-ordering remain important in the (Pythagoreanizing) cosmology of Plato, who, however, also constantly calls for empirical testing.

According to the testimony of Aristotle's disciple Eudemus, Anaximander of Miletus was the first to determine quantitatively the sizes of the planets and the distances between them. The Pythagoreans, who according to the same source were the first to attempt to clarify the sequence of the planets, probably relied on Anaximander's conclusions in offering their explanation of the harmony of the spheres, in which these distances play an important role. In their view, stars, which as very large, very swiftly moving bodies, must necessarily produce a sound, revolve at distances and at speeds proportional to each other. But since the resulting sound is correlated with speed and distance and corresponds to the numerical proportions of musical concords, the revolution of the stars produces a harmonious sound.[211] Whether Pythagoras had already explained the cosmic harmony in this way must remain a matter of debate. At least, he may very well have been familiar with the teaching of his neighbor Anaximander of Miletus.

Arithmogony and Cosmogony

The doctrine of the origin of numbers, which within the Pythagorean system runs entirely parallel to the cosmogony, strikes scholars as being ancient. For if numbers are by their very nature the first of all existing things, then it is obvious that their "elements" and "origins" are also the "origins" of the world and of all the things contained within it.[212] According to Aristotle, the Pythagoreans defined as "elements" of number "the even and the odd," of which they said "one to be limited, the other unlimited." If we recall that in his dialogue *Philebus,* Plato identifies the knowledge of the fundamental distinction between "unlimitedness" and "limit," which are innate in all ever existing things, as a gift of the gods passed on by "the ancients, being superior to us and dwelling nearer to the gods,"[213] we may presume that the superhuman Pythagoras had already taught such a doctrine. Philolaus would then be a good Pythagorean on this point as well, for it is attested for him to have maintained that "limiters" and "unlimited things," both of which are evidently the components of the cosmos, had existed ever since.[214] Still, it would have been impossible for them to get together to form a world order (*kósmos*), if harmonic "fitting together" (*harmonía*) had not supervened[215] (as the following section shows, for Philolaus, *harmonía* meant the musical numerical proportions of the diatonic octave, which contains within itself particularly the fifth and fourth harmonic intervals and determines the structure of the cosmos). At the origin of the world, first of all the central fire—Philolaus' "hearth"—was "fitted together." It is being equated with the number one (*hén*) or the unity (*monás*),[216] which consists of both the basic elements of number, the even and the odd, and is therefore called the "even-odd";[217] as a proof of this is adduced the fact that the number one is able to "generate" both even and odd numbers, "for if it is added to an even number, it produces an odd number, [and if it is added to] an odd number, [it produces] an even number."[218]

The beginning of the "fitting together" of the world thus precisely corresponds to the construction of the number one out of the even and the odd. The coincidence is further emphasized by the Pythagorean definition of the even as the "unlimited" and the odd as the "limited," as it emerges for example from the series of ten pairs of opposites (understood as "principles," according to Aristotle) developed by "some Pythagoreans": In the first position stands the certainly old binary opposition "limit-unlimited," followed by "odd-even," "one-plurality," "right-left," "male-female," "resting-moving," "straight-crooked," "light-darkness," "good-bad," and "square-oblong."[219] Clearly, here we once again encounter hierarchical thinking: Positive values are opposed to inferior ones. In passing let us note that these Pythagoreans—as well as the natural philosopher Alcmaeon of Croton, who according to Aristotle posited an undetermined number of opposites structuring human affairs[220]—could in a certain sense be considered forerunners of modern structuralism, which is primarily concerned with hierarchical chains of binary oppositions in texts and other objects of analysis.

The Use of Counting Pebbles

The higher rank of the "odd" becomes easier to understand if we consider that the Pythagoreans were accustomed to visualize numbers by means of counting pebbles (*psêphoi*). If such pebbles are laid out in a series of "carpenter's squares," or *gnomons*, around the smallest even number or the smallest odd number, the result is always a square in the case of odd numbers—because of the equality of its sides the square is considered "perfect"—whereas even numbers result in a rectangle:[221]

○	○	○	○		○	○	○	○	○
●	●	●	○		●	●	●	●	○
○	○	●	○		○	○	○	●	○
●	○	●	○		●	●	○	●	○

Against this background, the mystification of the *tetraktýs* also acquires an additional point, for if counting pebbles are used to represent the series of the first four numbers, a "perfect" equilateral triangle emerges:

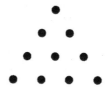

Among the Pythagoreans, visualization by means of counting pebbles did not remain an abstract mathematical game, but rather seems at least in part to have played a role in finding out the precise number of which individual things consist according to Pythagorean doctrine. Thus tradition tells us that Eurytus (born 450/440 B.C.E.?), who is said to have been Philolaus' pupil, used counting pebbles to form the outlines of living creatures and plants, and by counting the number of pebbles required, determined the numbers for man and horse, for instance.[222] This kind of procedure may seem to us naive. Nonetheless it fits with Aristotle's remark that although the Pythagoreans were the first to speak about formal causes and to make determinations, in doing so they proceeded all too "simply" and "superficially." According to him, they supposed that "the first subject to which a given determination"—that is, for the Pythagoreans probably a certain number or its property—would befit was the substance of the thing determined."[223] When in a fragment Philolaus speaks of the many "forms" of the even and the odd, which each thing "indicates" by itself,[224] this also reminds us of the figured representation of things by means of counting pebbles. It seems entirely conceivable that the Pythagoreans (and with them Pythagoras?) tried to demonstrate by means of counting stones and other means that in fact all things are numbers—a very similar mental attitude led to the taboo on eating beans being illustrated "experimentally." Just as counting stones, and also geometrical figures, set limits on a "limitless" surface and thereby make the contours of a thing first visible, so according to Philolaus number brings about the limitation of the "limitless" and thus creates the presupposition for anything at all being known, "for it is impossible to perceive or recognize anything without this [number]."[225]

The Identity of Numbers and Things

To understand Pythagorean doctrine correctly, one must always keep in mind that numbers and their elements represented for the Pythagoreans not merely a kind of analogy (different from perceptible reality) by means of which the structure of things can most easily be described. On the contrary, numbers *are* the existing things themselves. Like other pre-Socratics, too, the Pythagoreans considered everything that exists to be likewise material, perceptible through the senses.[226] They merely replace water, the "unlimited" (conceived as matter), air, earth, and fire by number. For, the "peculiarity" of their natural philosophical doctrine of number consists in the fact that they

> thought that the limited and the unlimited and the number one were not some different natures, like fire or earth or anything else of this kind, but that the unlimited and number one for itself were the substance of the things of which they are predicated, and that for this reason also number is the substance of all things. (Aristot. Metaph. 987a14–19)

Existing things, Aristotle notes in another passage, "are composed of numbers, and they *are* [in their essence] certain numbers."[227] Aristotle recognizes one of the main difficulties of this doctrine of nature to lie precisely in the fact that the Pythagoreans—unlike Plato later on—drew no distinction between the mathematical and the corporally realized numbers, but instead equated them with each other; yet how, Aristotle asks, could natural bodies ever emerge from mathematical numbers, which have neither weight nor magnitude?[228]

Pythagorean and Orphic Cosmogony; Pythagorean Doctrine of Numbers and Ionian Natural Philosophy

For the Pythagoreans, who are on this point typical pre-Socratics, this was obviously still not a problem. The origin of the One and the origin of the central fire at the beginning of the world coincide. Cosmogony is arithmogony. The unlimited (and even) is outside the heavens. If the unlimited is taken up (into the heavens) and limited by the odd, then it provides existing things with limitlessness.[229] The cosmic "limitless" becomes thereby associated with the "void" (better known from ancient atomism), which proceeds out of the limitless into heaven:

> Like air, heaven is inhaling also the void, which distinguishes the natures of things, as if it were like what separates and distinguishes the terms of a series. This holds primarily in numbers, for the void distinguishes their nature. (Aristot. Phys. 213b22–27; cf. fr. 166 Gigon, where we read that the void constantly delimits "the places" of individual things)

The One, which first came into existence, "generates" the other numbers,[230] and accordingly the central fire probably produces the other heavenly bodies, perhaps after it has replicated itself—for Philolaus "another fire" is attested, which is located "at the very top" and "comprehends" the world.[231] About the precise way in which the creation of the world further proceeds, the sources tell us hardly anything. However, it seems clear, among other things, that the Pythagoreans divided the heavens into right and left, the right side being considered as of higher rank, particularly if connected with "above."[232] In any case, according to Aristotle there is no doubt that they posited a coming into being (*génesis*):

> For they say plainly that when the One had been constructed, whether out of planes or of skin [colored surface] or of seed or of elements which they themselves cannot express, immediately the nearest part of the unlimited began to be constrained and limited by the limit. (Aristot. Metaph. 1091a13–18; transl. after Ross)[233]

Walter Burkert has pointed out similarities between this Pythagorean arithmo-cosmogony and an ancient Orphic account about the origin of the world.[234] In the latter, a shapeless unlimited stands at the beginning, and is called the "constantly flowing, unlimited depth of the sea." In it, all things were mixed together.[235] In the course of a spontaneously forming vortex, it takes on the form of an egg. This world-egg sucks the surrounding air (cf. the "void") into itself, becomes pregnant, and gives birth to a double-sexed creature called "male-female" (cf. the "even-odd" number One; in the Pythagorean series of ten pairs of opposites discussed above the odd correlates with "male" and the even with "female"). Because of its shining, fiery appearance Orpheus gives it the name *Phanes*, "shining, appearing" (cf. the central fire). This is the "origin of all." The "orderly arrangement (of the world)" (*diakósmesis*) follows, and in connection with it the keyword *harmonía*, familiar to us from the Pythagorean cosmogony, is also used.[236]

These remarkable parallels confirm the proximity of the Pythagorean account of the origin of the world to Orphic poetry in general. Moreover, its antique flavor indicates that the cosmic doctrine of numbers may go back at least in germ past Philolaus as far as Pythagoras (a more precise delimitation of its authentic elements, however, is not possible because of the state of the transmission). As was already considered in connection with the "oral sayings," Pythagoras could have developed his arithmo-cosmological thinking on the basis of "sacred discourses" attributed to Orpheus (or even such speeches composed by himself?). The number as being the wisest, the fourthness of numbers as the key to the cosmos and its harmony, the mysterious hints contained in the "oral sayings," which may well have been intentionally formulated in an enigmatic way, can at any rate be at least partly explained in light of Aristotle's observations and the fragments preserved from Philolaus. A quite coherent natural philosophy emerges, which testifies to a similar intellectual attitude as do the ritual rules for the conduct of life (cf. 87 above on the taboo on beans), and which should be seen, following Aristotle, in the context of pre-Socratic inquiry into the "origins" of nature. In this respect the Pythagoreans certainly used "stranger principles and elements" than did the other natural philosophers, principles and elements that would have been appropriate for moving beyond natural philosophy and advancing to the supersensible—in modern terms, their number philosophy would have given the Pythagoreans (and Pythagoras) an opportunity to become the founders of Western "metaphysics." But this decisive step was reserved essentially for Socrates' pupil Plato, who according to Aristotle however "closely" adhered to the "Italic philosophy." The Pythagoreans did not exhaust the potential of their intellectual approach, limiting themselves, as natural philosophers (*physio-lógoi*), to what "is perceptible by the senses and contained within the so-called 'heavens.' "[237]

The Beginnings of Western Mathematics?

Before concluding, one question must be at least briefly addressed: What role did Pythagoras and his followers play in the development of Greek mathematics? In the later tradition particularly, Pythagoras' contribution is exalted in a legendary way: He is supposed to have profited from stimulations he received during his travels in the Orient and especially in Egypt, and not only to have discovered the theorem named after him and perfected geometry, but to also be the founder of rigorous mathematics as a deductive science. Modern research is divided. Depending on the general assessment made of the figure of Pythagoras and his school, we find skepticism[238] or confidence.[239] Since the situation of the extant documents is particularly precarious on this point, this disagreement is hardly surprising. Stimuli coming from the East are most probable in the case of Greek mathematics. In Babylon, the technique of calculation had reached a remarkable level long before, and as with the Pythagoreans, mathematics went hand in hand with number mysticism (numbers were connected with divinities—witness, as mentioned at 81 above, seven as Athena's number—and their rank was determined in analogy with their status in mythology).[240] Pythagoras' theorem had been in use in Mesopotamia since 1500 B.C.E., even if it was never explicitly formulated.[241] Did Pythagoras bring this important theorem to Greece? Were "experimental" foundations for it first developed in his school? Was it under his influence that "concern with numbers" was first generally "taken away from the needs of tradesmen" and raised to a more theoretical level, as Aristoxenus—who is certainly sometimes not a wholly reliable witness—writes?[242]

One thing at least seems clear: Even a speculative theory of numbers with certain mythical traits as attested for Pythagoras and ancient Pythagoreanism represents a decisive attempt to structure reality in a comprehensive way and to bring it within a system of classification. It is therefore in the sense of Lévi-Strauss' *pensée sauvage* also a kind of science (the importance of number mysticism for the development of mathematics as an autonomous science is rightly stressed by Pichot).[243] Seen in this way, Aristotle's sweeping statement, which we have still not basically moved beyond, is justified: The Pythagoreans were the first to concern themselves with *mathémata*—that is, with arithmetic, geometry, astronomy, and music[244]—and "advanced" them.[245]

DID PYTHAGORAS INVENT THE WORD *PHILOSOPHY*?

In an "oral saying," the wisest (*sophótaton*)—in the superhuman realm—is designated, immediately after number, as that which—or the one who—"gives things names." The Pythagoreans probably thereby referred especially to their founding hero Pythagoras, who was admired for coining numerous words. Apart from the term "cosmos," the most successful of these was no doubt the composite *philó-sophos* ("loving wisdom, friend of wisdom"), without which and without whose nominal and verbal derivatives, *philosophía, philosophikós,* and *philosopheîn,* Western intellectual history is hard to imagine. Given the prestige this word family enjoys to date, it is not at all surprising that research has repeatedly sought to determine its origin—with variable results, however: Whereas some scholars are inclined to credit the unanimous ancient tradition, or at least not exclude the possibility that Pythagoras was the creator of the word *philosophy,* others have raised strong doubts about our main source, the Platonist Heraclides Ponticus (c. 390–after 322 B.C.E.), who in his lost dialogue "On the woman who is no longer breathing, or on illnesses" related an event in the course of which Pythagoras is supposed to have used the word for the first time. The following remarks are based on a fresh investigation into the question.[246] Before going into the arguments for and against the reliability of Heraclides' testimony, let us present the colorful, thought-provoking anecdote according to Cicero's Latin version, which adheres closely to the Greek original. In the fifth book of his *Tusculan Disputations,* after singing the praises of philosophy as *vitae dux,* Cicero seeks to refute the erroneous assumption that this wonderful power is something new. In doing so, he concedes that the name, in distinction from the thing, which he describes as *antiquissimam,* is recent, and that those who shifted all their efforts to the observation of things (*rerum contemplatio*) were earlier called "sages" (*sapientes,* Gk. *sophoí*):

> And this title of theirs penetrated to the time of Pythagoras who, according to Heraclides of Pontus, the pupil of Plato and a learned man of the first rank, came, the story goes, to Phlius and with a wealth of learning and words discussed certain subjects with Leon the ruler of the Phliasians. And Leon after wondering at his talent and eloquence asked him to name the art in which he put most reliance. But Pythagoras said that for his part he had no acquaintance with any art, but was a philosopher. Leon was astonished at the novelty of the term and asked who philosophers were and in what they differed from the rest of the world.

> (9) Pythagoras, the story continues, replied that the life of man seemed to him to resemble the festival which was celebrated with most magnificent games before a concourse collected from the whole of Greece. For at this festival some men whose bodies had been trained sought to win the glorious distinction of a crown, others were attracted by the prospect of making gain by buying or selling, whilst there was on the other hand a certain class, and that quite the best type of free-born men, who looked neither for applause nor gain, but

came for the sake of the spectacle and closely watched what was done
and how it was done: So also we, as though we had come from some
city to a kind of crowded festival, leaving in like fashion another life
and nature of being, entered upon this life, and some were slaves of
ambition, some of money; there were a special few who, counting all
else as nothing, ardently contemplated the nature of things. These
men he would call "lovers of wisdom" (for that is the meaning of the
word philo-sopher). And just as at the games it was most worthy of a
free man to watch while gaining nothing for oneself, so in life the
contemplation and discovery of nature far surpassed all other pur-
suits. (Cic. Tusc. 5,8s. = Heracl. Pont. fr. 88 Wehrli; transl. after King)

Let us immediately attach two explanations to the text: (1) To judge by parallel passages, the comparison most likely refers not to just any festival, but
to the Pan-Hellenic festivals *par excellence,* those that had regularly taken
place in Olympia every four years since 776 B.C.E. In this context, it is worth
mentioning that between the Olympic shrine to Zeus on the Peloponnesus
and Pythagoras' center of activity in southern Italy there were particularly
close relations in the sixth century B.C.E.—at this time no other city produced as many Olympic winners as did Croton.[247] (2) A linguistic effect of
the new coinage may have consisted for Heraclides in the fact that the word
sophós, which in Greek denotes initially any kind of practical skills and clev-
erness, especially musical ability, and then is also used in the transferred
sense of "prudence, wisdom," was presumably present in Leon's question
in the original version: "In what art (*téchne*) are you skilled (*sophós*)?" he
must have asked Pythagoras and received the answer that he is not in any
téchne sophós, but rather a *philó-sophos.*

Heraclides, to whom most of the ancient testimony can be traced back
(either directly or indirectly), is also named as a source by Diogenes Laertius in the proem to his lives of the philosophers:

Pythagoras was the first to use the term "philosophy," and he [called]
himself a "philosopher" when he was talking with Leon in Sicyon, the
tyrant of the Sicyonians—or of the Phliasians, as Heraclides Ponticus
says in his work "On the woman who is no longer breathing." For no
one is actually wise except God. (Diog. Laert. 1,12 = Heracl. Pont. fr.
87 Wehrli)

Differently from what we find in Cicero, here the city of Sicyon, which lies
north of Phlius, is given as the place where the conversation occurred, and
Leon therefore appears only in second place as the tyrant of the Phliasians.
Since Cicero gives no hint of uncertainty in this regard, and since Phlius is

otherwise constantly named, it can be presumed that Sicyon was not mentioned in Heraclides (the actual quotation of Heraclides would then be limited to "of the Phliasians").

What is new with regard to Cicero is primarily the explanation of the coining of the word by the hint that only God is wise. This statement represents one of the main grounds for those who are skeptical about the ancient tradition and assume that the etiological story was invented in the Platonic Academy.[248] In fact it is characteristic of Plato to reserve the attribute "wise" for the divine and to assign philosophy, understood as "striving for wisdom," a position intermediate between *sophía* and *amathía* ("ignorance, stupidity").[249] It seems, however, extremely questionable whether this addition really stems from Heraclides.[250] Setting aside the fact that as noted, the reference may be valid alone for the alternative information, the explanation does not fit well into the argumentative drift of the anecdote. In the encomiastic comparison of life to an Olympic festival gathering, the philosophers correspond to the third group of participants in the festival, who certainly achieve their goal, looking on with a desire to learn. How then could this be fundamentally denied to the philosophers? Furthermore, the larger context of the dialogue, so far as it can be deduced from the fragments, speaks against the authenticity of the addition. In Heraclides, Empedocles' disciple Pausanias seems to have recounted his master's reviving of a woman who had lain motionless for days, apparently dead. Whereas the "scientific physicians" considered her actually dead, Empedocles recognized—probably on the basis of his unique insight into the nature of things—that her soul had simply left her body for a while in a kind of ecstasy. The miraculous resuscitation of the woman was probably described as the triumphal, crowning achievement of Empedocles' life work, which directly led to the rapture and deification of the natural philosophical thaumaturge. Pythagoras may have been introduced by Heraclides as Empedocles' teacher and model, who had, just like Empedocles, reached the limits of a more than human perfection. In this context, the humble definition of philosophy as an ongoing effort to achieve something that ultimately cannot be attained is hardly conceivable. Instead, this explanation was probably a later, Platonizing addition.

Conversely, of course, we cannot immediately conclude that Heraclides' account is reliable in all respects. As the literary genre chosen suggests, the dialogues of this talented writer, who incidentally served as an important model for Cicero's own dialogues, will also have developed their own mimetic dynamics and have mixed history with fiction. In the case of Pythagoras, Heraclides' way of proceeding can be seen, for example, in his treatment of the various reincarnations, in which he seems to have "elaborated on older legends, to which Euphorbus at least belonged . . . by bringing in independent traditions."[251] Something similar probably holds for his account of the coining of the word *philosophy/-er*: It will neither be freely invented nor wholly authentic. Thus the difficult task is to discern as far as possible within Heraclides' narrative fabric the ancient, authentic thread of the story.

The localization of the conversation in Phlius is subject to considerable doubt. Ancient accounts do not indicate that Pythagoras spent time in this city on the northeastern Peloponnesus. On the other hand, it is attested that after the anti-Pythagorean uprisings in southern Italy new centers of Pythagoreanism in Greece were established in the second half of the fifth century B.C.E., amongst other places, in this city. The local community would have had every reason to want to assert an ancient connection between themselves and the master. The dialogue between Leon and Pythagoras also sounds fictitious. The confrontation between a sage and an autocrat is a narrative topos on which many variations were rung in antiquity (cf. below on Solon and Croesus in Herodotus). The suspicion that this element is fictitious is further strengthened by the fact that except for this episode, nothing is known of Leon (the name, however, crops up among the presumably Pythagorean addressees of the natural philosopher Alcmaeon of Croton[252] and in Iamblichus' catalog of Pythagoreans,[253] which probably goes back to Aristoxenus). In a disciple of Plato, moreover, the tripartite classification of people into servants of money, fame seekers, and philosophers makes us prick up our ears, since in the Platonic *Republic* three main types of people are deduced from the three parts of the soul, the desiring part, the impetuous part, and the part that is capable of reason: Depending on which of them is prevailing, the human being representing the profit-seeking type, the type who loves to win, and the type who loves wisdom may be discerned.[254] However, on this point Plato could also be following an older tradition, and all the more so because the three goods—money, reputation/honor, and intellectual activity—also appear in his work independently of his theory of the soul.[255] Herodotus was familiar with a comparable distinction between three groups of persons,[256] and in early Greek lyric poetry and pre-Socratic philosophy there are numerous examples that show that long before Plato people had pondered over the differing motives for humans' actions.[257]

In the Old Academy and in the Peripatetic school there were keen debates about which of the two ways of life—the *vita activa* devoted to politics and practical activity or the *vita contemplativa* devoted entirely to knowledge and philosophical reflection—was the better, and some scholars therefore thought to find evidence for the academic origin of the episode also in Heraclides' praise of disinterested contemplation of the world as an activity far superior to any other. However, this tends to neglect the fact that decades before Plato, *historía*, the contemplative search for knowledge and inquiry into nature and all things, was already considered the pre-Socratic natural philosophers' ideal way of life, to which they wanted to make everything subordinate. The tragedian Euripides (485/480–406 B.C.E.) gave this attitude impressive expression:

> Blessed he who knowledge gains
> through inquiry (*historía*),
> neither turning to offending the citizens
> nor committing unjust acts,
> but rather contemplating the ageless world order (*kósmos*)
> of immortal nature, by which way it came into existence
> and out of what and how.
> To such men never cleaves
> care for shameful acts.
>
> (Eur. fr. 910 N²= Incert. fab. fr. 3, p. 168 Diggle,
> with Wilamowitz's emendation in v. 7)

These verses sound as though Euripides wanted to elicit understanding for a way of life that was seen by the average citizen as provocative and threatening, and that was particularly connected with the name of the natural philosopher Anaxagoras, whose famous claim that the sun was merely a fiery clump of earth was likely to offend contemporaries' religious sensibilities (the sun was generally held to be a divinity). In his lost tragedy *Antiope* the same tragedian seems to have taken as his subject the later so intensively discussed opposition between a musical-intellectual life directed toward *sophía*, which seemed to outsiders "useless" and lazy, and the political-practical life, presenting the Theban twins Amphion and Zethus as exemplifying these two ways of life.[258]

In some important respects, even the colorful, comically distorted picture of contemporary intellectuals that appears behind the mask of Socrates in Aristophanes' *The Clouds* (produced in 423 B.C.E. and reworked between 420 and 417) comes quite close to the philosophical existence outlined in Heraclides' fragment. With the exception of sophistical rhetoric, which, by the way, becomes truly important only in the second part of the comedy, the residents of the "Thinkery" practice nothing other than the "ardent contemplation of the nature of things" (Heraclides). Central to their efforts are cosmological, astronomical, and meteorological phenomena, for which they seek "scientific" explanations. In our context, not the least interesting thing is that Aristophanes has given this form of existence a few unmistakably Orphic-Pythagorean characteristics, including especially the practice of keeping the doctrine secret and leading an ascetic life.[259]

As for the word *theoría* ("viewing, contemplation"), which for Heraclides and the Academy defines philosophical activity, it is first of all used for the envoys of a city or community who participate in a religious celebration taking place elsewhere, or who are making a pilgrimage to an oracle. The word continued to be used in this way later on, so that basically the comparison between visitors to a festival (who in fact had much to look at in Olympia, for instance—apart from the religious ceremonies and athletic competitions, there were also splendid edifices and artworks) and "spectators" (*theoroî*) of the universe experienced as a wonderfully ordered whole was easy to make at any time. The expression eventually came to resemble the usual word for "seeing, looking at" (*théa*), and this could be connected with the fact that for the Greeks legations to festivals probably represented in early times the most important opportunity to see foreign places.[260] However, as opposed to *théa*, *theoría* initially still connoted a change of place. Thus in Herodotus we read that after his laws were decreed, the Athenian statesman and "sage" Solon (c. 640–560/559 B.C.E.) traveled for ten years "for the sake of *theoría*"—or, to follow Walter Marg's translation, "in order to see and to learn."[261] The journey took Solon to Egypt and Sardis, where Herodotus has him meet the king, Croesus—an early example of the topos, which returns in Heraclides, of the encounter between a powerful man and a sage. At the beginning of their conversation, Herodotus' Croesus characterizes Solon in the following way:

> Guest from Athens—for we have heard a great deal about you, both because of your wisdom (*sophía*) and because of your wanderings, how "out of love for wisdom" (*philosophéon*) you have traveled over large parts of the Earth, in order to see and learn. (*theorías heíneken*) (Hdt. 1,30,2)

Wandering about and wanting to see many things out of a healthy curiosity: This is obviously considered a presupposition for the achievement of *sophíe*. We recall that according to ancient tradition, Pythagoras also traveled extensively. In any case, in Herodotus *theoría* and *philosophía* are very closely connected. Moreover, the natural way in which Herodotus speaks of practising philosophy indicates that the word was hardly first coined only in the twenties of the fifth century B.C.E.—the decade during which Herodotus' history was presumably published—but instead had been in use for some time. There are good grounds for assuming that it had already been employed by Heraclitus: "Men who love wisdom (*philósophoi*) must see and know (*hístores*) many things," we read in a fragment whose original extension, however, is a matter of dispute.[262] The statement may contain a jibe against the Pythagoreans,[263] whose founder, according to Heraclitus, was characterized by an exceptionally intensive if fruitless *historía*.

In the oldest testimonies going back as far as Pythagoras' own lifetime, there emerges thus a link between contemplative inquiry into the world (*historía*, *theoría*) and a particularly eager effort to acquire wisdom (*philosophía*) that seems to confirm the core of Heraclides' account. In addition, what Heraclides says seems to fit very well with the personal profile of the thoroughly self-conscious charismatic: Contrary to what the Platonic definition of the word might suggest, it is not self-moderation that is supposed to have allowed Pythagoras, who was equipped with unique abilities and celebrated by his followers as a being intermediate between humans and God, to describe himself as a *philósophos*. What was decisive was probably rather the need to distinguish his own superior prudence and insight from the many other kinds of "skills"—this was the original meaning of *sophía*[264]—and perhaps also to distinguish himself from earlier "sages" who had not attained the same heights, and who were probably named in the immediately preceding section of Heraclides' work. From the point of view of word formation, at any rate, *philó-sophos* in Greek does not denote a downgrading in comparison with *sophós*, but rather an intensification: A philosopher is a person who is engaged in particularly intensive dealings with *sophía* and who truly and exceedingly loves the latter.[265] Also, the choice of *theoría* to describe his own activity makes sense against the background of Pythagoras' personality: This word, which denotes first of all official visitors to festivals and those consulting oracles, and also later on retains its religious ring, seems not only in general highly applicable to the Pythagorean way of life and the self-conception of the "Hyperborean Apollo," but also is particularly appropriate to the festive self-staging through which Pythagoras, like Empedocles and modern charismatics, indicated the special status he claimed also by the externals. And is it an accident that according to ancient tradition the Olympic festivals were the place where Pythagoras once—no doubt as an envoy (*theorós*) of his city of Croton—rose and showed the spectators his golden thigh?

Thus it is not least on the basis of Pythagoras' appearance that it seems well possible that Heraclides' representation is in the essence accurate, and that not only his self-designation as a *philó-sophos*, which was later to become so influential, but also the description of this way of life as *theoría*, goes back to the charismatic founder of a politico-religious community in Croton.

3. THE PYTHAGOREAN SECRET SOCIETY

WERE THE PYTHAGOREANS AN ANCIENT "SECT"?

Definition of the Term

Before trying to answer the question in our heading, it seems necessary to attempt a brief clarification of the term *sect*. It is well known that this loan-word comes from the Latin noun *secta*, which by way of the intensive form *sectari* derives from the verb *sequi*, "to follow, to follow after," and hence denotes first of all the direction/line one "follows." Unlike the current modern use of the word, no value judgment is initially attached to this term. Thus, for example, in antiquity people spoke of the *secta* of the Stoics, of the Peripatetics, or of the Academics, and the word was also used to refer to different schools within Roman jurisprudence and political groups. The same holds for the corresponding word in Greek, which is based, however, on a different idea: The verbal abstract noun *haíresis* derives from *hairéomai*, "to take for oneself, choose, or prefer," and its literal meaning is thus "choice." From it developed in the Hellenistic period the meanings "a certain system of philosophic principles, a philosophical school" and "those who belong to this school"—and, of course, in this sense the term also applies to the Pythagoreans. Yet according to the evidence, it was in connection with the rise of Christianity that the shift in meaning to "false doctrine, heresy"—a shift which was to become so influential—gradually happened. When Christians were said by their opponents to belong to the "*haíresis* of the Nazoreens,"[1] the expression must have already carried an undertone of suspicion. For its part, the early church did not hesitate to describe, from at least the second century C.E. onward, as "heretics" the "false brothers" who split off from the congregation, although the neutral usage of *haíresis* survived for some time afterward.[2]

This history of *haíresis* and *secta* has shaped our own use of the word. In colloquial speech, it has for the most part negative connotations: "Sect" generally serves as a clearly derogatory designation of the "others," and commonly implies a deviation from a norm respected as valid as well as unethical forms of behavior such as the psychological and economic exploitation of the group's members. On the other side, scholars in the field of modern religious studies would prefer not to give up the concept of "sect," but abstain as far as possible from any value judgment and attempt to envisage "sect" as a certain religio-sociological phenomenon. In the following discussion, the word is used in this neutral, descriptive sense. Drawing freely on modern sociology of religion,[3] we shall try to determine to what extent the Pythagoreans—as an exclusive group that markedly stood out in various respects from the surrounding society—can be described as a "sect."[4]

Features of a Sect

What features amongst others can be seen as characteristic of sects of every kind? To approach the phenomenon from the outside: (1) the quantitative criterion is of a certain importance: As a rule, people speak of sects only with regard to minority groups that stand in some kind of strained relationship with the larger part of the society. If such a group becomes the majority, it loses more or less automatically the status of a sect (a favorite example of this is Christianity, which basically began as a Jewish sect and then became the dominant religious community). (2) As a rule, sects recognize a charismatic founder, an enlightened, holy master with extraordinary authority who is worshiped almost as a deity (there is no lack of examples also in the modern age; we have only to think of Bhagwan Osho or Sun Myung Moon). (3) Sects are distinguished by a clearly recognizable form of organization, often having hierarchical and centralized structures of power, and sometimes also a kind of communal property or at least close financial cooperation. Regular meetings of the membership are part of the external structure. The acceptance of candidates for membership depends on each individual's decision and the agreement of the accepting organization. (4) Sects usually are characterized by a high degree of spiritual integration. One can speak of genuine communities of belief, though their beliefs need not differ in every respect from those of the surrounding society (cf., e.g., Christian sects). An essential component of the coherent ideology is an idea of salvation, or "the promise of salvificatory goods" (*Heilsgüter*) as Gerhard Schmidtchen puts it:[5] According to the group's self-conception, only its members are in a position to evaluate correctly and master the contingencies of human life and its transitory nature.

Often they are given guarantees not only of earthly happiness but also for the Beyond. (5) Belief finds its expression in a regulated way of life that deviates at least in part from the usual one and may involve prescriptions regarding, for example, diet and clothing, and must be strictly followed. (6) From the common belief and the new way of life emerges at the same time a sense of superiority: The members see themselves as a specially chosen elite. The distinction between "we" and "they" becomes the primary frame of reference in judging real life. With this way of seeing things goes a sealing-off from the environment. Sects often break not only with the bases of the surrounding religious community, but also with those of the civil community. Tensions and social conflicts with the environment result, and members of the sect frequently become stigmatized by the external world. Conversely, sects commonly stigmatize renegade members and take action against them.

Application to the Pythagoreans

For the most part, the aforementioned sociological criteria for a determination of sects in general can be applied without further ado to the Pythagorean community, although we must qualify this by saying that the latter can be reconstructed only in outline because of the unfavorable state of the documentation (nonetheless, Heraclitus alludes to the existence of this group).

(1) So far as quantitative relationships are concerned, we must distinguish between true Pythagoreans and loosely associated followers (in later sources, the latter are also called "Pythagorists"). Toward the end of the sixth century B.C.E. the majority of the population of Croton probably belonged to the latter group. According to some testimonies, however, the inner circle consisted of not many more than three hundred persons.[6] As a group that initially consisted chiefly of aristocratic "young people," this inner circle also reminds us of politico-military followings of the kind that were particularly widespread in archaic and classical Greece.[7] In any case, these Pythagoreans represented only "a small part of the city."[8]

(2) Charismatic authority: That in the Pythagorean community "there was an extremely asymmetrical power relationship between an enlightened leader and a following,"[9] and that the latter had an extravagant respect for the founder, proceeds not only from their belief that Pythagoras possessed a superhuman form of existence, but also from the fact that in their circle the phrase "he himself said it" (*autòs épha*, Lat. *ipse dixit*) was proverbial and constituted for each and everything an unquestionable justification.[10] According to Iamblichus, Pythagoras' authority, which was confirmed by the miracles he performed, was so overpowering that the

Pythagoreans attributed everything, even their personal discoveries, to their master and hardly ever "claimed fame of their own."[11]

(3) Special structures: Interested persons' admission to the group was made anything but easy—in contrast to the practice of some modern sects.[12] Tests of physiognomic and ethical suitability are mentioned[13] (on physiognomics, see 18f. above). Admission was followed by a long probationary period during which the new member's ability to keep quiet, among other things, was tested:

> And whomever he examined in this way, he subjected to contempt for three years, to test how he was disposed to stability and true love of learning, and if he was sufficiently equipped against popular repute so as to despise honor. After this, he ordered a five year silence for those coming to him, testing how they were disposed to self-control, since more difficult than other forms of self-control is mastery of the tongue, as is revealed to us by those who instituted the mysteries. At this time, then, the things belonging to each, that is, their possessions, were held in common, given to those disciples appointed for this purpose who were called "politicians," and experienced in household management and skilled in legislation. The candidates themselves, then, if they appeared worthy of sharing in his teachings, having been judged by their way of life and other virtuousness, after the five year silence, became "eso-terics" [i.e., members of the "inner" circle] and heard Pythagoras within the curtain, and also saw him. Before this, they shared his discourses through mere hearing, being outside the curtain and never seeing him, while submitting over a long period to a test of their characters. (Iambl. VPyth. 72; transl. after Dillon and Hershbell)

In its details, this description is surely autonomously shaped and embellished by Iamblichus. Yet according to our sources, a few elements may have a core of authenticity. This holds in particular for the years of silence, which was considered throughout antiquity as almost the defining characteristic of the Pythagoreans. The oldest certain witness for this is the orator of the late fifth and early fourth century B.C.E., Isocrates. But the subject of one of the ancient "oral sayings" is also silence: "Master your tongue more than anything else [or: in front of the others?], following the gods!"[14] and the verse handed down to us by Heraclides Lembus, "Young people, venerate with silence all these things"[15] could very well be just as old. In addition, this verse suggests that the Pythagoreans saw the practice of silence not only as a way of achieving ascetic self-mastery but also as training for the duty to keep the teachings secret, which had to be strictly observed in the Pythagorean community, on the model of the mystery cults (in Greek, we often find in this context the composite *echémythos* [literally "withholding speech"], along with its verbal and nominal derivatives; according to Iamblichus, this expression was a *vox Pythagorica*).[16] Among the contents subject to secrecy were, as Aristotle tells us, the master's marvelous status intermediate between humans and God,[17] and certainly also the material foundation of taboos like that on beans, and perhaps also the doctrine of numbers, which has some mystical characteristics. Moreover, Iamblichus' mention of a community of property seems trustworthy (the "communism of love or comradship" is, incidentally, according to Weber another characteristic of the charismatic form of domination).[18] According to the Sicilian historian Timaeus, the beautiful proverb "What belongs to friends [is held in] common," quoted several times by Plato, owes its origin to precisely this institution:

> Now when young people came to him and wanted to live with him, he did not allow them [to do so] immediately, but rather told them that all the property of those who conversed [with each other] had to be held in common, too. . . . And because of them [the Pythagoreans], it was first said in Italy that "What belongs to friends [is held in] common." (Timaeus FGrHist 566 F 13)

In general, the Pythagoreans seem to have attached the greatest value to the cult of friendship. The word *friend* occurs in the oldest ever testimony: It is the voice of a friend that Pythagoras—in Xenophanes' satirical verses—heard in the whining of a dog as he was passing by. But friendship was limited to members of the secret society. From their opponents' point of view, it was accompanied by contempt for other people. The instruction to "worship friends as you do gods, but subjugate others as you do animals" was alleged to be Pythagoras,' and correspondingly, his disciples are supposed to have said in verses about him that

> His friends he considered equal to the blessed gods,
> the others were hardly worth mentioning, and counted nothing at all.
>
> (Apollonius FGrHist 1064 F 2,259)

This is surely a polemical exaggeration. But the story about the pledge, too, illustrates the Pythagoreans' tendency to "avoid friendship with other people."[19] Obviously, for them, as for other sects, the distinction between "we" (i.e., the initiates, the members) and "they" (i.e., the outsiders, the unenlightened) was the primary frame of reference (see below, criterian 6).

(4) A community of belief and (5) a regulated way of life: Further evidence that these two criteria apply to the Pythagorean community is hardly necessary. With their detailed and very extensive set of rules regarding purity, diet, and ritual behavior, the Pythagoreans were sharply distinguished from their contemporary environment, and in their total vegetarianism they even cut themselves off from the rest of society. The "spiritual unification" of the group was achieved not only by their reverence for the master and the mystification of numbers but especially by the doctrine of reincarnation. The Pythagoreans' hope of "salvation" in the Beyond was based on both the "purity" of their way of life and their master's advice as to what was to be observed regarding "moving away from here."[20]

(6) Conflicts between the elite secret society and the people around them did in fact occur. We have already mentioned the rebellion of Cylon, whom Pythagoras refused to admit to the community in Croton. A few decades after Pythagoras' death, the public discontent that had apparently been building up for a long time was vented in arson attacks on the Pythagoreans' meeting places in southern Italy. As for the Pythagoreans themselves, they show a behavioral pattern characteristic of a sect insofar as they not only punished by exclusion apostates and members who broke the rule of secrecy, but also, especially in the case of those on probation who in the five-year trial period had shown themselves, contrary to expectations, unworthy of participating in the doctrine. These unworthies were subjected to a true ritual of separation: Those who were rejected were given back the possessions they had handed over to the community during the probationary period, and indeed, they were given even twice as much (a gesture one would look long and hard to find in modern sects); then the Pythagoreans erected a gravestone and made a burial mound for them on the school's grounds, as if they were dead; and if one of them was ever encountered again afterward, he was treated, according to Iamblichus, as if he were not the same person, for the former member was actually considered by the Pythagoreans to be dead[21] (the community's reaction to Hippasus' betrayal of a mathematical secret is detailed at 108 below).[22] Similar ways of reacting are also found in modern movements (for instance, Jehovah's Witnesses seem to know a communication ban).[23]

As a result, we can record that in the community that Pythagoras founded in Croton, probably around the middle of the second half of the sixth century B.C.E., we encounter for the first time in the Western world a religious group that can on good grounds be described from the point of view of the sociology of religion as a "sect" *avant la lettre*. To judge on the basis of the fragmentary documents that have come down to us, it shows amazingly many of the traits now considered characteristic of this phenomenon, including the "emotional bonding as a community" (*emotionale*

Vergemeinschaftung),[24] and especially the orientation toward the charismatic leader whose self-confidence no doubt spread to the individual members of this community of the religiously and morally "pure."

THE PYTHAGOREANS IN THE FIFTH AND FOURTH CENTURIES B.C.E.

Problems with the Outside World: The Anti-Pythagorean Rebellions and their Consequences

Deviations from the societal norm, especially when combined with an ideologically underpinned feeling of superiority, are always regarded as provocative by the surrounding social environment. In the case of the Pythagorean community that is all the more true insofar as on the one hand it probably exercised considerable political influence, and on the other hand admission to the elite, aristocratic group was strictly regulated and remained closed to many people. Antagonistic reactions could hardly fail to result. Whereas the first rebellion was started, as we have seen, by a rejected candidate for membership who belonged to Croton's upper crust and led to Pythagoras' leaving Croton and moving to Metapontum, a later rebellion that damaged the Pythagorean community far more seems to have been politically motivated and involved essentially the common people (*dêmos*). Although the extant documents are particularly muddled on this point—most sources blend the two events together—the connection with the democratic movement can be quite clearly discerned, at least in Apollonius' account (paraphrased by Iamblichus, and probably going back to Timaeus), no matter how much the details of the latter may have been shaped by literary concerns. According to Apollonius, among the opponents' demands were that public offices and the public assembly be open to all, and that the rulers be obligated to justify their activities before a committee chosen by lot from the citizens at large; on the other hand the Pythagoreans, who were accused of having contempt for other people, an oligarchic attitude, and even wanting to become tyrants, insisted on retaining the existing constitution.[25]

A clear distinction between these two revolts occurring at different times is found only in Aristoxenus, who regards Cylon as at least indirectly responsible for the second revolt as well,[26] since after Cylon's "war" against Pythagoras his followers, "the so-called Cylonites," remained hostile to the Pythagoreans; yet "for a certain time" at least, the Pythagoreans' ethical excellence and the cities' desire to put them in charge of the polity won out. However, an attack was finally made: According to Aristoxenus, as the Pythagoreans had gathered in Milon's house in Croton and were discussing political affairs, the Cylonites set fire to the house and killed all the Pythagoreans but two men, Archippus and Lysis, whose youthful strength allowed them to fight their way out. According to other sources, anti-Pythagorean arson attacks were carried out not only in Croton, but all over Magna Graecia, throwing the whole region into bloody chaos (not until Greek legations were sent from the homeland did the situation calm down, and in time, moderately democratic constitutions based on the Achaean model were introduced).[27] In contrast, Aristoxenus limits the event to the city of Croton, which is hardly accurate. Only "if the leading men from each city died so senselessly"[28] can it be explained why these attacks represented such a major turning point for the Pythagorean community. That it was such a turning point seems undeniable even to Aristoxenus: In his account, the event resulted in the Pythagoreans' general withdrawal from political responsibility. As reasons for this withdrawal, he mentions first that the cities didn't at all care about the mischief that had been done (which probably means that to the surviving Pythagoreans' disappointment, the ringleaders were not brought to trial), and second, that the Pythagoreans had lost their men most gifted for political leadership—and this certainly not solely in Croton.

We lack established points of reference that would allow more precise dating of the arson attacks. Modern scholars' estimates vary between 450 B.C.E.[29] and the period between 440 and 415 B.C.E.[30] Subsequently, the Pythagorean community was spatially dispersed, which must surely have been accompanied by an internal disintegration. In accord with his alignment with the Pythagorean "home city," Aristoxenus first finishes telling the whole story of the two surviving men from Croton: Archippus withdrew to his hometown of Tarentum, but Lysis, embittered by the public officials' negligence, moved to Greece. At first, Lysis is said to have resided in Achaea in the Peloponnesus, and then to have gone to Thebes, where the major Theban commander of the first half of the fourth century B.C.E., Epaminondas, was among his pupils. In the sequel of his account, Aristoxenus abandons the purely Crotonian perspective and tells what happened to the "rest of the Pythagoreans": First, they assembled in Rhegium, but when the political situation there, too, became worse and worse, they all left Italy, with the sole exception of Archytas of Tarentum.

Aristoxenus then gives the names of the "most important" of these Pythagoreans: Phanto, Echecrates, Polymnastus, and Diocles—all from Phlius—as well as Xenophilus from Chalcidice. With Plato's friend Archytas and the Pythagoreans just mentioned, we are already in the first half of the fourth century B.C.E. According to Aristoxenus, whose father Spintharus seems to have been well acquainted with Archytas,[31] we are dealing with the "last" of the Pythagoreans altogether:

They, then, preserved their original customs and instructions, while
their school dwindled, until, maintaining their nobility, they disap-
peared. (Aristox. fr. 18, p. 13,32–34 Wehrli = Iambl. VPyth. 251,
transl. Dillon and Hershbell)[32]

According to this moving scenario, the Pythagorean school would have ceased
to exist around 360 B.C.E. However, that is demonstrably untrue. We know of
a Pythagorean called Lycon of Iasus, who made a polemical attack on Aristotle's lavish lifestyle and so probably lived primarily in the second half of the
fourth century B.C.E.[33] Moreover, "Pythagorists," whose typically Pythagorean
lifestyle is emphasized, are a favorite target of comedians' ridicule. The idea
suggests itself that the "enlightened" Pythagorean Aristoxenus, who also
turned completely upside down the Pythagoreans' vegetarianism and taboo
on beans for instance, did not recognize these "traditionalist" Pythagoreans
whose characteristic mode of behavior included vegetarianism and silence
(Timaeus must have rejected Diodorus of Aspendus, whom we will take up at
108 below, for similar reasons).[34] By having the "true" Pythagorean school
abruptly die out, Aristoxenus created the room for maneuver he needed to
reinterpret Pythagoreanism in a rationalistic way.[35]

On the other hand, the information provided by Aristoxenus regarding
the geographical dispersion of the Pythagoreans after the catastrophe
seems largely reliable. No later than at the turn from the fifth to the fourth
century B.C.E., the city of Tarentum became one of the most important
Pythagorean centers in southern Italy—this is shown not only by Archippus, Archytas, and Aristoxenus, but also, for example, by Middle Comedy
plays targeting the Pythagoreans and bearing titles such as "People from
Tarentum." Moreover, there are references to the presence of Pythagoreans on the Greek mainland, particularly in Thebes and Phlius, which were
allied with Athens' rival Sparta during the Peloponnesian War (431–404
B.C.E.) (see 10ff. for information about Philolaus, Lysis, Echecrates).[36] It
remains wholly uncertain whether the conciliatory conclusion of Apollonius' story has a historical basis: According to his account, "many years"
after the arson attack the people of Croton changed their minds and called
back the remaining Pythagoreans, all of whom are then said to have died
defending the city against Thurii.[37]

Internal Tensions: "Acousmatics" versus "Mathematicians"

Apart from the conflicts between the Pythagoreans and the surrounding society, the sources also tell us about conflicting tendencies within the school
itself. The names of the opposing groups suggest what the issue was: In
Greek, "acousmatic" is derived from "oral saying" (*ákousma*), while "math-

ematician" derives from "science" (*máthema*). Acousmatic Pythagoreans are therefore those for whom the master's "oral sayings," primarily concerning sacrifice and worship, were central, and who urged scrupulous observance of the various ritual rules and taboos that drastically regulated the members' everyday life.[38] The mathematicians, on the other hand, will have accorded this aspect less importance and considered their chief task to penetrate Pythagoreanism scientifically and to further develop it. As we can infer from Iamblichus, the mathematicians recognized the "conservative" acousmatics as true Pythagoreans, whereas conversely they were regarded by the latter as apostates and were associated with Hippasus, who is supposed to have betrayed a mathematical secret by publishing it. However, the mathematicians considered themselves Pythagoreans "to an even greater degree," and in order to justify this inequality they referred back to the situation in Croton when Pythagoras arrived there: Since the elders were completely absorbed with political tasks, he communicated his doctrine to them without further explanation, because he was convinced that they would also profit from it if they knew what to do, even if they were ignorant of the reasons for doing it—just as patients who were not also told why they must do something would nonetheless get well again; but he used scientific proofs in teaching young people who could still bear additional burdens and were capable of learning; they (that is, the mathematicians) were descended from these latter, while the others were descended from the elders.[39]

The temporal relationship between this internal split and the anti-Pythagorean attacks cannot be determined with certainty. Only this much is clear: The mathematicians, whose argument is summarized by Iamblichus (Aristotle?), looked back on Pythagoras' teaching in Croton as a quite distant event. One possible scenario is that first signs of a separation within the sect began to appear before 450/440–415 B.C.E., that these, however, were further deepened in connection with the organizational weakening and spatial dispersion that followed the catastrophe, and the gap between the two orientations ultimately became insuperable in the fourth century B.C.E. A significant factor in this development was no doubt the fact that with the progress of science and philosophy since the fifth century B.C.E., the old-fashioned prescriptions embodied in the "oral sayings" had become increasingly obsolete (later on, Iamblichus also emphasized the archaic character of the oral sayings, while at the same time praising their inexhaustible meaning-potential).[40]

In any case, the opposition between mathematicians and acousmatics appears to be particularly marked in the fourth century B.C.E. To the first, "mathematical" group seem to have belonged, among others, Archytas of Tarentum, who continued along the path set out by the natural philosophical Pythagoreans Philolaus and Eurytus, as well as the "last Pythagoreans" listed by Aristoxenus, to whom Aristoxenus himself seems to have felt close. Over against them stand figures such as Diodorus of Aspendus and Lycon as well as the nameless "Pythagoreans" and "Pythagorists" who are the butt of general ridicule in Middle Comedy.[41] Thus the poet Alexis (c. 375–c. 275 B.C.E.), for instance, represents them on stage as complete down-at-heels whose lifestyle is characterized by "eating little, by filth, frost, silence, gloominess, and being unwashed," and whose "sacrificial feasting" consists of dried figs, the pulp of pressed olives, and cheese.[42] According to Aristophon (middle of the fourth century B.C.E.?) again, the true reason for the asceticism of the "Pythagorists," whose sole garment is a worn cloak (the *tribon* of the Cynics), is their sheer lack of means;[43] they eat only vegetables and drink water, and in the Underworld Pluto messes solely with them because of their piety.[44] If we take all these characteristics together, even in the distorted image offered by comedy, it is clear that we are dealing with adherents of Pythagoras who were trying to follow consistently the ritual prescriptions in the "oral sayings" and therefore also hoped to have privileged status in the Underworld.

The "people from Tarentum" come off somewhat better in the comedies Alexis and Cratinus the Younger (second half of the fourth century B.C.E.?) wrote bearing this title: True, these Pythagoreans also eat neither meat nor creatures with souls, and are the only ones who drink no wine—their meals consist instead of bread and a glass of water ("you're talking about a prison life," one of the characters interjects on this). But apart from that they are also characterized as "intellectuals" whose nourishment consists in "Pythagoreanisms, fine speeches, and sophisticated ideas."[45] The comparison between human life and a feast, which we have already encountered in connection with Pythagoras' coinage of the word *philosophy* also finds an echo in Alexis: We the living are on a journey, for a festive gathering, as it were, set free from death and darkness in order to stay in this light; whoever in the time allotted him has most laughed and drunk and shared in Aphrodite—this is the comic twist given the original thought—goes home having had an exceptionally delightful feast.[46] In any case, the fact that in addition to vegetarianism and abstention from wine, intellectual activity is also attributed to these Pythagoreans from Tarentum basically confirms Iamblichus' (Aristotle's?) statement that the mathematicians recognized the acousmatics' lifestyle as Pythagoric, but considered their own "scientific" version of Pythagoreanism to be superior.

Prosopography of the Most Important Members

In this section the most important Pythagoreans—both male and female—of the fifth and fourth centuries B.C.E. shall be briefly presented one by one in chronological order (insofar as this is possible given the exceptionally fragmentary records). Regarding the oldest members of the community, we know little more than their names (on MYLLIAS see 2, 37 above). In the case of figures such as the athlete MILON and the physician DEMOCEDES we are unsure, moreover, how closely they were associated with Pythagoras. As for THEANO, who later became the type of the wise woman and to whom various ethical writings were falsely attributed, the sources waver: she is variously described as Pythagoras' wife, his daughter, or simply as his pupil,[47] and in general, family relationships in the legendary stories about Pythagoras seem still largely undetermined (a daughter named MYIA—according to Iamblichus,[48] she was Milon's wife—and a son named MNESARCHUS are mentioned). BRO(N)TINUS OF METAPONTUM also remains a rather shadowy figure to us, whose wife is sometimes said to be Theano, and sometimes Deino, about whom nothing else is known.[49] In any case, it seems clear that Bro(n)tinus existed, since a man by that name is one of the three presumed Pythagoreans to whom Alcmaeon of Croton addressed his work of natural philosophy. Interesting in addition is the report of a certain Epigenes (early fourth century B.C.E.) that Bro(n)tinus was the true author of two of the poems that circulated under the name of Orpheus.[50]

HIPPASUS OF METAPONTUM (end of the sixth century B.C.E./early fifth century B.C.E.?) is the first Pythagorean to emerge more strongly from the murkiness of the extant documents. Aristotle mentions him along with Heraclitus of Ephesus as a natural philosopher who considered fire to be the original matter of the world.[51] In the case of a Pythagorean, one is tempted to see in the background of this statement the Pythagorean cosmogony with its assumption of a central fire whose coming-into-being initiates cosmogony and which is identified with the One. Aristoxenus reports that Hippasus carried out sound experiments with bronze discs of equal size and varying thicknesses in the ratios 4:3, 3:2, and 2:1.[52] In contrast to the experiments narrated in connection with Pythagoras' discovery of the numerical proportions involved in musical concords, this test is physically possible.[53] Hippasus' name is also encountered in connection with the three means (taken over from Babylon?),[54] and especially with the so-called harmonic mean,[55] from which the basic concords of the octave, the fifth, and the fourth emerge almost automatically. (The harmonic mean between 12 and 6 [= 2:1 = octave] is 8; these three numbers include the fifth [12:8 = 3:2] and the fourth [8:6 = 4:3]. If the arithmetical mean, that is, 12:9:6, is also taken into account, then we get in addition the numerical relationship of the whole tone 9:8. The neo-Pythagorean Nicomachus terms the series 12, 9, 8, 6 "the first *tetraktýs*, which includes the source of the concords").[56] In view of these testimonies, it is hardly surprising that the "acousmatics" later saw Hippasus as the originator of the "mathematical" trend in

Pythagoreanism. The "mathematicians" for their part seem to have denied him any originality (all his teachings would stem instead from Pythagoras himself) and simply accused him of having betrayed the school's mathematical secrets—as examples are given the "solid consisting of twelve pentagons," that is, the dodecahedron (according to Plato's dialogue *Timaeus*, this is the form of the universe),[57] and the irrational numbers.[58]

The little we know about ARCHIPPUS and LYSIS has been detailed at 104 above. One of the most interesting Pythagoreans is PHILOLAUS OF CROTON (c. 470 B.C.E.–390/380 B.C.E.), about whose life, however, not much is known either. It may be that he came to Greece after the anti-Pythagorean unrest. In any case, he seems to have made at least a short stay in Thebes: sometime before 399 B.C.E. (the year of Socrates' death), Simmias and Cebes, Socrates' main interlocutors in Plato's dialogue *Phaedo*, heard him speak in their homeland about the prohibition on suicide.[59] He is mentioned as the teacher of the atomist Democritus, of the Pythagoreans Eurytus and Archytas, and in collaboration with Eurytus, of those whom Aristoxenus calls the "last Pythagoreans,"[60] whether the latter heard him in Tarentum—where Plato could also have met him during his first trip to southern Italy and Sicily (around 388 B.C.E.)[61]—in Phlius, or elsewhere.

In contrast to his life, Philolaus' doctrine is quite well-documented. As explained at 77 and 83 ff., it coincides to a large extent with the natural philosophy that Aristotle attributes to "Pythagoreans," whom he does not precisely define. We can therefore forego here a further sketch of his cosmogony and cosmology. Let us note only that in his book, Philolaus obviously offered a comprehensive explanation of the world comparable to Plato's *Timaeus*. Thus he discussed the creation of the central fire and the "ten divine" heavenly bodies that revolve around it;[62] the glasslike nature of the sun, which receives light and heat from the cosmic fire and passes it on to us through pores;[63] and the plants and living creatures on the moon, which are in his opinion much larger and more beautiful.[64] He also explored medical questions (embryology and the causes of illnesses),[65] distinguished four different psycho-physical forces of living creatures, and related them to certain parts of the body and different forms of existence: (1) head—intellect (humans), (2) heart—having a soul and sensation (animals), (3) navel—growth (plants), (4) member—procreation (all).[66] One wonders whether it is an accident that in Pythagorean dietary regulations the brain, heart, and sexual organs were forbidden: Was Philolaus perhaps offering in this passage a "scientific" explanation for these taboos?

Ethical questions seem also to have occupied him. We have already mentioned his prohibition of suicide (which probably took up Orphic teaching).[67] Moreover, a fragment that has come down to us without any context refers to "certain motives that are stronger than we are."[68] Finally, I believe that fragment B 14 (whose authenticity is contested), in which the "old 'theo-logians' and seers" are cited to show that "because of certain punishments, the human soul is yoked to the body and buried in it as in a tomb," finds its confirmation in the old Pythagorean "oral saying" according to which we "have come for punishment."[69] In any case, if the foregoing interpretations of 44 B 13s. D.-K. are correct, then Philolaus of Croton is a particularly instructive example for how, in Pythagoreanism, the thoroughly ritualized Pythagorean lifestyle could go hand in hand with "scientific" natural philosophy.

We have discussed Philolaus' pupil EURYTUS from Croton, Metapontum, or Tarentum (the sources differ on this point). He is also mentioned as the teacher of Archytas and Plato,[70] and probably lived from about 450/440 B.C.E. until sometime in the first two decades of the fourth century B.C.E.

In Philolaus' and Eurytus' tradition we find the multitalented and, apart from Philolaus, probably most important Pythagorean, ARCHYTAS OF TARENTUM, who was a near-contemporary of Plato's (c. 429–347 B.C.E.).[71] The two probably came in contact with each other as early as Plato's first journey to southern Italy and Sicily (c. 388 B.C.E.) and remained friends over the years. Archytas, who was famous for his high morals and self-command,[72] combined the "theoretical" life of the *philósophos* oriented toward the contemplative investigation of the world with the "practical" life of the politician, and served seven terms as his hometown's official military commander (*strategós*)[73] without suffering a single defeat.[74] To judge on the basis of fragment 47 B 3 D.-K., his political activity was guided by Pythagorean ideas: In that fragment we read that the presupposition for ending unrest and for the growth of civil harmony is the discovery of the (appropriate) "calculation" (*logismós*)—by which we have probably to understand the right (harmonic) proportion, the mathematically "mediated" balance between the various groups composing a polity. (Archytas' interest in the "three means in music"—the arithmetic, the geometrical, and the harmonic means—is shown by their precise definition in fragment 47 B 2 D.-K.) If the right measure is found, Archytas goes on, there will be no "greedy desire for always having more" (*pleonexía*), but instead equality will reign—we recall the saying attributed to Pythagoras, "Friendship [is] equality." Archytas apparently did not limit himself to philosophical theories about numbers, but seems to have also realized at Tarentum a kind of redistribution between rich and poor:

> Through this [the appropriate calculation] the poor receive from the rich and the rich give to those in need, both believing that they would thereby acquire that which is equal. (Archytas 47 B 3 D.-K.)

This is confirmed and at the same time illuminated by Aristotle, who in his *Politics* praises the inhabitants of Tarentum for having made their possessions available to the poor for common use and thereby won the good will of the masses.[75]

It is not surprising that as a Pythagorean scientist, Archytas considers astronomy, geometry, arithmetic, and music "sister sciences"—surely because of their numerical nature.[76] He also seems to be a good Pythagorean when he places at the beginning of his work *Harmonikós* a paean to his predecessors, whose insight into the nature of the universe had allowed them to attain accurate knowledge regarding all individual things as well.[77] Drawing on these older "mathematicians," he explains musical pitch as connected with the differing speeds at which the sound, caused by things striking each other, spreads (rapid movement = higher pitch and vice versa).[78] In addition, there is firm evidence that Archytas carried out calculations regarding the numerical proportions of the intervals of the three musical scales enharmonic, chromatic, and diatonic.[79] His main achievement in mathematics consists in his solution of the problem of the doubling of the cube.[80] Moreover, by proving that a superparticular proportion—that is, $(n+1) : n$—cannot be divided by a mean proportional, he paved the way for a general number theory such as we find later in Euclid.[81] He is also considered the first to have practiced mechanics "methodically, using mathematical principles."[82] Mentioned as his chief mechanical achievement is a wooden dove that could fly.[83]

About another Pythagorean named HICETAS OF SYRACUSE (perhaps end of the fifth or beginning of the fourth century B.C.E.?) all we know is that on the one hand, in agreement with Philolaus and Aristotle's "Pythagoreans," he postulated a Counter-Earth in addition to the Earth, and on the other, that he differed from them in maintaining that all the other heavenly bodies stood still, and only the earth turned on its axis, whence proceeded the same impression of the changes in the heavens.[84] ECPHANTUS OF SYRACUSE (about the same period as Hicetas?) seems to have been influenced by atomism. According to him, the first things—that is, probably the original matter—are "indivisible bodies" that can change in size, shape, and force, and from which the objects perceivable by the senses originate; according to our source, these bodies are moved by a "divine power" that Ecphantus called "intellect" and "soul." Like Hicetas (was the latter his teacher?) and Heraclides Ponticus,[85] Ecphantus further assumed that the Earth was in the middle of the spherical cosmos and turned on its own axis in an easterly direction.[86]

For the Syracusans DAMON and PHINTIAS, see 39f. ECHECRATES OF PHLIUS (end of the fifth, beginning of the fourth centuries B.C.E.) is counted by Aristoxenus, along with the Phlians PHANTO, POLYMNASTUS, and DIOCLES, as well as XENOPHILUS FROM CHALCIDICE—according to the Suda Aristoxenus' teacher[87]—among the "last" Pythagoreans of the "mathematical" direction. Echecrates owes his fame mainly to Plato's *Phaedo*. The fictitious venue of this dialogue is probably the gathering place of the Pythagoreans in Phlius, where at Echecrates' bidding Phaedo, presumably returning from Athens to his home in Elis, reports on the death of his friend Socrates. In *Phaedo* 88d, Plato has Echecrates express his sympathies with the (Pythagorean?) doctrine of the soul as a *harmonía*.

Like Archytas, the presumably more or less contemporary CLEINIAS FROM TARENTUM is famous in the sources for his outstanding morals. When he became angry at someone, he calmed himself by playing the lyre before rebuking the offender.[88] Once, when he learned that a fellow Pythagorean in Cyrene in Africa had lost his possessions as a result of political conditions and was in extreme need, he is said to have traveled from Italy to Cyrene, carrying a great deal of money with him, and restored the man's property to him, "without having ever seen him before, and solely because he had heard that he was a Pythagorean."[89] A statement of his about the (negatively valued) pleasure of love has also come down to us,[90] and it is mentioned that together with AMYCLAS, Cleinias dissuaded Plato from trying to burn all the books by Democritus he could lay his hands on (for these books, they argued, were already in wide circulation).[91]

With DIODORUS OF ASPENDUS in Pamphylia (first half of the fourth century B.C.E.) we finally have an example of a Pythagorean of the "acousmatic" orientation, who after training in southern Italy returned to Greece and there is said to have spread "the Pythagorean sayings"—by which probably the "oral sayings" are meant.[92] He seems to have adhered to a strict vegetarianism,[93] and because of his humble appearance—shabby cloak (*tríbon*), rucksack, and walking stick, long beard, long hair, and bare feet—which at least partly must have been new for Pythagoreans, he can be considered a forerunner of the Cynics.[94] In addition to the "Pythagorists" mocked in Middle Comedy, another Pythagorean of the second half of the fourth century B.C.E., LYCON OF IASUS in Caria, should probably be counted among the "acousmatics" too. In his work *On the Pythagorean Life*, Lycon emphasizes, among other things, Pythagoras' "temperate way of life."[95]

Of numerous other Pythagoreans of the fifth and fourth centuries, at least the names remain, thanks to the catalog that was handed down by Iamblichus and that may go back to Aristoxenus.[96]

4. THINKERS INFLUENCED BY PYTHAGORAS AND HIS PUPILS

PRE-PLATONIC THINKERS

Xenophanes and Heraclitus

There can be no doubt that with his personality and doctrines, the charismatic Pythagoras made an extremely strong impression on his immediate environment. It is harder to gauge, though, whether and to what extent his opinions had an effect outside the Pythagorean community (in the narrower and in the wider senses). It is tempting to assume that after the near-complete dissolution of the organizational structures resulting from the anti-Pythagorean riots, this influence became more widespread as the surviving members of the community were dispersed and people were more likely to come into contact with Pythagoreans, especially in Greece. However, as the oldest sources show, even before these events, Pythagoras was the subject of discussion among intellectuals not only in Italy but elsewhere. In view of the uncertainties that hinder our reconstruction of his teachings, we can hardly get beyond mere plausibilities in trying to determine his possible influence on other thinkers and writers. A few suggestions may therefore suffice. Although it is difficult to say for sure, it seems rather unlikely that XENOPHANES, who had been wandering around in southern Italy and Sicily since about 540 B.C.E., opposed in his theology the Pythagorean idea that the heavens "inhaled" the surrounding void "into" themselves. According to 21 A 1 D.-K., he advocated the view that the divine (conceived as spherical) did not "draw breath."[1] In HERACLITUS, on the contrary, it is not only the praise of the "invisible *harmonie*" that seems to echo Pythagorean ideas; in his doctrine of the soul and in his "eschatology," too, he may well have been influenced by Pythagoras when he questions the distinction between the immortal and the mortal,[2] maintains that the process of dying is reversible, and extends it to every fundamental change of state, thereby generalizing the doctrine of reincarnation,[3] as Kahn has aptly observed ("Thus Heraclitus has extended the Pythagorean cycle of rebirth to the general Milesian conception of elemental coming-to-be and passing-away expressed in the fragment of Anaximander").[4]

Parmenides, Alcmaeon, Empedocles, Democritus, Socrates

In scholarly research, there is a considerable difference of opinion regarding the relation of PARMENIDES (c. 520–after 450 B.C.E.?) to Pythagoras. The geographical proximity—Parmenides came from the city of Elea in southern Italy, which is located on the Tyrrhenian coast, about 150 kilometers from Metapontum—suggests that he might have been acquainted with the "Italic philosophy." Ancient sources make him a pupil of a Pythagorean called Ameinias[5] and indicate common points in their teaching.[6] However, the latter are difficult to prove in individual cases.[7] The journey to the abode of the goddess, described in the prologue, could have been influenced by Pythagoras. At the end of this journey, which transcends human limits of space and time and reminds one of a journey into the Beyond, the poet-philosopher, like an initiate, is introduced by the goddess to "truth" and to the erroneous "opinions of mortals."[8] Moreover, like Orphics and like Pythagoras, Parmenides seems to have had a negative view of human existence (compare "hateful birth").[9] In addition, the following aspects of Parmenides' doctrine, for example, can be compared with Pythagorean ideas: the fundamental dichotomy of truth/insight/being and meaning;[10] the origin of the world out of the "ethereal flame of fire" and the "night"[11] (cf. the Pythagorean central fire and the void inhaled by the heavens at the beginning of the development of the world mentioned in chapter 2); the emphasis on the limitation of being, without which it would be incomplete[12] (see 84f. above on the higher rank of limit among the Pythagoreans).

Whereas in the case of the natural philosopher ALCMAEON OF CROTON, Pythagorean influence is entirely conceivable,[13] the playful allusion made by the Sicilian comic poet EPICHARMUS (first half of the fifth century B.C.E.) to odd and even numbers and their alteration when a counting pebble is added, probably remains too general to conclude that it indicates a close relationship to the Pythagoreans.[14]

For EMPEDOCLES OF ACRAGAS, whom the sources quite often associate with Pythagoras and his school, see various references at 36ff., 54f., 67ff. above; for DEMOCRITUS OF ABDERA, see 58; and for SOCRATES, see 12ff. and 90ff.[15]

PLATO AND THE OLD ACADEMY

Plato's Relationship to the Pythagoreans; Aristotle on Plato's Theory of Principles

A superficial glance at the dialogues of PLATO (428/7–348/7 B.C.E.) on the whole could lead us rashly to conclude that Pythagoras was not particularly important for this outstanding philosopher. For as opposed to Heraclitus, Parmenides, Anaxagoras, the Sophists, let alone Socrates, Pythagoras' name is mentioned not more than once in Plato's published works, and that is in the context of the critique of poetry in the *Republic:* Unlike Homer, we read there, during his lifetime Pythagoras was highly respected primarily for the special way of life he founded (the *bíos pythagóreios*), through which his followers are "even now" still markedly distinguished from their environment.[16] That sounds like a recognition, even if rather reserved, of the Pythagorean way of life regulated by ritual prescriptions and taboos, to which perhaps neither the main speaker in the dialog, Socrates, nor Plato would have really subscribed. And yet there are good reasons for assuming that Pythagorean philosophy was of considerable importance for Platonic thought and action (cf., in addition to what will be said below, references at 12 to rhetoric and the Academy as a shrine to the Muses; at 82 and 84 on the harmony of the spheres, the world year, and the fundamental distinction "unlimited/limit"; and at 108 and 100 on the dodecahedron as the form of the universe and the proverbial saying about friends).[17]

Informative is another passage in the *Republic,* where an agreement in content with "the Pythagoreans"—this term again occurs in all the dialogues only once—is stated: Socrates explicitly endorses their idea that astronomy and music are "sciences somehow related to each other."[18] This idea, which as such is common Pythagorean property—according to Aristotle, "the whole heaven is harmony and number" in the eyes of the Pythagoreans—was also formulated in particular by Archytas, with whom Plato has probably been in close contact ever since his first journey to southern Italy and Sicily (c. 388 B.C.E.).[19] In Plato's Seventh Letter, whose authenticity is in doubt but which was at least composed by a well-informed writer from his entourage, we learn that Archytas and other friends from Tarentum saved Plato from the dangerous situation into which he had gotten himself at the court of Dionysius II in Syracuse during his third voyage to Sicily (361/360 B.C.E.).[20]

These close personal relationships suggest that there were also significant intellectual exchanges; the influence may well have worked in both directions (the Seventh Letter seems to emphasize Plato's intellectual independence in a slightly anti-Pythagorean tendency;[21] Philodemus makes

Archytas one of Plato's pupils).[22] That there were points on which their views coincided is implied by the title of a lost work of Aristotle's, in which "excerpts from Plato's *Timaeus* and works of Archytas" were compared.[23] However, apart from specific points such as the three means, which a fragment of Archytas' defines with precision and which are given practical application in Plato's *Timaeus*,[24] we cannot determine the relationship between the two thinkers more exactly, because of the fragmentary character of the extant works of Archytas (Barker offers interesting attempts at reconstruction in relation to harmony and music).[25]

Still, it is probably no accident that the (fictive?) main speaker of this most "Pythagorean" of all Plato's dialogues, Timaeus, comes from southern Italy: He is introduced as a distinguished citizen of Locri, where he is both a highly respected politician and an outstanding astronomer and naturalist[26]—a description that would also fit Archytas extremely well.[27] Moreover, on the level of its themes, Plato's *Timaeus* shows undeniable similarities with Philolaus of Croton's book on natural philosophy.[28] For this reason, Plato was early on accused of plagiarism: While he was at Dionysius II's court in Syracuse, Plato was said to have bought for a great deal of money—allegedly 40 minas of silver—(the recently deceased) Philolaus' book from the latter's relations, and to have "rewritten" his *Timaeus* out of it,[29] or, in the words of Timon of Phlius, an author of satirical verse:

You too, Plato! For you too were seized by the desire to learn from a
   teacher;
for a great deal of money you bought yourself a little book;
by it you were taught how to "write Timaeus" (*timaiographeîn*).

(Timon fr. 828 SH)

That is no doubt a malicious insinuation.[30] Yet ARISTOTLE'S judgment of Plato's unwritten theory of principles turns out not to be very different in substance.[31] He speaks of a close affiliation with the philosophy of the "Italics." Certain aspects of Plato's teaching were certainly peculiar to him. Aristotle mentions (1) the Ideas, which Plato was led to assume on the one hand by the Heraclitean doctrine of the constant change of everything perceptible by the senses, and on the other by the Socratic striving to arrive at conceptual definitions in ethics whose universal validity could be guaranteed only in the supersensible realm; (2) the attribution to mathematical entities of a status intermediate between the sensible and the Ideas (for the Pythagoreans, in contrast, as has been mentioned at 87 above, numbers and things perceptible by the senses coincide); (3) the replacement of the "unlimited" as a unity by an "unlimited dyad" (*ahóristos dyás*) of the large and the small, because in this way the coming-into-being of the other numbers can be more easily explained.

However, according to Aristotle the points of agreement are clearly predominant in the structure of Plato's thought: Whereas in the Pythagoreans' view things are an "iconic imitation" (*mímesis*) of numbers, Plato speaks of their "participation" (*méthexis*) in the Ideas, "[merely] using a different term." Aristotle notes critically that both the Pythagoreans and Plato failed to define more precisely the nature of this "participation" or "imitation." "Like the Pythagoreans," as Aristotle goes on to say, Plato describes the One as "beingness" or "essence" (*ousía*) and defends, "like the former," the view that (ideal) numbers are the causes of being for everything else.[32]

Speusippus, Xenocrates, Theophrastus, Heraclides Ponticus

Aristotle is not the only student of Plato's who assumes that the Pythagoreans had a significant influence on his teacher's philosophy. Indeed, the Pythagorean interpretation of Plato seems to have been quite widespread in the Academy.[33] As a mirror image to this, an increasing Platonization of Pythagoreanism may be observed. Because of the state of the documents, details once again remain largely obscure to us: The writings of Plato's first two successors, his nephew SPEUSIPPUS (head of the Academy 347–339 B.C.E.) and Xenocrates (head of the Academy 339–314 B.C.E.), who would be particularly important in this context, have been lost apart from a few fragments. How great the uncertainty is can be seen by the fact that in the case of Speusippus, who, incidentally, accompanied Plato on his last voyage to Sicily, we do not even know whether the work in which he discussed in detail the number 10, which in the Pythagorean view is "perfect," actually bore the title *On the Pythagorean Numbers,* as Iamblichus' excerpt suggests.[34] In the case of another fragment that apparently transfers Platonic principles to the Pythagoreans, it remains highly doubtful whether it actually reproduces Speusippus' opinion or is merely a Neoplatonic interpretation of Speusippus or of Plato and Pythagoreanism.[35] Nonetheless, it seems clear that in his explanations Speusippus liked to refer back to Pythagorean precursors, even if he did not follow their number philosophy in every respect (thus for instance he rejected the notion shared by Plato and the Pythagoreans that the principles of numbers are also the principles of things; in his opinion, different kinds of being require different principles).[36]

XENOCRATES, who is known to have written a book on "Pythagorean [matters]"[37]—incidentally, this book also contains some entirely accurate information about Pythagoras—seems in his Pythagorizing exegesis of the *Timaeus* to have at least partly shaped the later image of Pythagorean philosophy. Thus his definition of the soul, developed out of the creation of the world soul in the *Timaeus*, as a "self-moving number"[38] is found again in the doxographies under Pythagoras' name[39] (in view of the points of contact between Plat. Tim. 36b-d and the doctrine of the soul proposed by Alcmaeon of Croton 24 A 12 D.-K., whom ancient sources often describe as close to the Pythagoreans in certain respects, and in view of the importance of number philosophy for the Pythagoreans, caution, however, is certainly called for here, too; the heart of the doctrine at least might just as well be an older Pythagorean view).

It is worth noting that no later than with Aristotle's colleague and successor THEOPHRASTUS OF ERESUS (c. 371–c. 288 B.C.E.), the differences between Plato and the Pythagoreans become blurred and both are seen as endorsing, for instance, the "One" and the "unlimited dyad" as principles,[40] even though according to Aristotle's unambiguous testimony the latter is Plato's innovation. Against the background of this result, it is hardly surprising that in the later doxographies, which in essence probably go back to Theophrastus' *Natural Philosophical Opinions*, only a few traces of the older Pythagoreanism not yet overlaid by Platonic thinking are to be found.[41] At the same time, however, later Pythagoreans were probably not wholly unjustified in accusing Plato, Aristotle, Speusippus, Aristoxenus, and Xenocrates of having appropriated, with minimal reworking, what was fertile in Pythagoras' teaching[42] (even though this accusation seems to presuppose the existence of Pythagorean pseudepigrapha, where Platonic-Aristotelian philosophical themes have been unscrupulously projected back into Pythagoras). For despite all the uncertainties regarding details, no one denies that these thinkers, as well as HERACLIDES PONTICUS, another of Plato's and Aristotle's students, drew inspiration from Pythagorean philosophy.

HELLENISTIC "FORGERIES" AND NEO-PYTHAGOREANISM

Pythagoreanism in the Hellenistic Period

What happened to Pythagoreanism in the Hellenistic period remains in large part an open question. On the one hand, surrounding the Academy, we can observe a clear intensification of the literary analysis of Pythagoras and his school: Plato's own students Aristotle and Xenocrates (and perhaps also Speusippus?), as well as a few of Aristotle's students in the fourth century B.C.E., such as Heraclides Ponticus, Dicaearchus of Messana, and Aristoxenus of Tarentum, all wrote one or even several works on this topic. In addition, the founder of Stoicism, Zeno of Citium (335–263 B.C.E.) is supposed to have written a book on "Pythagorean [matters]." In the third century B.C.E., the Peripatetic Hermippus of Smyrna followed with a work, *On Pythagoras*, that contained not a few critical remarks.[43] Moreover, since Theophrastus, the philosopher from Samos had had an established place in doxography, and he is discussed in some detail in the numerous works on the history of philosophy written during the last three centuries B.C.E.—including Hippobotus (end of the third century B.C.E.), Satyrus (end of the third century B.C.E.), Sotion (second century B.C.E.), Heraclides Lembus (second century B.C.E.), Sosicrates (around 150 B.C.E.), and Alexander Polyhistor (around 110–40 B.C.E.). In historiography the picture is much the same: Theopompus of Chios and Neanthes of Cyzicus mention Pythagoras; the Sicilian historian Timaeus of Tauromenium and Duris of Samos pay him special attention in their works, evidently out of local patriotism.

On the other hand, this strong presence of Pythagoras in philosophical and biographical-historical literature contrasts with almost the complete silence of the sources regarding the actual continued existence of the school in the Hellenistic period. Were there perhaps still scattered followers who practiced the typical Pythagorean way of life, in the "acousmatic" tradition? On the basis of the allusion to a dirty, "pale, and shoeless 'Pythagorist'" from Athens in Theocritus of Syracuse,[44] one might presume that there were—unless the early third century B.C.E. bucolic poet adopted the type of the follower of Pythagoras from the literary tradition of comedy. However, Theocritus' contemporary, the outstanding Hellenistic poet and philologian Callimachus of Cyrene, seems still to have had a vivid idea of this kind of Pythagoreanism.[45]

Pseudo-Pythagorica

A certain continuity or at least an ongoing interest in Pythagoreanism is, moreover, indicated by the flowering of Pythagorean pseudepigrapha, which were presumably composed as early as from the late fourth century B.C.E. onward, in various places (including southern Italy, Rome, and Alexandria?) and at various times (probably at least into the first or second century C.E.), and which were attributed not only to Pythagoras but also to many of his pupils. From this wide-ranging body of writings let us select two examples that enjoyed great popularity in antiquity as well as later on: Lysis' letter and the so-called Golden Verses.[46] Lysis' letter, which may have been written in the second half of the third century B.C.E.,[47] probably owes its popularity chiefly to the circumstance that it pretends to offer an inside view of the Pythagorean community. Lysis, the fictitious writer, is familiar to us from Aristoxenus' description of the anti-Pythagorean arson attacks, where he is described as one of the two survivors, the other being Archippus. In this letter—cited by Copernicus, among others—Lysis reminds a certain Hipparchus (otherwise unknown to us; perhaps confused with Archippus?) of the master's "divine and venerable instructions" not to communicate by any means the treasures of wisdom to those whose souls are still entirely impure. For making available to just anyone what has been earned with such effort is as great an infraction of divine law as recounting the Eleusinian mysteries to the uninitiated.[48] After some remarks concerning purification, to which they themselves were subjected in the old days by Pythagoras as preparation, and after a drastic description of the devastating ethical consequences that would ensue when this is omitted, Lysis accuses his addressee of having betrayed the Pythagorean ideal under the influence of Sicilian luxury[49] and of practicing philosophy, it is said, even in public,

> a thing which Pythagoras forbade—he, who had entrusted to his daughter Damo the [written] "memories" (*hypomnémata*) and instructed her not to pass them on to anybody outside the house. Although she could have sold the words for a great deal of money, she did not wish to do so, but rather put poverty and her father's admonitions above gold. It is said that when she was dying, Damo gave her daughter Bistala the same instruction. (Ps.-Lysis Epist. 7)

These remarks, which are followed by another warning addressed to Hipparchus, show how "genuine" works of Pythagoras could theoretically have survived. The hypothesis that Lysis' letter was made up in order to legitimate the fictitious "memories" mentioned in it and published together with them, therefore has much to be said for it[50] (these "memories" or "records" may well be identical with the work by Alexander Polyhistor, bearing the same title, mentioned at 20 above).[51]

A collection of Pythagorean ethical maxims—today almost unknown, but quite popular in Greco-Roman antiquity, in Islam, and in the early modern period—acquired around 200 C.E. the well-justified title "GOLDEN VERSES" (*chrysâ épe*, Latin *carmen aureum*). The poem, consisting of seventy-one hexameters, some of them rather clumsily formulated, contains a multitude of interesting "golden" rules, which include advice about how to deal with gods and heroes; with parents, friends, and fellow men; about self-mastery and self-respect; speaking and acting in an absolutely virtuous way; and mental training and healthcare. It recommends that an "examination of conscience" be carried out each evening. The poem concludes with a promise that assiduous efforts to lead such a life will result in insight into the construction of the world, liberation from all suffering, and even apotheosis. In order to give an idea of this work, I quote the beginning and a few selected verses:

(1) Honor the immortal gods first, in the order appointed by custom,
and revere your oath. Pay reverence next to the noble heroes
and the divinities of the Underworld by performing the prescribed rites.
Honor your parents as well as your closest relatives.
(5) Among others, choose as your friend him who excels in virtue.
Yield to gentle words and useful actions,
and do not hate your friend for a small fault,
for as long as you are able to do so, for ability lives near necessity.
[which means "a very long time" in the opinion of Hierocles of Alexandria, a late-Antiquity commentator on the "Golden Verses" (fifth century C.E.);[52] for when compelled, everyone shows that he can do more than he thought he could.]
. . .

(27) Deliberate before the deed, lest foolish things result from it.
It is typical of a worthless man indeed to do or to say senseless things.
But bring that to completion which will not distress you afterwards.
(30) Do not do even one thing of what you do not understand, but learn
what is necessary, and thus you will lead a most enjoyable life.
You should not be careless about your physical health,
but you should practice due measure in drinking, eating, and physical exercises. By due measure I mean that which will not distress you.
(40–42)

(49) When you have mastered these things,
you will come to know the [numerical?] essence of immortal gods and mortal men,
how it pervades each thing and how each thing is ruled [by it].
You will come to know, as is right, nature, alike in everything,
so that you do not expect what is not to be expected, nor anything escapes your notice.
You will come to know that the miseries men suffer are self-incurred,
(55) the wretched people, who do not see the good even though it is near,
nor do they hear it. Few understand the deliverance from their troubles.

(Carmen Aureum 1–8, 27–39, 49–56; transl. Thom)

Many aspects of these rules of life are traditional and characteristic of Greek ethics (and not solely Greek ones) in general. Thus, for instance, respect for the gods and for parents is among the generally recognized "unwritten laws," which were at best more expressly required by the Pythagoreans,[53] and the duty to observe (the right) measure is found in the oldest Greek poetry as well as in Plato's and Aristotle's ethical reflections. On the other hand, some aspects are specifically Pythagorean: for example, the "examination of conscience" and mental training, the hint at the numerical structure of everything, and the allusion to specific dietary prohibitions at the end.[54]

The date of composition of these doubtless post-Platonic "Golden Verses," whose original title is unknown, can hardly any longer be determined with precision. Modern scholars' estimates vary between the second half of the fourth century B.C.E. (Thom) and the fourth century C.E. (Nauck).[55] We should like to know whether the Stoic Chrysippus (c. 280–207 B.C.E.), who cites verse 54 as an "expression of the Pythagoreans,"[56] had the poem before him in its present form. In any case, it is not disputed that older material went into the poem, which was frequently cited beginning with the Empire (the most obvious of this older material is the oath on the discoverer of the *tetraktýs*, whose original Doric dialectal form has been retained;[57] on the oath, see 27ff. and 82f. above).

Nigidius Figulus as the "Reviver" of Pythagoreanism?

The modern *communis opinio*, according to which in the first century B.C.E. there was a revival of Pythagoreanism in Italy, essentially adopts the assessment offered by Cicero, who in the foreword to his translation of Plato's *Timaeus* introduces his friend the naturalist and grammarian NIGIDIUS FIGULUS (c. 100–45 B.C.E.), as the "reviver" of Pythagorean teaching:

> Finally, it is my view that after those noble Pythagoreans whose teaching has more or less died out after having flourished for a long time in Italy and in Sicily, this [man] appeared to revive that [teaching]. (Cic. Tim. 1)

Wherein the Pythagoreanism of this Roman senator and savant consisted is not easy to determine from a modern point of view. A connection with Nigidius' known astrological and mantic interests may be hypothesized, especially since at that time the idea of occult prophetic practices could also be associated with the word *Pythagorean*.[58] However, skepticism with regard to Cicero's account is elicited first by the fact that it unmistakably follows Aristoxenus, who has the Pythagorean school "honorably die out" around

360 B.C.E., which is, as was mentioned at 104 above, demonstrably false, and second because there is no lack of evidence showing that the "Italic philosophy"—as Pythagoreanism had been called since Aristotle—for quite some time had been enjoying considerable sympathy in Rome, on grounds of local patriotism. Aristoxenus mentions the Romans as being among the Italic peoples who had sought political advice from Pythagoras.[59] The legendary second king of Rome, Numa Pompilius (according to the tradition, 715–673 B.C.E.), whose sacred legislation was considered exemplary and whose reign supposedly established harmony, is so reminiscent of Pythagoras that he was simply declared to have been the latter's pupil.[60] True, Cicero saw that this was impossible on chronological grounds.[61] But he, too, was basically of the opinion that "in their institutions" the Romans had "taken over many things" from the Pythagoreans.[62] When during the Samnite Wars the Pythian Apollo demanded that a statue both of the strongest and of the wisest of the Greeks be erected in a prominent location, the Romans placed Alcibiades and Pythagoras at the far ends of the Comitium.[63]

In short, in the first century B.C.E. the veneration of Pythagoras had become traditional in Rome, which awakens certain doubts about Cicero's account and the *communis opinio* influenced by it, even if it is true that for us today, it is first at this period that persons once again come into view who describe themselves as Pythagoreans or at least consciously follow Pythagoras on particular points, such as vegetarianism: The latter is attested for a Roman philosopher of the Augustan period, Q. Sextius, and for his pupil Sotion, Seneca's teacher.[64]

It remains similarly uncertain whether the interest in Pythagoreanism shown by the Middle Platonist Eudorus (first century B.C.E.) and Philo, the important Judeo-Hellenistic allegorist (15/10 B.C.E. [?]-after 40 C.E.), announces a "new" Pythagoreanism in Alexandria, or instead an old Academic and Peripatetic tradition is simply being continued.[65]

Neo-Pythagoreanism: Apollonius of Tyana, Moderatus of Gades, Nicomachus of Gerasa, Numenius of Apamea, Iamblichus of Chalcis

Be that as it may, the flowering of so-called Middle Platonism starting in the first century B.C.E. seems to have been accompanied by an increasing tendency to turn back to Pythagoras and his philosophy. "Neo-Pythagoreanism" and "Middle" or "Neoplatonism"—all terms that were coined but by modern scholars—differ from each other only in minor ways regarding their basic philosophical assumptions and especially their theories of principles, and this is ultimately a consequence of the Platonization of the Pythagorean tradition that began in the Academy. In a certain sense, neo-Pythagoreanism can be seen as a variety or even as a "denomination" within the Platonism of the imperial age. Its most important representatives shall be briefly described here.[66] They all come from the borderlands of the Roman Empire: Apollonius from Tyana (in Cappadocia, now eastern Turkey), Moderatus from Gades (today Cádiz in Spain) and Nicomachus from Gerasa (today Jarash in Jordan, north of Amman).

A particularly interesting figure is APOLLONIUS OF TYANA, who died during the reign of Nerva (96–98 C.E.), and who lived his life entirely in accord with Pythagoras' model.[67] Like Pythagoras, he traveled far and wide and sought to combine the ritual piety (including vegetarianism) and modesty of the "acousmatic" Pythagoreans with the master's thaumaturgical feats. As a result, outsiders regarded him as a magician and a charlatan.[68] Conversely, Philostratus, the author of a biography written in 217 C.E. at the behest of the Empress Julia Domna that clearly tends toward hagiography,[69] defends Apollonius—as a "holy man" (*theîos anér*) par excellence[70]—against precisely this accusation and explains his miraculous feats by his extraordinary "wisdom" (*sophía*). The Emperor Caracalla (198–217 C.E.) is reported to have erected a *heroon* for Apollonius,[71] and another emperor, Alexander Severus (222–235 C.E.), is said to have put Apollonius' image in the Lararium, together with those of Christ, Abraham, and Orpheus.[72] It was in particular his miracles, including healing the sick[73] and raising the dead,[74] that encouraged comparison with Christ. In his anti-Christian work *The Friend of Truth,* the high Roman official Sossianus Hierocles, a driving force behind the persecution of Christians in 303 C.E., placed Apollonius above Christ, a view against which Eusebius of Caesarea (before 264/5–339/40 C.E.) stood up in his refutation *Against Hierocles*.[75] It is not clear whether the writer of the same name who composed a life of Pythagoras[76] is identical with Apollonius of Tyana.

In contradistinction to Apollonius, we know little about the life of MODERATUS OF GADES (second half of the first century C.E.). A few aspects of his teaching can be reconstructed on the basis of later paraphrases (especially in Porphyry) and two fragments cited by Stobaeus (probably early fifth century C.E.). He explains the Pythagorean theory of numbers in Platonic terms as a symbolic illustration of ideal realities with a didactic intent. Positioning a "first One over being and every existence," to which the second One, which is equated with the Ideas, is subordinated, followed by the realm of beings with souls and the nature of things perceptible by the senses, Moderatus seems to anticipate Plotinus' system of hypostases.[77] Like Ecphantus, he probably understood the soul as a kind of mathematical harmony.[78]

Of NICOMACHUS FROM GERASA, a mathematician and musicologist of the early second century C.E., two complete works are extant, namely the *Manual of Harmonics* and the *Introduction to Arithmetic,* in which the ancient theory of numbers is represented in full (the Western Middle Ages became acquainted with this knowledge through Boethius). The extent that Neopythagoreanism and Platonic philosophy were melded in Nicomachus' thought can be seen in the beginning of the *Introduction to Arithmetic:* After reminding the reader by way of introduction that Pythagoras coined the word *philosophy,* Nicomachus attributes to Pythagoras a completely Platonic understanding of "wisdom"—"scientific knowledge of the truth in existing things" that "always remain the same" and are "immaterial"—and to confirm this he quotes the often-cited *locus classicus* for Plato's ontological dichotomy between being and becoming, Tim. 27d-28a.[79] A further Platonic element consists in the fact that like Moderatus, Nicomachus aligns the alterity with the dyad and the identity with the monad, and presents these alignments as the doctrine of the old Pythagoreans.[80] In addition to the two works just mentioned, he also wrote, among other things, a work of number mysticism (*arithmetikà theologoúmena*) whose outlines are still discernible to some extent, and in which, following old Pythagoreanism, the first ten numbers are identified, on the basis of their structure and properties, with certain divinities and/or with ethical and physical concepts[81] (on old Pythagoreanism, see 80ff. above). Moreover, Nicomachus is the author of a life of Pythagoras that is among the main sources used by Porphyry[82] and Iamblichus.[83]

NUMENIUS OF APAMEA (on the Orontes in Syria) (second century C.E.) is also frequently counted among the Neopythagoreans. Since in his works, to judge by the extant fragments, neither Pythagorean number theory nor the Pythagorean way of life seems to play a major role (however, a book *On Numbers* has been lost), and because his philosophy is based chiefly on Plato, he might better be called a "Pythagorizing Platonist" rather than a "Platonizing (neo-)Pythagorean"[84] (in antiquity Numenius was described both as a Pythagorean and as a Platonist; this wavering confirms the basic proximity of the two philosophical tendencies). In fragments 24 (in a general respect) and 52 des Places (concerning the theory of principles), Numenius stresses—not unlike Aristotle—the Pythagorean component in Plato's philosophy, but at the same time notes a difference in style: Plato, Numenius says,[85] occupies a middle position between the excessively august Pythagoras and the all too playful Socrates (according to Numenius, Socrates is secretly also a Pythagorean).

Plato's theory undergoes, one might say, a certain relativization by being connected back to Pythagoras.[86] However, much the same happens to the "great Pythagoras":[87] He, too, is only a representative of that old wisdom and truth that was possessed by non-Greek peoples such as the (Indian) brahmins, the Jews, (Persian) magi, and Egyptians.[88] In assuming an original wisdom, Numenius coincides with another Middle Platonist of the second century C.E., Celsus, who in his anti-Christian polemical work *True Logos* advocates the same theory, although he omits the Jews (as forerunners of the Christians he is attacking), while in the case of Numenius, the following statement has also come down to us: "What after all is Plato [other] than a Moses who speaks Attic Greek?"[89] (this famous statement probably regards the coincidence of LXX Exodus 3:14, "I am the one who is" and Plato's "that which always is," in e.g. Tim. 27d).[90] That this old truth was not retained after Plato and his immediate students in the Academy, but instead skepticism prevailed, Numenius explains by saying that Plato—out of fear that he could suffer the same fate as Socrates—deliberately avoided showing openly his Pythagorean convictions, and by obscuring them he inadvertently and without any evil intention provided the bases for the later dissent.[91] According to Numenius, the task of interpreters of Plato is therefore to lay bare again the genuine, that is, the Pythagorean Plato.[92]

Finally, the Neoplatonist IAMBLICHUS OF CHALCIS (in the province Coele Syria) (c. 240–c. 325 C.E.) went particularly far in Pythagorizing Platonism. Iamblichus is best known as the founder of the theurgic tendency in Neoplatonism (in contrast to Plotinus and Porphyry, he taught that even the highest part of the soul was completely connected with the body, so that the liberation of the soul and its reunion with the gods was possible only through magical-ritual practices). Of his ten-volume magnum opus, *On the Pythagorean School of Philosophy* (*Perì tês pythagorikês hairéseos*), the first four books at least are extant: (1) The essay *On the Pythagorean Way of Life*, which is most important for the Pythagorean tradition and which is regularly cited in the present introduction to Pythagoras (*Perì toû pythagoreíou bíou*; on its construction, see 34ff. above; on its anti-Christian tendency, see 2, 5, and 30ff.);[93] (2) an *Exhortation* to study philosophy (*Protreptikós*); (3) *On the General Science of Mathematics*, (4) a commentary *On Nicomachus' Introduction to Arithmetic*. The other books were titled (5) *Arithmetical Science in Physics*, (6) *Arithmetical Science in Ethics*, (7) *Arithmetical Science in Theology*, (8) *Geometry among the Pythagoreans*, (9) *Music among the Pythagoreans*, and (10) *Astronomy among the Pythagoreans*.

Thus Iamblichus' work was a comprehensive Pythagorizing of the (Neoplatonic) philosophy, in which stimuli provided by Nicomachus and Numenius are taken up and systematically developed. In the foreword, Pythagoras' teaching is viewed programmatically as gift from the gods, a kind of revelation whose beauty and magnitude exceeds human capabilities (only with divine help can the treasures of this wisdom be appropriated).[94] This is not the place to embark on a detailed discussion of this rich work, which has recently attracted a lot of scholarly attention.[95] Let us add only that it was presumably composed as an introductory course in philos-

ophy for Iamblichus' students in Apamea. In any case, the first book, *On
the Pythagorean Way of Life*, shows that the author was not trying to write biography or source-critical historiography, but rather an "ethical propae-
deutic for philosophy" centered on the figure of Pythagoras.[96] These
elementary introductions to the quadrivium of arithmetic, geometry,
music, and astronomy, widened to include "arithmetical" ethics, physics,
and theology, seem to have been followed by metaphysical works (now
lost), which were wholly devoted to the highest realities, true being and the
gods.[97] Moreover, in Iamblichus' school the exegesis of Plato's dialogues,
individual works of Aristotle, and the Chaldean oracles—the latter certainly in connection with theurgy—played a large role.[98] The extant fragments of his commentaries on Plato and Aristotle also show a clear
Pythagorizing tendency.[99] For Iamblichus, not only Plato and the later
"true" Platonists are basically Pythagoreans, but also Aristotle, insofar as he
remained true to Pythagorean-Platonic teaching. The most important dis-
tinguishing characteristic of such a philosophy Iamblichus sees in the concern with supersensible realities. Not least of these is mathematics, through
which in his view the intellect is exercised and prepared for the highest theological insights.[100]

PYTHAGORAS AS AN IDEA IN THE MIDDLE AGES
AND MODERNITY—A PROSPECT

Latin Middle Ages

Had Pythagoras and his teachings not been since the early Academy overwritten with Plato's philosophy, and had this "palimpsest" not in the course
of the Roman Empire achieved unchallenged authority among Platonists,
it would be scarcely conceivable that scholars from the Middle Ages and
modernity down to the present would have found the pre-Socratic charismatic from Samos so fascinating. In fact, as a rule it was the image of
Pythagoras elaborated by s and Neoplatonists that determined the idea of
what was Pythagorean over the centuries. For the Latin Middle Ages,
Boethius (c. 480–524 C.E.), a Roman savant and administrator under
Theodoric the Great, played an important mediating role. His discussion
of the quadrivium begins with *De institutione arithmetica*, a Latin reworking
of Nicomachus' *Introduction to Arithmetic*. In this work he passes on the
image of Pythagoras as a metaphysician who considered the study of numbers, their proportions, and harmony as the royal road not only to a correct understanding of the sciences as a whole, but also to the knowledge
of the unchanging, supersensible realities.[101] Through Boethius' five-vol-
ume *De institutione musica* (another reworking of a lost treatise by the same

Nicomachus), which in combination with the *Introduction to Arithmetic* became for the Middle Ages the standard work on musical theory, was spread in Western Europe the knowledge of Pythagoras the musician who was supposed to have discovered in the smithy the numerical proportions of musical harmonies and to have invented the monochord to test them experimentally.[102] It came to be taken for granted that the harmony of the spheres of the planets was part of the *Musica mundana.*[103] Echoes of these ideas are found in numerous authors of the Latin Middle Ages, including Guido of Arezzo (c. 992–after 1033), Jacques de Liège (c. 1260–after 1330), and Jean de Muris (c. 1300–c. 1350).[104]

Yet, the main lines of Pythagoras' biography and of his teaching, as sketched by the Latin authors Cicero, Ovid, Valerius Maximus (first half of the first century C.E.), Gellius (second century C.E.), and Iustinus (around 390 C.E.?) in his popular epitome of the historian Pompeius Trogus (early Empire), as well as the Church Fathers St. Jerome (c. 347–420) and St. Augustine (354–430), also remained alive among the learned. This is testified to not least by the historical-doxographical works of Vincent de Beauvais (before 1200–1264) and Pseudo-Burleius (early fourteenth century), in each of which a substantial section is devoted to Pythagoras.[105]

Renaissance; Reuchlin's Synthesis of Christianity, Pythagoreanism, and Kabbala

Through the reencounter with the Greek sources, the Neoplatonic image of Pythagoras flourished anew in the works of the Renaissance Platonists Marsilio Ficino (1433–1499), Giovanni Pico della Mirandola (1463–1494), and others.[106] Ficino regarded Pythagoras, along with the Persians, the Egyptians, Orpheus, and Plato as representatives of "ancient wisdom" and translated, for example, Pythagorean pseudepigrapha into Latin. In a modern study the Pythagorean view of the world as a divine order (cosmos) is judged to be the central concept of Renaissance culture as a whole, as it manifested itself in literature, art, music, and science.[107] In any case, ancient writings from the domain of Pythagoreanism enjoyed great popularity. This is particularly true for the "Golden Verses," which were among the Greek poems most often read in the Renaissance and which were also often printed as exercise text in schoolbooks.[108]

In connection with Renaissance Pythagoreanism, the German humanist and Hebraist JOHANNES REUCHLIN (1455–1522) is worthy of special mention. Influenced by Pico della Mirandola to adopt a positive view of the Jewish Kabbala, he undertook an interesting attempt to combine this secret doctrine, which had been developed in the thirteenth and fourteenth centuries in southern France and Spain on the basis of older Jewish and

Neoplatonic-Gnostic traditions, with Pythagorean philosophy and Christian theology. In his dialogue *De verbo mirifico* (published in Basel in 1494 by Johann Amerbach), he compares the best of all God's names, the "miracle-working," unspeakable tetragram "JHVH" (as the four consonants of the name Yahweh), with Pythagoras' *tetraktýs*. In doing so, he attributes to each of the letters, which are also used in Hebrew as in Greek as number characters, a secret, symbolic meaning. For example, he interprets the first "*He*"—the numerical character for the number five, which for the Pythagoreans symbolizes wedding—as the unification of the triune God with nature, which is conceived as twoness (dyad) in the sense of that term in Platonized Pythagoreanism. With the incarnation of the logos, fourness develops into fiveness, and the tetragram becomes a pentagram, thus creating "JHSVH," which Reuchlin considers Jesus' true name; the latter, unlike the tetragram, can be spoken, and has worked many miracles. For Reuchlin, the philosophical interpretation of the meaning of the world culminates in this name.[109]

In his *Three Books on the Art of the Kabbala*, published in 1517, in which an Alanian Pythagorean with the significant name of Philolaus junior appears alongside Simon the Jew and Marranus the Mohammedan, Reuchlin again seeks to prove the basic identity of the doctrines of the Kabbala and those of Pythagoras. According to Reuchlin, both Pythagoras and the Kabbala took their inspiration from the Mosaic tradition, and therefore Pythagoras can in a certain sense also be called a kabbalist.[110] Kabbalism and (Neoplatonic) Pythagoreanism, which are discussed in detail in the second book of this work, agree, Reuchlin maintains, amongst other things in their assumption of two worlds, their secret knowledge regarding numbers and letters, and in the goal of detaching the human mind from earthly things and leading it toward apotheosis.[111]

Copernicus and Kepler

At about the same time, namely in the years between 1507 and 1514, the multitalented Polish canonist and astronomer NICHOLAS COPERNICUS (1473–1543) elaborated the basic outline of his heliocentric system, which was gradually to replace the geocentric worldview of Ptolemy (second century C.E.), which had been canonical in the Middle Ages. A revolutionary event, without any doubt. Yet, Copernicus, the initiator of this radical change hardly saw himself as an innovator; rather, he was far more interested in restoring the old, pre-Ptolemaic astronomy. Uncomfortable with the obvious defects in the current astronomical system, he studied, as he explains in the letter dedicating his magnum opus, *De revolutionibus orbium caelestium* (1543), to Pope Paul III, all the philosophical writings he could lay his hands on, in order to check whether no one of them had defended a different view—and promptly came across various Pythagoreans who had taught that the Earth moved. In Cicero, he found Hicetas of Syracuse (whom Copernicus mistakenly calls "Nicetus"),[112] and in (Pseudo-)Plutarch he found Philolaus, Heraclides Ponticus, and Ecphantus (Copernicus considered Heraclides to be also a Pythagorean). By these philosophers he was led, according to his own statement, to "reflect on the mobility of the Earth." In them he found the ancient authorities (which at that time were still absolutely required) for his heliocentric theory. He names the same thinkers again in the fifth chapter as well as in the concluding part (later omitted) of the first book, where in addition Lysis' letter is cited to explain why this Pythagorean teaching was not more widespread (oral transmission and the secrecy outside the circle of friends and relatives prevented it from becoming more widely known).

Whereas the Pythagorean influence on Copernicus remains mainly limited to the movement of the Earth,[113] JOHANNES KEPLER (1571–1630) was far more thoroughly imbued with Pythagorean ideas. In his *Mysterium cosmographicum* (1596), in which the idea of "world harmony" that was to become so important for him is still lacking, he tries to connect speculatively the Copernican system with the five Platonic bodies traced back to Pythagoras that since Plato's *Timaeus* had been related to the elements. It was on them that God had looked when creating the world and ordering the heavens as planned; the distances between the planets turning around the sun and their respective speeds he had arranged "in accordance with their nature."[114] Kepler explains the spheres of the planets as the circles circumscribed and inscribed in these bodies, and thereby also attributes to them the properties of the elements (supplemented by the quintessence), which could also be exploited astrologically and alchemically.[115]

The title of Kepler's main work, *Harmonices mundi libri V* (1619) shows that in it he was concerned with far more than sober empirical-mechanistic science. His declared goal is to prove from a Christian-Pythagorean perspective the "world harmony" in God's creation. In the first four books he assembles the necessary geometrical, architectonic, musical, and metaphysical-psychological-astrological[116] bases for this cosmic vision before bringing them together in the fifth, "astronomical and metaphysical" book, and demonstrating—according to this book's heading—"THE MOST PERFECT HARMONY OF THE HEAVENLY MOTIONS, and . . . the origin from the same of the Eccentricities, Semidiameters, and Periodic Times."[117] In this Pythagorizing context, he formulates in chapter 3 the famous "Third Law" named after him, according to which "the proportion between the periodic times of any two planets is precisely the sesquialterate proportion of their mean distances, that is, of the actual spheres"[118] (thus the ratio is 3:2, that is, the proportion of the fifth)—a law that was to stimulate Newton to develop the law of gravitation. On the basis of the observations made by Tycho Brahe (1546–1601), Kepler also attributes to the planets, as much as possible, speeds whose proportional numbers correspond to those of simple musical intervals. From the various orbital values he calculates the tonics, scales, melodies, and harmonies. Triple harmonies of Mars, Earth, and Mercury would still appear relatively often, Kepler tells us, while four- or even five-voiced harmonies would be produced much more rarely. In his view, the most perfect harmonic polyphony of all six planets might have rung out at the beginning of the Creation.[119] In a letter, he expressly appeals in this context to Pythagoras: If something should not quite work out, Pythagoras must rise from the dead again who would be able to teach him; yet the latter does not come, "unless perhaps his soul has transmigrated into me."[120] Kepler as Pythagoras *redivivus*.

"Harmonical Pythagoreanism"

From Kepler, to whom Paul Hindemith erected a musical monument in his opera *Die Harmonie der Welt* (1957), one might draw a line to Gottfried Wilhelm Leibniz (1646–1716), in whose theory of monads the concept of harmony plays an important role. In any case, in the twentieth century the adepts of the "HARMONICAL PYTHAGOREANISM," who see in the musical numerical proportions of the series of harmonic overtones the true, universally valid law of the world, have also appealed to Pythagoras, Kepler, and Leibniz. In their view, this law structures not only music and art, but also nature as a whole, as well as the psycho-physical disposition of man and his emotional capacities to experience things. The jurist and politician Albert Freiherr von Thimus (1806–1878) tried in his two-volume work *Die harmonikale Symbolik des Altherthums* (1868 and 1876) to prove that the acoustical phenomena on which music is based were the core of the ancient wisdom teachings of China, Egypt, Greece, and Israel. The true founder of this intellectual trend, the German musician and art historian HANS KAYSER (1891–1964) took up von Thimus' ideas and systematically elaborated them. Kayser, a student of Humperdinck and Schönberg who emigrated to Switzerland in 1933 together with his Jewish wife, brought recent scientific research to bear on the question and tried to use harmonic proportions to explain the growth of crystals and the orbits of the planets as well as, for instance, quantum theory.[121] In view of this combination of modern theory of nature and musical number mysticism, it cannot be denied that Kayser's efforts proceeded from a genuine Pythagorean impulse.

Many further traces of Pythagoras could be found in European culture. Of course, the memory of Pythagoras' earliest proven teaching, the transmigration of the soul, even into animals, remained alive over the centuries through the mediation of Ovid and other ancient classical writers—we have only to think of Shakespeare, who in *The Merchant of Venice* and two other plays wittily alludes to it[122] (the harmony of the spheres is also mentioned in *The Merchant of Venice*).[123] Not only was Plato probably modeling the structure of his Academy after the community which Pythagoras had founded in Croton, but also the freemasons apparently derive their origin at least in part from Pythagoras and his secret society.[124] In more recent times, Pythagoras has been the subject of an English comedy (Dannie Abse 1979) as well as a historical novel (T. Vos-Dahmen von Buchholz 1995/ 1997). Interest in this fascinating figure seems to continue down to the present day.

CHRONOLOGY

Bold: Everything related to Pythagoras himself
Indented: Cultural and intellectual environment
Italics: Discussions of and important sources for Pythagoras and/or Pythagoreanism

Sixth century b.c.e.

Milesian natural philosophers: Thales, Anaximander (for example, first map of the earth and first celestial globe), and Anaximenes
Theogonic and other writings under Orpheus' name
Xenophanes of Colophon (ca. 580–ca. 475): *poet and rhapsode, natural philosopher; moved to Elea (southern Italy) ca. 540*

ca. 570? Birth of Pythagoras in Samos
Ibycus of Rhegium: lyric poet, comes to Samos in 564/1
Amasis: Pharaoh of the late twenty-sixth dynasty in Egypt (570–526)
Hecataeus of Miletus (ca. 560/550–480): improved map of world, description of the world; historical rationalization of myths

Pythagoras' travels, including journey to Egypt (?)

Pythagoras' teachers: the cosmogonist Pherecydes of Syros (?) and the Samian Homeride Hermodamas (?)
ca. 550 Construction of the Eupalinos tunnel on Samos
538–522 Polycrates reigns in Samos
Theodorus of Samos: a multitalented, innovative artist (the ring of Polycrates, etc.)
Anacreon of Teos (born ca. 575?): poet at Polycrates' court
Democedes of Croton: physician in Polycrates' service

ca. 530 (?) Arrival of Pythagoras in southern Italy (Croton)

    ca. 530 (?) Founding of Dicaearchia (modern Pozzuoli) by Samians
522 Death of Polycrates
Milo of Croton: uniquely successful wrestler (thirty-two victories in the
Pan-Hellenic Games)
Croton's political and military superiority (victory over neighboring city
of Sybaris, 510)

    ca. 503/500 fl. Ionian natural philosopher *Heraclitus of Ephesus*
Hippasus of Metapontum (end of the sixth, beginning of the fifth centuries): experiments with sound, mathematical interests, fire as the original material

FIFTH CENTURY B.C.E.

ca. 500 (?) Cylonian rebellion against Pythagoras (proceeding from the
Crotonian upper class) ➤ Pythagoras' emigration to Metapontum
    Alcmaeon of Croton (early fifth century): physician and naturalist
    Epicharmus: poet of Doric comedy
    Parmenides of Elea (520–ca. 450): philosophy of being
Theano (wife, sister, or pupil of Protagoras?)
Bro(n)tinos of Metapontum
Archippus and Lysis
    Empedocles of Acragas (ca. 494–ca. 434): Sicilian natural philosopher
    close to Orphism and Pythagoras
    Ion of Chios (ca. 490–422): many-sided writer active in Athens

ca. 480 (?) Death of Pythagoras

    Herodotus (ca. 485–424): Historian; moved to Thurii (southern
    Italy) 444/3
Spread of Pythagoreanism to Locri, Rhegium, Tarentum (already before
Pythagoras' death?)
ca. 450 or between 440 and 415: anti-Pythagorean rebellions (probably
democratically motivated)
➤ geographical dispersion of the Pythagoreans; growth of new centers in
the Greek homeland (Phlius, Thebes, etc.)

Philolaus of Croton (ca. 470–after 399): comprehensive explanation of
the world in terms of natural philosophy, also ethics
    Democritus of Abdera (born ca. 460?): "*Pythagoras*" (ethical work)
Eurytus (born 450–440?): pupil of Philolaus
Increasing split of Pythagoreans into "acousmatics" and
"mathematicians"

Archytas of Tarentum (ca. 429–347): Pythagorean of the "mathematical" orientation and politician
    Aristophanes (born ca. 450–ca. 386): "The Clouds" (423; reworked between 420 and 417)

FOURTH CENTURY B.C.E.

Other Pythagoreans of the "mathematical" orientation at the end of the fifth century/beginning of the fourth century B.C.E.: Hicetas, Ekphantus of Syracuse, Damon, Phintias, Echecrates of Phlius
    ca. 400 *Anaximander the younger of Miletus: "Interpretation of Pythagorean Symbols"*
Cleinias of Tarentum
    399 Death of Socrates
    Antisthenes (ca. 445–ca. 365): Socratic philosopher
Diodorus of Aspendus: "acousmatic"
    Isocrates (436–338): *"Busiris"*
    Plato (428/7–348/7):
    ca. 388 First journey to southern Italy and Sicily, contacts with Archytas and the Pythagoreans
    366/5 Second journey to Sicily, to the court of Dionysius II of Syracuse (367– 357)
    361/0 Third journey to Sicily
    "Timaeus" as the most "Pythagorean" dialogue

    Speusippus (ca. 407–339): *"On Pythagorean Numbers"* (?)
    Middle Comedy (*Alexis, Aristophon, Cratinus the younger*)
    Xenocrates (ca. 396/5–314): *"Pythagorean [Matters]"*
    Eudoxus of Cnidus (ca. 390–ca. 340): mathematician
    Heraclides Ponticus (ca. 390–after 322): *"On the Pythagoreans," "On the woman who is no longer breathing,"* etc.
    Aristotle (384–322): *"Against the Pythagoreans," "On the Pythagoreans,"* and *"Metaphysics"*
    Andron of Ephesus: "Tripod" (book on the seven wise men)
    Theopompus of Chios (378/7–after 320): historian
    Dicaearchus of Messina (born ca. 375?): *Biography*
    Theophrastus of Eresus (ca. 371–288): successor of Aristotle, founder of the *Doxography*
Aristoxenus of Tarentum (ca. 370–after 322): *"On Pythagoras and his Friends," "On the Pythagorean Life," "Pythagorean Sentences"*
    Eudemus of Rhodes (born before 350): pupil of Aristotle

Lycon of Iasus (second half of the fourth century?): "*On the Pythagorean Way of Life*"

    Neanthes of Cyzicus (late fourth century): "*On Famous Men*"

    Androcydes (? certainly before the first century): "*On Pythagorean Symbols*"

    Timaeus of Tauromenium (ca. 350–ca. 260): "*Sicilian History*"

    Duris of Samos (ca. 340–ca. 260): politician and local historian

    Zeno of Citium (335–263): "*Pythagorean [Matters]*"

From the end of the fourth century (?) on, increasing production of Pythagorean pseudepigrapha

    Timon of Phlius (ca. 320–230): *satirical verse*

    Callimachus of Cyrene (born 320/303): poet and philologist

THIRD CENTURY B.C.E.

    Hermippus of Smyrna: "*On Pythagoras*"

    Theocritus of Syracuse (early third century): poet (creator of bucolic poetry)

Pseudo-Pythagorean "Lysis' Letter" (second half of the third century?)

    Works on the history of philosophy by *Hippobotus* and *Satyrus* (both end of the third century)

    Antiphon (Hellenistic period?): "*On the Life of Persons of Outstanding Virtue*"

SECOND CENTURY B.C.E.

    Works on the history of philosophy by *Sotion, Heraclides Lembus, and Sosicrates*

"Golden Verses," a Pythagorean collection of ethical maxims (precise dating uncertain)

    Apollonios (the Paradoxographer): "*Wondrous Stories*"

FIRST CENTURY B.C.E.

    Alexander Polyhistor (ca. 110–after 40): "*Sequence of the Philosophers*"

Nigidius Figulus (100–45): Flourishing of Pythagoreanism in Rome

    Cicero (106–43): *Tusculanae disputationes,* etc.

    Beginning of Middle Platonism: Eudorus, Philo of Alexandria; interest in Pythagoreanism

    Ovid (43 B.C.E.–18 C.E.): "*Metamorphoses*"

So-called **neo-Pythagoreanism**

FIRST CENTURY C.E.

Valerius Maximus (first half of the first century): *Facta et dicta memorabilia*
Apollonius of Tyana (died 96/98)
Moderatus of Gades

SECOND CENTURY C.E.

Nicomachus of Gerasa (beginning of second century): neo-Pythagorean mathematician and musicologist, *Life of Pythagoras*, etc.
Antonius Diogenes: "Marvels beyond Thule" (romance)
Aulus Gellius: Noctes Atticae
Numenius of Apamea: Pythagorizing Middle and Neo-Platonist
Alexander of Aphrodisias: Commentary on Aristotle's Metaphysics

THIRD CENTURY C.E.

Hippolytus (died 235/6): *"Refutation of all Heresies"*
Porphyry of Tyros (234–ca. 305): *Life of Pythagoras* (from "History of Philosophy")
Diogenes Laertius (middle of the third century?): *Lives of the Philosophers*
Neoplatonism
Iamblichus of Chalcis (ca. 240–325): *"On the Pythagorean Life"* (= book I of *"On the Pythagorean School of Philosophy"*).

FOURTH CENTURY C.E.

Iustinus (ca. 390?): *Epitoma historiarum Philippicarum Pompei Trogi*
Hieronymus (ca. 347–420) and *Augustine* (354–430)

SIXTH CENTURY C.E.

Simplicius (ca. 490–560): *Commentary on Iamblichus' "On the Pythagorean Life"*

LATIN MIDDLE AGES

Chiefly via *Boethius* (ca. 480–524), reflections of the Neoplatonic image of Pythagoras, e.g., in Guido of Arezzo (ca. 992–after 1033), Jacques de Liège (ca. 1260–after 1330), Jean de Muris (ca. 1300–ca. 1350); more detailed presentation of the life and teaching of Pythagoras on the basis of ancient Latin sources in Vincent of Beauvais (before 1200–1264) and Pseudo-Burleius (early fourteenth century).

RENAISSANCE

Marsilio Ficino (1433–1499): Translation of Pythagorean pseudepigrapha
Giovanni Pico della Mirandola (1463–1494)
Johannes Reuchlin (1455–1522): Connection between Pythagoreanism and Kabbala
Nicholas Copernicus (1473–1543): Heliocentric image of the universe
Johannes Kepler (1571–1630): World harmony

MODERN AGE

Harmonical Pythagoreanism: Hans Kayser (1891–1964)

ABBREVIATIONS

Aelian.	Aelianus
Var. hist.	*Varia historia*
Alex. Aphr.	Alexander of Aphrodisias
Alex. Polyhist.	Alexander Polyhistor
Apollon.	Apollonius of Tyana
Hist. mir.	*Historia mirabilium*
Apul.	Apuleius
De Plat.	*De Platone*
Aristot.	Aristotle
Anal. post.	*Analytica posteriora*
De cael.	*De caelo*
De sens.	*De sensu*
Ethic. Nic.	*Ethica Nicomachea*
fr.	*Fragments*
Metaph.	*Metaphysica*
Oecon.	*Oeconomica*
Phys.	*Physica*
Probl.	*Problemata*
Aristox.	Aristoxenus
Athen.	Athenaeus
Bernabé	A. Bernabé, *Poetarum epicorum Graecorum testimonia et fragmenta*, Part 1. Stuttgart-Leipzig 1996.
Boeth.	Boethius
Inst. arithm.	*De institutione arithmetica*
Inst. mus.	*De institutione musica*
CAG	*Commentaria in Aristotelem Graeca* (18 vols.), Berlin 1885–1909.
Cic.	Cicero

Div.	*De divinatione*
Phil. fr.	*Librorum philosophicorum fragmenta*
Rep.	*De re publica*
Tim.	*Timaeus*
Tusc.	*Tusculanae disputationes*
Vatin.	*In P. Vatinium testem interrogatio*
Corp. Hippocr.	*Corpus Hippocraticum*
Morb. sacr.	*De morbo sacro*
Diggle	Diggle, J. *Tragicorum Graecorum Fragmenta selecta.* Oxford 1998.
Diod.	Diodorus
Diog. Laert.	Diogenes Laertius
D.-K.	H. Diels and W. Kranz, eds. *Die Fragmente der Vorsokratiker.* Berlin 1951–52.
Emp.	Empedocles
Eudem.	Eudemus
Eur.	Euripides
FGrHist	F. Jacoby, ed. *Die Fragmente der griechischen Historiker.* Leiden 1923–1958 (continued: 1994ff.).
FHG	C. and Th. Müller, eds. *Fragmenta Historicorum Graecum.* Paris 1878–1885.
Gigon	O. Gigon, *Aristotelis opera III: Librorum deperditorum fragmenta.* Berlin 1987.
h. Cer.	*Hymnus ad Cererem*
Hdt.	Herodotus
Hecat.	Hecataeus Milesius
Heinze	R. Heinze, *Xenokrates. Darstellung der Lehre und Sammlung der Fragmente.* Leipzig 1892 (= Reprint Hildesheim 1965).
Heracl. Pont.	Heraclides Ponticus
Heraclit.	Heraclitus
Hes.	Hesiod
Op.	*Opera et dies*
Theog.	*Theogony*
Hippol.	Hippolytus
Ref.	*Refutatio omnium haeresium*
Hygin	
Fab.	*Fabulae*
Iambl.	Iamblichus
Protr.	*Protrepticus in philosophiam*
VPyth.	*Vita Pythagorica*
Isnardi	M. Isnardi Parente, *Senocrate-Ermodoro. Frammenti.* Naples 1982.
Isocr.	Isocrates

Or.	*Oratio*
Jan	C. Jan, *Musici scriptores Graeci*. Leipzig 1895.
K.-A.	R. Kassel and C. Austin, *Poetae Comici Graeci* (PCG), Berlin 1983ff.
LXX	Septuagint
Ex.	*Exodus*
Lyd.	Johannes Lydus
De mens.	*De mensibus*
Macrob.	Macrobius
Somn.	*Commentarii in Ciceronis somnium Scipionis*
Mirhady, Dicaearchus	Mirhady, D. C. "The Sources, Text and Translation." In W. W. Fortenbaugh and E. Schütrumpf, eds. *Dicaearchus of Messana. Text, Translations and Discussion.* New Brunswick and London 2001, 1–142.
N^2	A. Nauck, *Tragicorum Graecorum fragmenta*, Leipzig 1926.
Neanth.	Neanthes
Nicom.	Nicomachus of Gerasa
Enchir.	*Enchiridium harmonicum*
Intr. arithm.	*Introductio arithmetica*
NT	New Testament
OF	O. Kern, *Orphicorum fragmenta*. Berlin 1922.
Ov.	Ovid
Met.	*Metamorphoses*
Pont.	*Epistulae ex Ponto*
Parm.	Parmenides
Pfeiffer	R. Pfeiffer, *Callimachus*, vol. 1: *Fragmenta*. Oxford 1949; vol. 2: *Hymni et Epigrammata*. Oxford 1953.
Philodemus	
Academ.	*Academicorum index*
Philol.	Philolaus
Philostrat.	Philostratus
VApoll.	*Vita Apollonii*
des Places	E. des Places, *Numénius. Fragments*. Paris 1973.
Plat.	Plato
Epist.	*Letters*
Lys.	*Lysis*
Phaid.	*Phaedo*
Phileb.	*Philebus*
Rep.	*Republic*
Symp.	*Symposium*
Tim.	*Timaeus*

Plin.	Pliny the Elder
Nat. hist.	*Naturalis historia*
Plut.	Plutarch
Sept. sap.	
conviv.	*Septem sapientium convivium*
Porph.	Porphyry
VPyth.	*Vita Pythagorae*
Abst.	*De abstinentia*
Ptolem.	Ptolemy
Harm.	*Harmonica*
Pythag.	Pythagoras
Hier. log.	
hex.	*Hieros logos in hexameters* (Thesleff 1965, 158f.)
Quint.	Quintilian
Inst. orat.	*Institutio oratoria*
Radt	S. Radt, *Tragicorum Graecorum fragmenta*, vol. 4: *Sophocles*. Göttingen 1977.
Schibli	H. S. Schibli, *Pherekydes of Syros*. Oxford 1990.
Schol. in	
Hom. Il.	*Scholia in Homeri Iliadem*
Schol. in	
Theocr.	*Scholia in Theocritum*
Sext. Emp.	Sextus Empiricus
Adv. math.	*Adversus mathematicos*
SH	H. Lloyd-Jones and P. Parsons, *Supplementum Hellenisticum*. Berlin 1983.
Smith	A. Smith, *Porphyrii philosophi fragmenta*. Stuttgart and Leipzig 1993.
SSR	G. Giannantoni, *Socratis et Socraticorum reliquiae* (Elenchos 18). Rome 1990.
SVF	J. von Arnim, *Stoicorum veterum fragmenta*. Stuttgart 1903–1905, Index 1924 (Reprint 1978–1979).
Tarán	L. Tarán, *Speusippus of Athens. A Critical Study with a Collection of the Related Texts and Commentary*. Leiden 1981.
Thesleff	H. Thesleff, *The Pythagorean Texts of the Hellenistic Period*. Åbo 1965.
Xenocr.	Xenocrates
Xenoph.	Xenophanes
Wehrli	F. Wehrli, *Die Schule des Aristoteles. Texte und Kommentar*. Basel and Stuttgart 1967–1969.

NOTES

CHAPTER 1

1. Dicaearch. fr. 40 Mirhady.
2. Cf. West 1971, 218 Anm. 31; Kingsley 1999, 14s.
3. Aelian Var. hist. 12,32.
4. Iambl. VPyth. 135 and 140, commenting on Aristotle, cf. fr. 171; 173s. Gigon.
5. Plat. Phileb. 272b–c considers the capacity to communicate with animals as a distinctive feature of men under Kronos' rule.
6. Nicom. FGrHist 1063 F 1.
7. Luke 5:1–11; cf. John 21:1–14.
8. Cf. also Fauth 1987, 38s.
9. Iambl. VPyth. 36; similarly now also Dillon 2002, 297.
10. Andron FGrHist 1005 F 3 = Porph. fr. 408,24–29 Smith.
11. On the latter, Apollon. Hist. mir. 6,2c = Aristot. fr. 171 Gigon.
12. Ibid., Aelian. Var. hist. 2,26 and 4,17 = Aristot. fr. 171 and 173s. Gigon.
13. Aelian. Var. hist. 4,17 = Aristot. fr. 174 Gigon; cf. Federico 2000.
14. Porph. VPyth. 26 ≈ Iambl. VPyth. 63.
15. Cf. Iliad, 16,849s.; Mühlestein 1987.
16. Cf. Skutsch 1959. See 67ff. below.
17. Iliad 17,51s.
18. Diod. 10,6,2–3; Schol. in Hom. Il. 17,29s.; also Ov. Met. 15,160–4.
19. Zimmer 1969, 185.
20. Heracl. Pont. fr. 89 Wehrli.
21. Porph. VPyth. 28s. ≈ Iambl. VPyth. 135.
22. Aristot. fr. 171s. Gigon.
23. Aristipp. IV A 150 SSR.
24. His identification with the neo-Pythagorean Apollonius of Tyana has recently been questioned: cf. Gorman 1985; Flinterman 1995, 77–79; and now also Staab 2002, 228–237.
25. Iambl. VPyth. 6s.
26. Porph. VPyth. 1.
27. Cf. Neanth. FGrHist 84 F 29; Aristot. fr. 155 Gigon; Aristox. fr. 11 Wehrli.

28. Among others, by Diog. Laert. 8,1.
29. Hermippus FGrHist 1026 F 23, with commentary; cf. Demand 1973.
30. Neanth. loc. cit.
31. Cf. Burkert 1992 and 2003a; West 1997.
32. Plat. Tim. 22b.
33. Diodorus 1,69,3s. and 96,2.
34. Antiphon FGrHist 1096 F 1b.
35. Ibid., 1096 F 1a.
36. Cf. Porph. VPyth. 6; Iambl. VPyth. 19; 151; 154; Diodorus of Eretria FGrHist 1103 F 1; Aristox. fr. 13 Wehrli; Guthrie 1962, 253s., and Kingsley 1990.
37. Porph. VPyth. 6.
38. Hermippus FGrHist 1026 F 21.
39. Antonius Diogenes in Porph. VPyth. 11.
40. Philostr. VApoll. 8,7, p. 320 Kayser.
41. Iambl. VPyth. 151.
42. Antonius Diogenes in Porph. VPyth. 12.
43. Cf. Detienne 1962, 13s. and Burkert 1972d.
44. Theopompus FGrHist 115 F 71.
45. Apollon. Hist. mir. 6.
46. For instance, by Andron FGrHist 1005 F 4; according to Diog. Laert. 8,2, the instruction took place on the island of Lesbos.
47. Iambl. VPyth. 184.
48. Cf. Iambl. VPyth. 252 = Nicom. FGrHist 1063 F 2; the mere fact that Pythagoras buried Pherecydes is already mentioned in Aristoxenus fr. 14 Wehrli.
49. In Iambl. VPyth. 251.
50. Schibli 1990, 6–10.
51. Dicaearch. fr. 41A Mirhady.
52. Duris FGrHist 76 F 22.
53. Cf. also Breglia 2000, 169ss, and below 49–53.
54. Cf. also Riedweg 1997, 84. See 73ff. below.
55. Cf. Diog. Laert. 8,3.
56. A sort of odeum, or perhaps to be identified with the theater, which in Hellenistic times was used for assemblies? Cf. Shipley 1987, 306; in general Isler 1994.
57. Differs from Radicke in his commentary to Antiphon FGrHist 1096 F 1a.
58. Iambl. VPyth. 27s.
59. Cf. also Boudouris 1992; on Zalmoxis as Pythagoras' supposed slave and pupil on Samos, see 55ff.
60. Without naming Eurymenes, Heracl. Pont. [?] fr. 40 Wehrli = Porph. Abst. 1,26.
61. Theodorus of Hierapolis FHG IV 513 = Athen. 10,412e.
62. Among others, Strabo 6,1,12 and Iambl. VPyth. 267.
63. In general on Milon, Visa-Ondarçuhu 1997; Mann 2001, 175–177. See 104ff. below.
64. Diog. Laert. 8,13 and 46.
65. Cf. Ov. Met. 15,60–2; Hippol. Ref. 1,2,1.
66. Porph. VPyth. 16.
67. See Fauth 1987, 26–29.
68. Aristox. fr. 15 Wehrli.
69. Porph. VPyth. 17.
70. OF test. 42.
71. Cf. Corp. Hippocr. Morb. Sacr. 1,17.

72. Cf. Diod. 10,9,6; Alex. Polyhist. FGrHist 273 F 93,33; Aristot. fr. 157 Gigon: "White belongs to the nature of the good, black to that of the bad."
73. Diog. Laert. 8,2s. On Diogenes Laertius' description of Pythagoras and his teachings in general, cf. amongst others now also Staab 2002, 101–109.
74. Aristox. fr. 17 Wehrli.
75. Antisthenes fr. V A 187 SSR.
76. Cf. Phaedrus 277bc.
77. Cf. de Vogel 1966, 70–147; Centrone 1996, 28–32.
78. Iambl. VPyth. 44.
79. Ibid., 45.
80. Aristotle fr. 159 Gigon.
81. Porph. VPyth. 39.
82. Dicaearch. fr. 41A und B Mirhady. See 18ff. below.
83. Iambl. VPyth. 170, probably following Timaeus; cf. Vallet 1974.
84. Boyancé 1966, 105s, supports the former interpretation, on good grounds.
85. Iambl. VPyth. 46–49
86. Cf. on this topic Zoepffel 2001.
87. Cf. Iambl. VPyth. 84.
88. Cf. also Diodorus 10,9,1, Iambl. VPyth. 144 and Diog. Laert. 8,22. On similarities between the Pythagorean "oral sayings" and early Christian literature in general, cf. Thom 1994.
89. Already in the address to the young people of Croton, Heracles therefore was invoked as a model: Iambl. VPyth. 40.
90. Cf. Iambl. VPyth. 132 and 195.
91. Ibid., 50.
92. Ibid., 51–3.
93. Cf. Diodorus 8,17,1; on Myscellus' founding of the colony in general, Braccesi 1998.
94. Iambl. VPyth. 54–57.
95. Ibid., 132.
96. On the Pythagorean attitude to sexual activity in general, cf. Gaza 2000.
97. Cf. Tim. FGrHist 566 F 17.
98. Iambl. VPyth. 56.
99. Cf. Iustinus 20,4,11s.
100. Diodorus 10,9,6; cf. Iambl. VPyth. 153.
101. Tim. FGrHist 566 F 131.
102. Cf. also Iambl. VPyth. 30 and 166.
103. Cf. also Diodorus 10,3,2s.
104. de Vogel 1966, 218–231.
105. Iambl. VPyth. 46.
106. Cf. Ibid., 33 and 214.
107. Cf. Aristox. fr. 43 Wehrli; Bollansée 1999, 45, n. 83.
108. Cf. Tim. FGrHist 566 F 130, with Jacoby's commentary.
109. Iambl. VPyth 215–221.
110. Cf. Burkert 1998, 315, and Burkert 2000.
111. Neanth. FGrHist 84 F 31. See 37–41 below.
112. Dicaearch. fr. 41A Mirhady.
113. Musti 1990.
114. Theopomp. FGrHist 115 F 73; cf. Hermippus FGrHist 1026 F 27.
115. Diog. Laert. 8,39.

116. Apollon. FGrHist 1064 F 2 = Iambl. VPyth. 254–64, esp. 260.
117. Porph. VPyth. 54.
118. Ibid., 54.
119. Cf. Hippol. Ref. 1,2,5.
120. Antonius Diogenes in Porph. VPyth. 13
121. Aristox. fr. 18 Wehrli.
122. Dicaearch. fr. 41A und B Mirhady.
123. Neanth. FGrHist 84 F 31. See 37ff. below.
124. Diog. Laert. 8,39.
125. Hermippus FGrHist 1026 F 25.
126. Cf. *Golden Verses* 32–38.
127. Heraclides Lembus FHG III 169 = Diog. Laert. 8,40.
128. Plat. Phaed. 81d.
129. Plat. Rep. 7, 514a-517c.
130. Plat. Rep. 7, 522c-527c.
131. Aristot. Metaph. A 6, 987b and M 8, 1083b17.
132. Cf. also the detailed discussion of this work by Kahn 2001, 79–83.
133. Aristot. Metaph. A 6; cf. Burkert 1972a, 67–69; Centrone 1992, 4196s.
134. Aristot. Metaph. A 5, with the commentary by Alexander of Aphrodisias on this passage.
135. In Porph. VPyth. 48–52.
136. Moderatus in Porph. VPyth. 49s.
137. Plat. Rep. 6, 510d-e.
138. Xenocrat. fr. 54 and 68 Heinze = 154–158 and 188 Isnardi.
139. Cf. Baltes 1976.
140. Moderatus in Porph. VPyth. 51.
141. Aristot. De cael. 268a10–13.
142. Hippol. Ref. 1,2,2.
143. On geometry, cf. already Hdt. 2,109.
144. Hecataeus of Abdera FGrHist 264 F 25,98,2.
145. Anticleides FGrHist 140 F 1.
146. Iambl. De comm. math. sc. 21.
147. Ibid., sc. 22.
148. Ibid., sc. 23.
149. Ibid., sc. 24.
150. Iambl. VPyth. 88s., cf. De comm. math. sc. 25.
151. Iambl. De comm. math. sc. 25.
152. Diog. Laert. 8,12.
153. Cic. De nat. deor. 3,88.
154. Porph. VPyth. 36.
155. Emp. 31 A 11 D.-K.
156. Xenocr. fr. 9 Heinze = 87 Isnardi.
157. Cf. e.g., Diog. Laert. 8,12.
158. Iambl. VPyth 115.
159. Nicom. Enchir. 6s.
160. Iambl. VPyth. 121, transl. Dillon and Hershbell.
161. Cf. Burkert 1972a, 375s.
162. Ptolem. Harm. 1,8.
163. Aristox. fr. 90 Wehrli.
164. Cf. e.g., Porph. VPyth. 20.

165. Hippol. Ref. 1,2,2.
166. Cf. Iambl. VPyth. 65.
167. Porph. VPyth. 31 = Nicom. FGrHist 1063 F 1; transl. Radicke.
168. Iambl. VPyth. 66.
169. Aristox. fr. 26 Wehrli.
170. Porph. VPyth. 32; cf. Iambl. VPyth. 110s.; on Pythagoras and Hesiod, see chapter 2; in general, see Detienne 1962.
171. Cf. Iambl. VPyth. 224.
172. Cf. e.g., Cic. Phil. fr. X 3; Quint. Inst. orat. 1,10,32; Iambl. VPyth. 112.
173. Antonius Diogenes in Porph. VPyth. 32.
174. Cf. already Aristox. fr. 27 Wehrli.
175. Antonius Diogenes in Porph. VPyth. 34; cf. Diog. Laert. 8,19.
176. Diog. Laert. 8,3; Iambl. VPyth. 104 and 222 identifies Epimenides as a pupil of Pythagoras.
177. Hermippus FGrHist 1026 F 12.
178. Plut. Sept. sapient. conviv. 158ab.
179. Aelian. Var. hist. 4,17.
180. Iambl. Protr. 21, no. 38; cf. Iambl. VPyth. 109.
181. Cf. Epimenides FGrHist. 457 T 1.
182. Iambl. VPyth. 141; transl. Dillon and Hershbell.
183. Thom 1995, 35–58.
184. Seneca De ira 3,36,1.
185. Iambl. VPyth. 164–166; cf. also Diodor. 10,5,1.
186. On the structure of the work in general, cf. Dillon and Hershbell 1991, 14–29; and now Lurje 2002, 236–242; and Staab 2002, 238–242; 441–447; 478–487; on Iambl. VPyth. 134–240 in particular cf. id., 351–434.
187. Cf. Iambl. VPyth. 86; Isocr. Or. 11,28; Aristox. fr. 33 Wehrli.
188. Cf. Diog. Laert. 8,20 and 24.
189. Iambl. VPyth. 138; cf. also 163.
190. Cf. Hermippus FGrHist 1026 F 22.
191. Dicaearch. fr. 40 Mirhady.
192. Emp. 31 B 137 D.-K.
193. Ov. Met. 15,477s.
194. Eudoxus fr. 325 Lasserre.
195. Aristox. fr. 25 Wehrli.
196. Aristox. fr. 28 Wehrli.
197. Aristox. fr. 29a Wehrli; cf. also Iambl. VPyth. 150.
198. Ovid Met. 15,120–126.
199. Aristox. fr. 1 Wehrli; cf. Visconti 1999, 15.
200. Iambl. VPyth. 167.
201. Ibid., 174s. and 179.
202. Aristox. fr. 18 Wehrli.
203. Neanth. FGrHist 84 F 31 = Iambl. VPyth. 189–194; cf. 214.
204. Neanth. FGrHist 84 F 31 = Iambl. VPyth. 189, transl. Dillon and Hershbell.
205. Iambl. VPyth. 195, transl. Dillon and Hershbell; cf. also 72, 188 and 225.
206. Iambl. VPyth. 162.
207. Hygin Fab. 257.
208. Aristox. fr. 31 Wehrli; cf. Visconti 1999, 20s.
209. See his commentary on the passage.
210. Against this view, Gegenschatz 1981.

211. Diod. 10,4,3.
212. Wehrli on fr. 31; von Fritz 1963a, 174s.

CHAPTER 2

1. Cf., e.g., Centrone 1996, 24s. for further information.
2. Cf. Riedweg 1997.
3. Iambl. VPyth. 11s.; cf. Apollon. FGrHist 1064 F 1 and Antonius Diogenes in Porph. VPyth. 11. See 8f. above.
4. Cf. Hdt. 2,109,3.
5. Diog. Laert. 2,4s.
6. Eudem. fr. 146 Wehrli.
7. Cf. Hdt. 2,143.
8. Hecat. FGrHist 1 F 1.
9. Hdt. 3,60; cf. also Shipley 1987, 74–80.
10. Vitruv. 7 praef. 12.
11. Plin. Nat. hist. 7,198.
12. Kienast 1995, 187.
13. Cf. Käppel 1999.
14. Cf. Xenoph. 21 B 3 D.-K. regarding the people of Colophon.
15. Cf. Athen. 1,3a.
16. On this term cf. Musti 1986; Ameruso 1996; Mele 2000.
17. Apollon. FGrHist 1064 F 2 = Iambl. VPyth. 257 and 261.
18. Hdt. 3,137,5.
19. Cf. Accame 1980, 28–44, who wants to see the settlers as followers of Pythagoras.
20. Timo fr. 831 SH.
21. Cratinus iun. fr. 7 K.-A.
22. Xenoph. 21 B 10–12 D.-K.
23. Cf. Xenoph. 21 B 19 D.-K.
24. Cf. Xenoph. 21 B 27–29 and 33 and A 47 D.-K.
25. Xenoph. 21 A 1 and B 20 D.-K.
26. Xenoph. 21 A 52 D.-K.
27. Xenoph. 21 B 34 D.-K.
28. Porph. VPyth. 45.
29. Heraclit. 22 B 28a D.-K., perhaps in an eschatological context, cf. Kahn 1979, 211.
30. Heraclit. 22 B 42 D.-K.
31. Hesiod Theog. 55 and 98–103.
32. Heraclit. 22 B 57 D.-K.; cf. also B 106 D.-K. for more criticism of Hesiod.
33. On the criticism of Homer, cf. also Heraclit. 22 A 22 D.-K.
34. Heraclit. 22 B 104 D.-K., with Kahn's explications: Kahn 1979, 175; cf. also A 23 D.-K.
35. Pythag. Hier. log. hex. 2 Thesleff.
36. Cf. Riedweg 1997, 90–92.
37. Hermippus FGrHist 1026 F 24.
38. Cf. Kahn 1979, 212.
39. Cf. also Heraclit. 22 B 35 D.-K.
40. Cf. Shipton 1985, 129s.; somewhat differently, Kahn 1974, 184, who sees in the invisible harmony an allusion to the cosmic harmony; cf. also Kahn 2001, 37; Kahn 1979, 203s. and 285 on 22 B 10 D.-K.

41. Cf. for example Sandbach 1958/1959; others believe they discern a skeptical tone in these verses; cf. Leurini 1992, 129.
42. Cf. Kranz 1967 = 1934, 104.
43. Emp. 31 B 147 D.-K.
44. Cf., in general, Riedweg 1995.
45. On the latter, see van der Ben 1975, 181.
46. Cf. Emp. 31 B 112 D.-K.; cf. also Kahn 2001, 17s.
47. Ibid., 13s. D.-K.
48. Ibid., 128 D.-K.
49. Zuntz 1971, 209.
50. Wright 1981, 257.
51. Porph. VPyth. 30s.
52. Cf. Wright 1981, 258.
53. On Empedocles' relationship to Pythagoreanism in general, Musti 1989, 44–51.
54. Hdt. 2,123,2.
55. Cf. Demand 1973, 93s., and Kingsley 1994, 1–3.
56. Hdt. 4,95,2.
57. Gold Leaf A 4,6 Zuntz 1971 = L 8 Bernabé and Jiménez 2001.
58. Plat. Rep. 2,363c.
59. Cf. now also Ustinova 2002, 278–281.
60. Cf. Burkert 1972a, 155–161.
61. Hermippus FGrHist 1026 F 24.
62. Soph. Electra 62–64; cf. schol. ad 62.
63. Democritus 68 B 0a-c D.-K.
64. Cf. Democritus 68 A 1,38 D.-K.
65. Metzler 1971, 272; cf. also Schwabacher 1968.
66. Iambl. VPyth. 11 and 30; cf. Eratosthenes FGrHist 241 F 11.
67. Strocka 1992 (pl. 60).
68. Schefold 1997, 152–155, 276s., 412s., and 424s.; cf. moreover Smith 1991 for a late-antique portrait.
69. Porph. fr. 408 Smith.
70. This may well be an allusion to the (Pythagorizing) Old Academy, as Staab 2002, 56 n. 102 suggests.
71. Cf. Boudon and Bourricaud 1992, 60.
72. Macris 2003 has independently reached the same conclusion. For a different application of Weberian categories to describe Pythagoreans and Orphics, cf. Bremmer 1999. See also 67–73, and 100ff. below.
73. Cf. Accame 1980, 14–25.
74. According to Dicaearch. fr. 40 Mirhady; cf. Kahn 2001, 7s.
75. Cf. e.g. Iustinus 20,4; Giangiulio 1989, 305–308.
76. Cf. Sassi 1988, 571s. See 12ff. above.
77. Cf. Schol. in Theocr. 4,33b.
78. Cf. Diod. 12,9,5s.; Visa-Ondarçuhu 1997, 40–44. Cf. also the encouragement of warlike courage in 58 C 4,85 D.-K.; and in general Ellinger 1992.
79. Mele 1984, 57s.
80. Cf. de Vogel 1966, 55–57; Parise 1987, 310–314.
81. Cf. Berger 1992, 21.
82. Aristox. fr. 18 Wehrli (cf. Porph. VPyth. 54).
83. Apollon. FGrHist 1064 F 2 = Iambl. VPyth. 254.
84. Cf. also Giangiulio 1989, 310s.
85. Cf. Casadio 1991.

86. Cf. Pherecydes fr. 2 Schibli. An Indian influence is less likely: Karttunen 1989, 112–115; Casadio 1991, 140s.; Bremmer 2002, 24 (for an opposite view cf. Kahn 2001, 19); cf. also Burkert 2003b, 116.
87. Heracl. Pont. fr. 89 Wehrli; cf. also Alex. Polyhist. FGrHist 273 F 93,28, Schol. in Hom. Il. 16,857a.
88. Cf. Wright 1995, 138–141; Huffman 1993, 260 and 276–279.
89. Eudem. fr. 88 Wehrli; cf. Petit 1987; in general Kalogerakos 1996, 121s.
90. Cf. Hom. h. Cer. 480–482.
91. Sophocles fr. 837 Radt.
92. Cf. Plat. Rep. 2, 364e-365a.
93. Cf. Ibid., 2, 364b-366b.
94. Cf. e.g. Zeller 1919, 411; Redlow 1966, 47.
95. Iambl. VPyth. 82–86 = 58 C 4 D.-K.; cf. Burkert 1972a, 166–170, in the wake of Rose, Rohde, Hölk, and Böhm.
96. However, cf. Iambl. VPyth. 154s.
97. Iambl. VPyth. 86. On the judgment of souls in general, cf. Iambl. VPyth. 155 and 179.
98. Diog. Laert. 8,35 = Aristot. fr. 157 Gigon.
99. Cf. Riedweg 1998 and 2002; Bernabé and Jiménez 2001.
100. Transl. Dillon and Hershbell (for the most part).
101. Diog. Laert. 8,34 = Aristot. fr. 157 Gigon.
102. Iambl. Protr. 21, no. 1.
103. 1989, 149.
104. Cf. 58 C 5 D.-K., Iambl. VPyth. 48, and Aristot. [?] Oecon. 1344a9–13.
105. Cf. Zoepffel 2001, 171s.
106. Anaximander the Younger FGrHist 9 T 1.
107. Cf. Hölk 1894, 40–60.
108. Cf. Iambl. VPyth. 87.
109. Alexander Polyhistor FGrHist 273 F 94.
110. Porph. VPyth. 42
111. Cf. Böhm 1905; Parker, 1983, 291–296.
112. Cf. also Parker 1983, 296s.
113. Iambl. Protr. 21, no. 40.
114. Aristot. fr. 157 Gigon.
115. Cf. Iambl. Protr. 21, no.5.
116. Aristot. fr. 158s. and 177 Gigon. For a general prohibition to eat fish based on cosmogonical speculations, cf. Anaximander 12 A 30 and A 11,6 D.-K.
117. Iambl. (Aristot.?) VPyth. 85; cf. Hdt. 1,140,3 on the Egyptian priests.
118. Aristot. fr. 158s. and 177 Gigon.
119. Iambl. Protr. 21, no. 31.
120. Cf. Alex. Polyhist. FGrHist 273 F 93,33; Delatte 1922, 231s., and Burkert 1972a, 177s.; on the widespread special treatment of the head and feet, see Burkert 1972b, 121 and 125.
121. Cf. OF test. 212–215; Sfameni 1987.
122. Emp. 31 B 137 D.-K.
123. Iambl. VPyth. 85, probably following Aristotle.
124. Cf. Iambl. VPyth. 150; Detienne 1970.
125. Lipp 1995, 34.
126. Iambl. VPyth. 82, probably following Aristotle.
127. Cf. Emp. 31 B 128 D.-K.; OF test. 212.
128. Porph. VPyth. 44, following Antonius Diogenes in Lyd. De mens. 4,42.

129. Cf. also Heracl. Pont. fr. 41 Wehrli; Hippol. Ref. 1,2,14s.
130. Seelkopf in Marcovich 1964, 31.
131. Plin. Nat. hist. 18,118.
132. Cf. Cic. Div. 1,62; on India, Schroeder 1901, and in general Böhm 1905, 14–17.
133. Cf. e.g. Grmek 1980 and Scarborough 1981.
134. Schol. T on Hom. Il. 13,589.
135. Cf. also Delatte 1930.
136. Lipp 1995, 33s.
137. Iambl. VPyth. 148.
138. Cf. Weber 1976, 140.
139. Cf. Iambl. VPyth. 143s. and 255 (=Apollon. FGrHist 1064 F 2).
140. Aristot. fr. 497 Gigon.
141. Iambl. VPyth. 25 and 35; cf. Bruneau 1970, 161–164, and Detienne 1970, 150s., as well as Bruit-Zaidman 1993.
142. On all this, cf. Giangiulio 1989, 79–92 and 134–160; also Giangiulio 1994.
143. Burkert 1972a.
144. Zhmud 1997, 99.
145. Cf. e.g. Guthrie 1962, 181s.; Gladigow 1965, 25; Kahn 1974, 169s. and now also id. 2001, ix and 14ss.; Bremmer 1999, 71–78.
146. Plat. Phaed. 96a.
147. Cf. Iambl. VPyth. 82.
148. Burkert 1987, 78–84.
149. Kahn 2001, 21s. exaggerates the differences between Orphic and Pythagorean traditions.
150. OF test. 222 and 229.
151. Text now in Janko 2002; cf. Laks and Most 1997.
152. Aristot. fr. 174 Gigon = Aelian. Var. hist. 4,17.
153. Aristot. fr. 159 Gigon.
154. Aristot. Anal. post. 94b33.
155. Aristot. fr. 174 Gigon = Aelian. Var. hist. 4,17.
156. Hes. Theog. 482–491.
157. Cf. Ibid., 687–735.
158. Ibid., 780 and 784. See 30 above.
159. Hes. Op. 168–173.
160. Iambl. VPyth. 85.
161. Emp. 31 B 115,5 D.-K.
162. Thales 11 A 22 D.-K.
163. Cf. West 1971, 215.
164. Cf. Ibid., 216.
165. Anaxim. 13 A 18 D.-K.
166. Diog. Laert. 8,12.
167. Cf. Iambl.VPyth. 56.
168. Cf. Aetius 2,1,1; Finkelberg 1998, 107s.
169. Cf. e.g., Iambl. VPyth. 162.
170. Cf. Szlezák 1993, 173s.
171. Burkert 1972a, 13.
172. Diog. Laert. 8,85.
173. Burkert 1972a, 348, 400, and 478–480.
174. Cf. also Kahn 2001, 16s. See 49ff. above.
175. Cf. also Mann 2001, 173s.

176. Pythagoreans 58 C 1 D.-K., cf. fr. 158 and 175 Gigon.
177. Cf. also Zhmud 1998 and now Kahn 2001, 23–35.
178. Cf. Philol. 44 B 13 D.-K.
179. Philol. 44 B 14 D.-K.
180. Cf. Aristot. fr. 169 and 179 Gigon.
181. Philol. 44 A 16, cf. B 7 D.-K.
182. Cf. in general Petit 1992 as well.
183. E.g., Huffman 1993.
184. Hippol. Refut. 1,2,1. Cf. in general also Guthrie 1962, 147.
185. E.g., Aristot. Metaph. 986a22.
186. Cf. Ibid., 985b23 and 1078b21, with the commentary by Alex. Aphr. p. 37 CAG.
187. Cf. Aristot. Metaph. 1083b11s. and 17.
188. Cf. Ibid., 986a2s.; 1090a24s.
189. Ibid., 990a3–5; cf. 1091a18–20.
190. See von Fritz 1963b, 262.
191. Ross, W. D., *Metaphysica (Metaphysics) (complete)* in *The Basic Works of Aristotle,* ed. R. MacKeon (New York 1941), 681–926
192. = Aristot. fr. 162 Gigon.
193. Cf. also Aristot. Ethic. Nic. 1132b21–23.
194. See also Manthe 1996.
195. Cf. Ps.-Aristot. Probl. 910b31–34.
196. Iambl. VPyth. 162. Cf. on the *tetraktýs* quite in general, Delatte 1915, 249–268. See 27ff. above.
197. Cf. Sext. Emp. Adv. math. 7,94.
198. Burkert 1972a, 187.
199. Plat. Rep. 10, 617b-c.
200. Plat. Cratyl. 405d.
201. Aristot. Metaph. 986a2s.
202. Cf. Xenocr. fr. 9 Heinze = 87 Isnardi.
203. E.g., Iambl. VPyth. 162.
204. Cf. Aristot. Metaph. 985b32s.
205. Aristox. fr. 23 Wehrli.
206. Aristot. Metaph. 986a8–12
207. Cf. Aristot. De cael. 293a18–27 and fr. 162, p. 413b,35–414,3 Gigon.
208. Cf. also Kahn 2001, 26s. and 30.
209. Aristot. De cael. 293b1–4; cf. also Kahn 2001, 26s.
210. Philol. 44 B 7 D.-K.
211. Aristot. De cael. 290b12–29 and 291a7–9, as well as fr. 162, p. 414a, 3–16 Gigon.
212. Cf. Aristot. Metaph. 985b25–986a2 and fr. 162, p. 413b, 9–15 Gigon.
213. Plat. Phileb. 16c, cf. 23c; transl. Benardete; cf. also Kahn 2001, 13s.
214. Philol. 44 B 1s. and 6 D.-K.
215. Ibid., 44 B 6 D.-K.
216. Ibid., 44 B 7s.; cf. Schibli 1996 on these fragments.
217. Ibid., 44 B 5.
218. Aristot. fr. 162, p. 413b, 21–24 Gigon.
219. Aristot. Metaph. 986a22–26.
220. Ibid., 986a27–b3
221. Cf. Pythagoreans 58 B 28 D.-K.
222. Eurytus 45 A 2s. D.-K.
223. Aristot. Metaph. 987a 20–24.

224. Philol. 44 B 5 D.-K.
225. Philol. 44 B 4 D.-K., cf. B 3.
226. Cf. Aristot. Metaph. 990a3–5.
227. Aristot. fr. 162, p. 413b,7–9 Gigon.
228. Aristot. Metaph. 1090a30–35.
229. Aristot. Phys. 203a7–12.
230. Cf. Aristot. fr. 162, p. 413b,18–24 Gigon.
231. Philol. 44 A 16 D.-K.
232. Cf. Pythagoreans 58 B 30s. D.-K.
233. On color, cf. Aristot. De sens. 439a30s., on seeds, Porph. VPyth. 44.
234. Burkert 1968, 107–109; cf. also Pierris 1992, 136–139.
235. Cf. Porph. VPyth. 44.
236. OF 55s.
237. Cf. Aristot. Metaph. 989b29–990a8.
238. E.g., Burkert 1972a, 401–479; reservations also in van der Waerden 1979, 36–43.
239. E.g., Zhmud 1997, 156–170; more balanced von Fritz 1963b, 262–266, and Leszl 1988, 208s.
240. Cf. Pichot 1995, 92s.
241. Cf. Ibid., 80–85 and 360s., on Egypt 197s.; in general also Kahn 2001, 32s.
242. Aristox. fr. 23 Wehrli.
243. Pichot 1995, e.g., 92 and 94.
244. Cf. Archytas 47 B 1 D.-K.
245. Aristot. Metaph. 985b23s.
246. Cf. Riedweg 2004.
247. Cf. Giangiulio 1989, 99–130; Mann 2001, 164–191.
248. E.g., Jaeger 1960 = 1928 and Burkert 1960.
249. Cf. Plat. Phaedr. 278d; Symp. 204a; Lys. 218a.
250. Cf. also Gottschalk 1980, 23–36.
251. Wehrli in his commentary on Heracl. Pont. fr. 89.
252. Cf. Alcmaeon 24 B 1 D.-K.
253. Iambl. VPyth 267.
254. Plat. Rep. 9, 581c.
255. E.g., in Plat. Apol. 29de.
256. Hdt. 3,139.
257. Cf. Joly 1956, 12ss.
258. Cf. Festugière 1950, 34–41
259. Cf. Melero 1972, 83–90, Demand 1982, 183s., Patzer 1993, 75–77, and Bowie 1998, 60–65. See 12ff. above.
260. Cf. Koller 1958, 281–283; in general, also Rausch 1982, 9–47.
261. Hdt. 1,29,1.
262. Heraclit. 22 B 35 D.-K.; cf. Kahn 1979, 105.
263. Cf. Dixsaut 1985, 369.
264. Cf. above and Nicom. Intr. arithm. 1,1s.
265. On the word formation, see Cipriano 1990, 95–113.

CHAPTER 3

1. NT Acts 24: 5.
2. Cf. von Staden 1982, 96–100.

3. Cf. e.g., continuing the work of Max Weber and Ernst Troeltsch, Wilson 1970 and Rudolph 1979; on the theological debate about the phenomenon, Hemminger 1995.
4. Cf. Burkert 1982 (also on the difference between Orphism and Pythagoreanism in this respect); Leszl 1988, 197s.; Brisson and Segonds 1996, XXXVIss.
5. Schmidtchen 1987, 7.
6. Apollon. FGrHist 1064 F 2,254 and Iustinus 20,4,14; the figure of six hundred is mentioned in Diog. Laert. 8,15, Iambl. VPyth. 29, and Suda s. v. *gnórimoi* = γ 351.
7. Cf. Bremmer 1995, 65s.
8. Apollon. FGrHist 1064 F 2,254.
9. This is the definition of charisma in Boudon and Bourricaud 1984, 59.
10. Cic. De nat. deor. 1,10; Diog. Laert. 8,46; cf. already Callimachus fr. 61 Pfeiffer.
11. Iambl. VPyth. 198; cf. 88 and 158.
12. Cf. Schmidtchen 1987, 10.
13. Cf. Iambl. VPyth 71.
14. Iambl. Protr. 21, no. 6.
15. Pythagoras Hier. log. hex. 2 Thesleff.
16. Iambl. VPyth. 94.
17. Fr. 156 Gigon.
18. Weber 1976, 141.
19. Nicom. FGrHist 1063 F 3.
20. Cf. also Bremmer 1999, 77. See 52f., 55ff., 62–67 above.
21. Iambl. VPyth. 73s., probably following the historian Timaeus.
22. Iambl. VPyth. 246.
23. Cf. also Sorg 1991, 27s. on the "Verein für Psychologische Menschenkenntnis"; in general Wilson 1970, 27.
24. Weber 1976, 141.
25. Apollon. FGrHist 1064 F 2,257–260; cf. Centrone 1996, 34–43; on the Pythagoreans' "conservative" attachment to traditional laws, cf. also Aristox. fr. 33s. Wehrli, and the interpretations offered by Camassa 1976/1977.
26. Aristox. fr. 18 Wehrli.
27. See Polybius 2,39; on the spread of the uprisings, cf. also Dicaearchus fr. 41 A,17–19 Mirhady.
28. Polybius 2,39,2.
29. Cf., e.g., von Fritz 1963b, 215s.
30. Musti 1990, 62–65.
31. Aristox. fr. 30 Wehrli.
32. Cf. Aristox. fr. 19 Wehrli.
33. Lycon FGrHist 1110; cf. Burkert 1972a, 204.
34. Tim. FGrHist 566 F 16.
35. Cf. also Burkert 1972a, 198–205; on Aristoxenus in general, Kahn 2001, 69–71.
36. See Centrone 1996, 139–141.
37. Apollon. FGrHist 1064 F 2,263s.
38. Cf. Iambl. VPyth. 82.
39. Iambl. VPyth. 87–89; cf. 81 (with confusion of the two groups) and De comm. math. scient. 25; Burkert 1972a, 195–197 presumes, following Delatte, that Iamblichus' account goes in essence back to Aristotle.
40. Iambl. VPyth. 157 and 247; cf. 105 and Protr. 21, p. 106.
41. Cf. also Melero 1972, 65–70, and Sanchis 1995.
42. Alexis "The female follower of Pythagoras" fr. 201 K.-A.
43. Aristophon Pythagoristes fr. 10 K.-A.

44. Aristophon Pythagoristes fr. 12 K.-A.
45. Alexis "The people from Tarentum" fr. 223 K.-A.; cf. Cratinus iun. "The people from Tarentum" fr. 7 K.-A.
46. Alexis "The people from Tarentum" fr. 222 K.-A.
47. Cf. Burkert 1972a, 114, and in particular Montepaone 1993.
48. Iambl. VPyth. 267
49. Cf. Thesleff 1965, 54s.
50. Bro(n)tinus 17 D.-K.
51. Aristot. Metaph. 984a7.
52. Aristox. fr. 90 Wehrli.
53. Cf. also Comotti 1991.
54. Cf. Burkert 1972a, 440–442.
55. Hippasus 18 A 15 D.-K.
56. Nicom. Enchir. 7, p. 279 Jan.
57. Plat. Tim. 55c.
58. Cf. Hippasus 18 A 2 and 4 D.-K.; Burkert 1972a, 206s. and 459–461.
59. Plat. Phaid. 61d-e.
60. Philol. 44 A 2–4 D.-K.
61. Diog. Laert. 3,6; cf. Huffman 1993, 5.
62. Philol. 44 A 16 D.-K.
63. Philol. 44 A 19 D.-K. and Achill. Isag. 1,19, p. 46 Maass.
64. Philol. 44 A 20 D.-K.
65. Philol. 44 A 27s. D.-K., cf. A 11.
66. Philol. 44 B 13 D.-K.
67. Cf. Plat. Phaid. 62b.
68. Philol. 44 B 16 D.-K.
69. Iambl. VPyth. 85.
70. Apul. De Plat. 1,3; Diog. Laert. 3,6.
71. Cf. now also Kahn 2001, 39–48.
72. Cf. Aristox. fr. 30 Wehrli.
73. Archytas 47 A 1 D.-K.
74. Aristox. fr. 48 Wehrli.
75. Aristot. Pol. 1320b9–11. Cf. now also Huffman 2002, 260–262.
76. Archytas 47 B 1 D.-K. See 116ff. below.
77. Archytas 47 B 1 D.-K.; on its authenticity, cf. Huffman 1985.
78. Archytas 47 A 19a and B 1 D.-K.; cf. Bowen 1982, 92–99.
79. Archytas 47 A 16 D.-K.; cf. Barker 1989.
80. Eudem. fr. 141 Wehrli; cf. van der Waerden 1956, 249–253.
81. Archytas 47 A 19 D.-K.; cf. Burkert 1972a, 442–447.
82. Archytas 47 A 1 D.-K.; cf. Krischer 1995.
83. Archytas 47 A 10a D.-K.
84. Hicetas 50 A 1s. D.-K.
85. Heracl. Pont. fr. 104–110 Wehrli; on the relationship between the two, cf. Gottschalk 1980, 44s. and 142.
86. Ecphantus 51 A 1–5 D.-K.
87. Aristox. fr. 1 Wehrli
88. Chamaeleon fr. 4 Wehrli, in connection with Aristox. fr. 30 Wehrli.
89. Cleinias 54 A 3 D.-K.
90. Cleinias 54 A 5 D.-K.
91. Aristox. fr. 131 Wehrli.

92. Iambl. VPyth. 266.
93. Archestratus fr. 154,19s. SH.
94. Cf. Burkert 1972a, 202–204.
95. Lycon 57 A 3 D.-K. See 104ff. above.
96. Iambl. VPyth. 267; cf. Burkert 1972a, 105 n. 40, and Musti 1989, 34–39.

CHAPTER 4

1. Cf. Burkert 1972a, 280s.; more positively on a possible Pythagorean influence, Kahn 1974, 183s. and id. 2001, 36s.
2. Heraclit. 22 B 62 D.-K.
3. Heraclit. 22 B 36 and 88 D.-K.
4. Cf. Kahn 1979, 218ss. (the quotation is to be found on p. 221s.); see also 238 and now id., 2001, 37.
5. Parm. 28 A 1 D.-K., cf. A 4 and 12.
6. Parm. 28 A 44 D.-K., cf. A 1, 42 and 49.
7. Coxon 1986, 19, for example, is quite optimistic; Burkert 1972a, 281–285, is more reserved at least with regard to Parmenides' actual philosophy; cf. also Petit 1992 for a considerate evaluation, and Kingsley 1999 for a bold attempt at Pythagorizing, as it were, the mystic Parmenides.
8. Parm. 28 B 1 D.-K.; cf. Burkert 1969, 16–29.
9. Parm. 28 B 12,4 D.-K. On the Pythagorean assessment, cf. Iambl. VPyth. 85.
10. Esp. Parm. 28 B 1,28–32 and B 8,50–53 D.-K.; cf. Aristot. fr. 162, p. 413a, 6–12 Gigon on the Pythagoreans.
11. Parm. 28 B 8,56–59 D.-K.
12. Parm. 28 B 8,26–33 D.-K.
13. On Alcmaeon in general, cf. now Perilli 2001.
14. Epicharmus 23 B 2,1–3 D.-K. = 276,1–3 K.-A.; cf. Burkert 1972a, 438 n. 64 and generally 289 n. 58.
15. Cf. also Zoepffel 2001.
16. Plat. Rep. 10, 600b.
17. Cf. also Boyancé 1966, moreover, for other teachings, such as the recollection, the transmigration of the soul, and the importance of mathematics, cf. Kahn 2001, 49–62. Brisson 2002 seems to me to adopt an unwarranted critical attitude.
18. Plat. Rep. 7, 530d.
19. Cf. in general Mathieu 1987.
20. Plat. Epist. 7, 350a.
21. Cf. Lloyd 1990.
22. Philodem. Academ. col. 6,12s.
23. Cf. Diog. Laert. 5,25.
24. Plat. Tim. 31c-d and 36a.
25. Barker 1989 and 1994.
26. Plat. Tim. 20a and 27a.
27. Cf. similarly Kahn 2001, 40.
28. See also Robinson 1992, 186s.; in general Kahn 2001, 3s., who considers the *Phaedo* and the *Timaeus* "as emblems for what is most vital and lasting in the Pythagorean contribution to Western thought: on the one hand, a mathematical understanding of the world of nature; on the other hand, a conception of human destiny that points beyond

the visible world and beyond the mortal body to a higher form of life. It is the combination of these two conceptions that is distinctively Pythagorean, but also distinctively Platonic." See 108ff. above.

29. Hermippus FGrHist 1026 F 69.
30. For similar objections against Plato cf. Dörrie and Baltes 1990, sec. 37.
31. Aristot. Metaph. A 6; cf. also Dillon 2003, 17–20.
32. Cf. also Aristot. fr. 87; 92s. Gigon.
33. It could well have been prompted already by Plato himself, cf. Kahn 2001, 63s.
34. Speusippus fr. 28 Tarán, with Tarán's commentary.
35. Speusippus fr. 48 Tarán, with Tarán's commentary.
36. Speusippus fr. 29s. Tarán. Aristotle records two points of agreement between Speusippus and the Pythagoreans: Aristot. Metaph. 1072b30–34 and Ethic. Nicom. 1096b5–7.
37. Xenocr. p. 158 Heinze = fr. 2 Isnardi = Diog. Laert. 4,13.
38. Xenocr. fr. 60–65 Heinze = 165–194, 196–198 Isnardi.
39. Cf. Aetius 2,3s.
40. Theophrastus Metaph. 33.
41. Cf. in general the basic, if also partly overly critical, account given by Burkert 1972a, 53–96.
42. Porph. VPyth. 53.
43. See in general Bollansée 1999, 44–52.
44. Theocritus of Syracuse 14,4s.
45. Cf. Callimachus fr. 61; 191,58–63; 553 Pfeiffer; on these, see Ardizzoni 1965, 264–267.
46. For more details on the pseudepigrapha in general Centrone 1996, 148–163; cf. also Kahn 2001, 74–79 and Macris 2002, 79–85.
47. Cf. Burkert 1961, 24s., followed by Kahn 2001,75s.; Städele 1980, 212 and 215s. proposes a date in the early Empire.
48. Ps.-Lysis Epist. 1.
49. Ibid., 6.
50. Cf. Burkert 1961, 18s.
51. See Ibid., 26–28.
52. Cf. in general Schibli 2002.
53. Cf. Aristox. fr. 33 Wehrli.
54. "Carmen aureum" 67s.; cf. in general the commentary by Thom 1995.
55. See Thom 1995, 4s.
56. SVF II 1000.
57. "Carmen aureum" 47s.
58. Cf. Cic. Vatin. 14.
59. Aristox. fr. 17 Wehrli.
60. Cf., among others, Diod. 8,14, Ov. Met. 15,7ss. and Pont. 3,3,44.
61. Cic. Rep. 2,28.
62. Cic. Tusc. 4,4.
63. Plin. Nat. hist. 34,26.
64. Cf. in general Centrone 1996, 164–170; on the beginnings of Pythagoreanism in Rome also Humm 1996 and 1997; Storchi 2000; Kahn 2001, 86–93; for Pythagoreanism in Roman milieu in later times cf. Ternes 1998.
65. Cf. on both of them Kahn 2001, 94–104. See 118–119 above.
66. Cf. also Dillon 1977, 341–383; O'Meara 1989; Centrone 1996, 170–189; Gombocz 1997, 143–151; also Kahn 2001, 94–138 and Staab 2002, 75ss.
67. Cf. Philostr. VApoll., e.g., 1,7s.; 32. Cf. in general also Kahn 2001, 142–146.
68. Cf. e.g., Cass. Dio 78,18,4.

69. Cf. Flinterman 1995.
70. Cf. on this aspect du Toit 1997, 219–240.
71. Cass. Dio loc. cit.
72. Hist. Aug. Vita Alex. Sev. 29,2.
73. Philostr. VApoll. 4,10; 20.
74. Ibid., 4,45.
75. The authorship of Eusebius of Caesarea has recently been questioned by Hägg 1992.
76. Apollon. FGrHist 1064 F 1–2.
77. Simplicius In Aristot. Phys. CAG 9, p. 230s. Diels; cf. Centrone 1996, 178–180; a differentiated discussion of the passage in Tornau 2000; cf. on Moderatus in general also Kahn 2001, 105–110; and Staab 2002, 77–81.
78. Stob. 1,49,32.
79. Nicom. Intr. arithm. 1,1s.
80. Ibid., 2,17,1.
81. Cf. O'Meara 1989, 20–22.
82. On Porphyry's Vita Pythagorae, cf. now Macris 2001 and Staab 2002, 109–134.
83. Nicom. FGrHist 1063. On Nicomachus in general cf. now also Kahn 2001, 110–118 and Staab 2002, 81–91.
84. Cf. also M. Frede 1987, 1043–1049.
85. Numenius fr. 24,73ss. des Places.
86. Cf. also Numenius fr. 7 des Places.
87. Numenius fr. 24,19 des Places.
88. Numenius fr. 1 des Places.
89. Numenius fr. 8 des Places.
90. Cf. Merlan 1967, 99s., and Riedweg 1994, 91 n. 367.
91. Cf. Numenius fr. 23 and 24,57ss. des Places, discussed in Riedweg 1994, 87s.
92. Cf. O'Meara 1989, 10–14; Kahn 2001, 118–133; Staab 2002, 92–100.
93. Burkert 1982, 13s.; Edwards 1993, 168s.; Dillon 2002; Lurje 2002, 252s.; Staab 2002, 34 (cf. also 356 and 439).
94. Iambl. VPyth. 1.
95. Cf. O'Meara 1989, 30–105; Kahn 2001, 135–138; and in particular Lurje 2002 and Staab 2002. On the sources of Iambl. VPyth., cf. the information given by du Toit 1997, 220–222 and 241 passim., which should be complemented by Gorman 1985 and, above all, by Staab 2002, 12–14 and 217–237.
96. von Albrecht 1963, 9; cf. now also Lurje 2002 and Staab 2002 (in particular 462–477).
97. O'Meara 1989, 92–95; a different view in Brisson and Segonds 1996, XVI.
98. Cf. Dillon and Hershbell 1991, 21s.
99. Cf. O'Meara 1989, 97–100.
100. Cf. Ibid., 212.
101. Boethius Inst. arithm. 1,1; cf. also Inst. mus. 2,2.
102. Cf. Boethius Inst. mus. 1,10s.
103. Cf. Ibid., 1,2; 27.
104. Cf. Münxelhaus 1976.
105. Cf. Prelog 1990 (suggested to me by Marc-René Jung); in general also Biliński 1977, 16–18.
106. Cf. e.g., Biliński 1977, 19–22 and 94–123.
107. Heninger 1974; on the harmony of the spheres in the Renaissance, cf. also Stephenson 1994, 43–46; on the Pythagoreanism of this time in general Butler 1970, 47–79 and 94–105.
108. Cf. Heninger 1974, 55s. and 63s. n. 41.

109. Cf. Rupprich 1955, 17s.
110. Cf. the dedication to Pope Leo X; also Reuchlin, *De arte cabbalistica* Book 2, p. XXII A; Book 3, p. LII, etc.
111. Cf. Reuchlin, *De arte cabbalistica* Book 1, p. II E-F and VI F; Book 2, p. L; Book 3, p. LI E: on the Kabbala as a "symbolic theology"; in general, Rupprich 1955, 30–32, Idel 1993, Lloyd Jones 1993, and Beierwaltes 1994.
112. Cf. Biliński 1977, 111s.
113. Cf. Ibid., esp. 61–73; see now also Kahn 2001, 159–161.
114. Cf. the foreword in Heninger 1974, 140 n. 86.
115. Cf. Fleckenstein 1975, 433s.
116. See Ibid., 429s.
117. Aiton, Duncan, and Field 1997, 387.
118. Ibid., 411.
119. Kepler *Harmonices mundi* Book 5, chaps. 4–9; cf. Haase 1969, 83–88; Butler 1970, 80–93; Stephenson 1994; Kahn 2001, 161–172.
120. Cf. Caspar 1995, 109.
121. Cf. Kayser 1968, 10s.; on harmonical Pythagoreanism in general, Kayser 1984 and Haase 1969.
122. Cf. on this subject and in general Zander 1999, 321–323 and Index s.v. Pythagoras.
123. Cf. Heninger 1974, 4s. and in general 178–194.
124. Cf. Wedekind 1820; also Oliver 1875.

BIBLIOGRAPHY

Abse, D. *Pythagoras*. London 1979.

Accame, S. "Pitagora e la fondazione di Dicearchia." *Miscellanea Greca e Romana* 7 (1980): 3–44.

Aiton, E. J., A. M. Duncan, and J. V. Field, eds. *The Harmony of the World by Johannes Kepler*. Philadelphia 1997.

Albrecht, M. von, ed. *Iamblichos, Pythagoras. Legende, Lehre, Lebensgestaltung*. Zurich 1963.

———, J. Dillon, M. George, M. Lurje, and D. S. du Toit, eds. *Jamblich* ΠΕΡΙ ΤΟΥ ΠΥΘΑΓΟΡΕΙΟΥ ΒΙΟΥ. *Pythagoras: Legende—Lehre—Lebensgestaltung*. *Eingeleitet, übersetzt und mit interpretierenden Essays versehen*. SAPERE 4. Darmstadt 2002a.

———. "Das Menschenbild in Jamblichs Darstellung der pythagoreischen Lebensform." In Albrecht, Dillon, George, Lurje, and du Toit 2002b, 255–274 (*A&A* 12, 1966: 51–63.)

Ameruso, M. *Megále Hellás. Genesi, storia ed estensione del nome*. Studi pubblicati dall'Istituto italiano per la storia antica 61. Rome 1996.

Antico Gallina, M., ed. *I Greci nel sud dell'Italia*. Milan 1995.

Ardizzoni, A. "Echi Pitagorici in Apollonio Rodio e Callimaco." *RFIC* 93 (1965): 257–267.

Baltes, M. *Die Weltentstehung des platonischen Timaios nach den antiken Interpreten*, Part 1. Philosophia antiqua 30. Leiden 1976.

Barker, A. "Archita di Taranto e l'armonia pitagorica." In A. C. Cassio and D. Musti, eds., *Tra Sicilia e Magna Grecia. Aspetti di interazione culturale nel IV secolo a. C.*, 159–178. Atti del convegno, Napoli 19–20 marzo 1987 = AION filol. 11. Pisa 1989.

———. "Ptolemy's Pythagoreans, Archytas, and Plato's Conception of Mathematics." *Phronesis* 39 (1994): 113–135.

Barnes, J. *Presocratic Philosophers*. Oxford 1982. Reprint 1986.

Baumgarten, R. *Heiliges Wort und Heilige Schrift bei den Griechen. Hieroi Logoi und verwandte Erscheinungen*. ScriptOralia 110. Tübingen 1998.

Beierwaltes, W. "Reuchlin und Pico della Mirandola." *Tijdschrift voor Filosofie* 56 (1994): 313–336.

Ben, N. van der. *The Proem of Empedocles' Peri* Physios. *Towards a New Edition of All the Fragments. Thirty-one Fragments Edited.* Amsterdam 1975.

Benardete, S. *The Tragedy and Comedy of Life: Plato's Philebus.* Chicago 1993.

Berger, S. *Revolution and Society in Greek Sicily and Southern Italy.* Stuttgart 1992.

Bernabé, A., and A. I. Jiménez San Cristóbal. *Instrucciones para el más allá. Las laminillas órficas de oro.* Madrid 2001.

Biliński, B. *Il pitagorismo di Niccolò Copernico.* Accad. Pol. delle Sc. Bibl. e Centro di Studi a Roma Conf. 69. Wroclaw 1977.

Böhm, F. *De symbolis Pythagoreis.* Ph.D. diss., Berlin 1905.

Bollansée, J. *Hermippos of Smyrna and his Biographical Writings. A Reappraisal.* Louvain 1999.

Boudon, R., and F. Bourricaud. *Dictionnaire critique de la sociologie.* Paris 1984.

Boudouris, K. I. "The Pythagorean Community: Creation, Development, and Downfall." In K. I. Boudouris, ed., *Pythagorean Philosophy,* 49–69. Athens 1992.

Bowen, A. C. "The Foundation of Early Pythagorean Harmonic Science: Archytas, Fragment 1." *Ancient Philosophy* 2 (1982): 79–104.

Bowie, E. L. "Le portrait de Socrate dans les Nuées d'Aristophane." In M. Trédé and P. Hoffmann, eds., *Le rire des anciens,* 51–66. Actes du colloque international, Université de Rouen, 11–13 janvier 1995. Paris 1998.

Boyancé, P. "L'influence pythagoricienne sur Platon." In *Filosofia e scienze in Magna Grecia,* 73–113. Atti del quinto convegno di studi sulla Magna Grecia, Taranto 10–14 ottobre 1965. Naples 1966.

Braccesi, L. "Cronologia e fondazioni coloniarie, 2 (Miscello e le tre spedizioni a Crotone)." *Hesperia* 9 (1998): 9–17.

Breglia, L. "Ferecide di Siro tra orfici et pitagorici." In M. Tortorelli Ghidini, A. Storchi Marino, and A. Visconti, eds., *Tra Orfeo et Pitagora. Origini e incontri di culture nell'antichità,* 161–194. Atti dei seminari napoletani 1996–1998. Naples 2000.

Breglia Pulci Doria, L. "Le Sirene di Pitagora." In A. C. Cassio and P. Poccetti, eds., *Forme di religiosità e tradizioni sapienziali in Magna Grecia,* 55–77. AION filol. 16. Pisa and Rome 1994.

Bremmer, J. N. "Religious Secrets and Secrecy in Classical Greece." In H. G. Kippenberg and G. G. Strousma, eds., *Security and Concealment,* 61–78. Studies in the History of Mediterranean and Near Eastern Religions 65. Leiden 1995.

———. "Rationalization and Disenchantment in Ancient Greece: Max Weber among the Pythagoreans and Orphics?" In R. Buxton, ed., *From Myth to Reason? Studies in the Development of Greek Thought,* 71–83. Oxford 1999.

———. *The Rise and Fall of the Afterlife.* The 1995 Read-Tuckwell Lectures at the University of Bristol. London 2002.

Brisson, L. "Usages et fonctions du secret dans le Pythagorisme ancien." In Ph. Dujardin, ed., *Le secret,* 87–101. Roundtable March 5 and 6 1986: "Usages et fonctions du secret: approches comparées," organized by the Centre de Politologie Historique de l'Université Lumière Lyon II. Lyons 1987.

———, and A. P. Segonds, eds. *Jamblique, Vie de Pythagore.* Paris 1996.

———. "Platon, Pythagore et les Pythagoriciens." In M. Dixsaut and A. Brancacci, eds., *Platon, source des Présocratiques. Exploration,* 21–46. Paris 2002.

Bruit-Zaidman, L. "La piété pythagoricienne et l'Apollon de Délos." *Métis* 8 (1993): 261–269.

Brumbaugh, R. S., and J. Schwartz. "Pythagoras and Beans: A Medical Explanation." *CW* 73 (1980): 421–423.

Bruneau, Ph. *Recherches sur les cultes de Délos à l'époque hellénistique et à l'époque impériale.* Paris 1970.

Burkert, W. "Platon oder Pythagoras? Zum Ursprung des Wortes 'Philosophie.'" *Hermes* 88 (1960): 159–177.

———. "Hellenistische Pseudopythagorica." *Philologus* 105 (1961): 16–43, 226–246.

———. "Orpheus und die Vorsokratiker. Bemerkungen zum Derveni-Papyrus und zur pythagoreischen Zahlenlehre." *A&A* 14 (1968): 93–114.

———. "Das Proömium des Parmenides und die Katabasis des Pythagoras." *Phronesis* 14 (1969): 1–30.

———. *Lore and Science in Ancient Pythagoreanism.* Cambridge, Mass. 1972a. Revised translation of *Weisheit und Wissenschaft.* Nuremberg 1962.

———. *Homo Necans. Interpretationen altgriechischer Opferriten und Mythen.* Religionsgeschichtliche Versuche und Vorarbeiten 32. Berlin 1972b. Reprint 1997.

———. "Zur geistesgeschichtlichen Einordnung einiger Pseudopythagorica." In *Pseudepigrapha I*, 25–55.Entretiens de la Fond. Hardt 18. Geneva 1972c.

———. "Die Leistung eines Kreophylos. Kreophyleer, Homeriden und die archaische Heraklesepik." *MH* 29 (1972d): 74–85. Reprinted in Burkert, W., *Kleine Schriften I: Homerica*, ed. Ch. Riedweg in collaboration with F. Egli, L. Hartmann, and A. Schatzmann, 138–149. Hypomnemata suppl. 2. Göttingen 2001.

———. "Craft Versus Sect: The Problem of Orphics and Pythagoreans." In B. F. Meyer and E. P. Sanders, eds., *Jewish and Christian Self-Definition 3: Self-Definition in the Graeco-Roman World*, 1–22 and 183–189 (notes). London 1982.

———. *Ancient Mystery Cults.* Carl Newell Jackson Lectures. Cambridge, Mass. 1987.

———. *The Orientalizing Revolution: Near Eastern Influence on Greek Culture in the Early Archaic Age.* Revealing Antiquity 5. Cambridge, Mass., 1992. Revised translation of *Die orientalisierende Epoche in der griechischen Religion und Literatur*, Sitzungberichte der Heidelberger Akad. d. Wiss., Phil.-hist. Kl., 1984, 1.

———. "Pythagoreische Retraktationen. Von den Grenzen einer möglichen Edition." In W. Burkert, L. Gemelli Marciano, E. Matelli, and L. Orelli, eds., *Fragmentsammlungen philosophischer Texte der Antike*, 303–319. Atti del Seminario Internazionale Ascona, Centro Stefano Franscini 22–27 settembre 1996. Aporemata 3. Göttingen 1998.

———. "Neanthes von Kyzikos über Platon. Ein Hinweis aus Herculaneum." *MH* 57 (2000): 76–80.

———. *Die Griechen und der Orient. Von Homer bis zu den Magiern. Aus dem Italienischen ins Deutsche übertragen vom Verfasser.* München 2003a. Revised and expanded German translation of *Da Omero ai Magi. La tradizione orientale nella cultura greca*, ed. C. Antonetti. Venice 1999.

———. "'Seele,' Mysterien und Mystik. Griechische Sonderwege und aktuelle Problematik." In W. Jens, B. Seidensticker, eds., *Ferne und Nähe der Antike*, 111–128. Berlin 2003b.

Butler, Ch. *Number Symbolism*. London 1970.

Camassa, G. "Il mutamento delle leggi nella prospettiva pitagorica." *Annali della Facoltà di lettere e filosofia di Perugia* 14 (1976/77): 457–471.

Cameron, A. *The Pythagorean Background of the Theory of Recollection*. Menasha, Wis. 1938.

Casadio, G. "La metempsicosi tra Orfeo e Pitagora." In Ph. Borgeaud, ed., *Orphisme et Orphée*, 119–155. Geneva 1991.

Casertano, G. "Due note sui primi pitagorici." In *Filologia e forme letterarie. Studi offerti a F. della Corte* 5: 5–25. Urbino 1987.

Caspar, M. *Johannes Kepler*. Stuttgart 1995.

Centrone, B., ed. *Pseudopythagorica ethica: I trattati morali di Archita, Metopo, Teage, Eurifamo. Introduzione, edizione, traduzione e commento*. Elenchos 17. Naples 1990.

——. "L'VIII libro delle 'Vite' di Diogene Laerzio." In *ANRW* II 36.6 (1992): 4183–4217.

——. *Introduzione a i Pitagorici*. Rome and Bari 1996.

Cipriano, P. *I composti greci con ΦΙΛΟΣ*. Viterbo 1990.

Comotti, G. "Pitagora, Ippaso, Laso e il metodo sperimentale." In R. W. Wallace and B. MacLachlan, eds., *Harmonia mundi. Musica e filosofia nell'antichità*, 20–29. Biblioteca di Quaderni Urbinati di Cultura Classica 5. Rome 1991.

Coxon, A. H., ed. *The Fragments of Parmenides*. Assen 1986.

Delatte, A. *Études sur la littérature pythagoricienne*. Bibliothèque de l'École des hautes études, sciences historiques et philologiques 217. Paris 1915.

——. *La vie de Pythagore de Diogène Laërce*. Brussels 1922. Reprint Hildesheim 1988.

——. "Faba Pythagorae cognata." *Serta Leodiensia* 44 (1930): 33–57.

Demand, N. "Pythagoras, Son of Mnesarchos." *Phronesis* 18 (1973): 91–96.

——. "Plato, Aristophanes, and the Speeches of Pythagoras." *GRBS* 23 (1982): 179–184.

Detienne, M. *Homère, Hésiode et Pythagore. Poésie et philosophie dans le pythagorisme ancient*. Collection Latomus 57. Brussels 1962.

——. "La cuisine de Pythagore." *Archives de sociologie des religions* 29 (1970): 141–162. Cf. Detienne, M. "Le boeuf aux aromates." In M. Detienne, *Les jardins d'Adonis. La mythologie des aromates en Grèce*, 71–114. Paris 1972.

Dillon, J. *The Middle Platonists. A Study of Platonism 80 B.C. to A.D. 220*. London 1977. Rev. ed., Ithaca, N.Y., 1996.

——, and J. Hershbell, eds. *Iamblichus: On the Pythagorean Way of Life*. Atlanta, Ga., 1991.

——. "Die Vita Pythagorica—ein 'Evangelium'?" In Albrecht, Dillon, George, Lurje, and du Toit 2002, 295–301.

——. *The Heirs of Plato: A Study of the Old Academy (347–274 BC)*. Oxford 2003.

Dixsaut, M. *Le naturel philosophe. Essai sur les dialogues de Platon*. Collection d'études anciennes. Antiquité grecque 100). Paris 1985.

Dörrie, H. "Pythagoras 1 C: Der nachklassische Pythagoreismus." *RE* 24 (1963): 268–277.

——, and M. Baltes. *Der Platonismus in der Antike 2: Bausteine 36–72*. Stuttgart 1990.

Edwards, M. J. "Two Images of Pythagoras: Iamblichus and Porphyry." In H. J. Blumenthal and E. G. Clark, eds., *The Divine Iamblichus*, 159–172. London 1993.

Ellinger, P. "Guerre et sacrifice dans le mysticisme grec: Orphisme et Pythagorisme." In M.-M. Mactoux and E. Geny, eds., *Mélanges Pierre Lévêque 6: Religion*, 73–87. Paris 1992.

Fauth, W. "Pythagoras, Jesus von Nazareth und der Helios-Apollon des Julianus Apostata. Zu einigen Eigentümlichkeiten der spätantiken Pythagoras-Aretalogie im Vergleich mit der thaumasiologischen Tradition der Evangelien." *ZNTW* 78 (1987): 26–48.

Federico, E. "Euforbo/Pitagora genealogo dell'anima." In M. Tortorelli Ghidini, A. Storchi Marino, and A. Visconti, eds., *Tra Orfeo et Pitagora. Origini e incontri di culture nell'antichità*, 367–396. Atti dei seminari napoletani 1996–1998. Naples 2000.

Ferrero, L. *Storia del Pitagorismo nel mondo romano (dalle origini alla fine della repubblica)*. Turin 1955.

Festugière, A. J. *Contemplation et vie contemplative selon Platon*. Paris 1950.

Finkelberg, A. "On the History of the Greek *ΚΟΣΜΟΣ*." *HSPh* 98 (1998): 103–136.

Fleckenstein, J. O. "Kepler and Neoplatonism." In A. Beer and P. Beer, eds., *Kepler: Four Hundred Years*, 427–438. Oxford 1975.

Flinterman, J.-J. *Power, Paideia and Pythagoreanism: Greek Identity, Conceptions of the Relationship between Philosophers and Monarchs and Political Ideas in Philostratus' Life of Apollonius*. Dutch Monographs on Ancient History and Archaeology 13. Amsterdam 1995.

Frank, E. *Platon und die sogenannten Pythagoreer. Ein Kapitel aus der Geschichte des griechischen Geistes*. Halle 1923.

Frede, M. "Numenius." *ANRW* II 36, 2 (1987): 1034–1075.

Freyburger, G. "L'initiation pythagoricienne dans le livre XV des Métamorphoses d'Ovide." In A. Moreau, ed., *L'initiation. Les rites d'adolescence et les mystères*, 1:261–269. Actes du colloque international de Montpellier 11–14 avril 1991. Montpellier 1992.

———. "De l'*amicitia* païenne aux vertus chrétiennes: Damon et Phintias." In G. Freyburger and C. Pernot, eds., *Du héros païen au saint chrétien*, 87–93. Paris 1997.

Freyburger-Galland, M.-L., and G. Freyburger. *Sectes religieuses en Grèce et à Rome dans l'antiquité païenne*. Paris 1986.

Fritz, K. von. "Theano 5." *RE* VA (1934): 1379–1381.

———. *Pythagorean Politics in Southern Italy: An Analysis of the Sources*. New York 1940.

———. *Mathematiker und Akusmatiker bei den alten Pythagoreern*. Munich 1960.

———. "Pythagoras 1 A: Pythagoras von Samos." *RE* 24 (1963a): 171–209.

———. "Pythagoras von Samos 1 B: Pythagoreer. Pythagoreismus bis zum Ende des 4. Jhdts. V. Chr." *RE* 24 (1963b): 209–268.

Gallop, D. *Plato, Phaedo*. Oxford 1975.

Gaza, K. L. "The Reproductive Technology of the Pythagoreans." *CP* 95 (2000): 113–132.

Gegenschatz, E. "Die 'pythagoreische Bürgschaft'—zur Geschichte eines Motivs von Aristoxenos bis Schiller." In P. Neukam, ed., *Begegnungen mit Neuem und Altem*, 90–154. Klassische Sprachen und Literaturen 15. Munich 1981.

George, M. "Tugenden im Vergleich. Ihre soteriologische Funktion in Jamblichs *Vita Pythagorica* und in Athanasios' *Vita Antonii*." In Albrecht, Dillon, George, Lurje, and du Toit 2002, 303–322.

Giangiulio, M. *Ricerche su Crotone arcaica*. Pisa 1989.

———. ed. *Giamblico: La Vita pitagorica*. Milan 1991.

———. "Sapienza pitagorica e religiosità apollinea. Tra cultura della città e orizzonti panellenici." In A. C. Cassio and P. Poccetti, eds., *Forme di religiosità e tradizioni sapienziali in Magna Grecia*, 9– 27. AION filol. 16. Pisa 1994.

Gladigow, B. *Sophia und Kosmos. Untersuchungen zur Frühgeschichte von σοφός und σοφίη.* Spudasmata 1. Hildesheim 1965.

Gobry, I. *Pythagore ou la naissance de la philosophie. Présentation, choix de textes, bibliographie.* Philosophes de tous les temps. Paris 1973.

Gombocz, W. L. *Die Philosophie der ausgehenden Antike und des frühen Mittelalters. Geschichte der Philosophie,* ed. W. Röd, vol. 4. Munich 1997.

Gorman, P. *Pythagoras: A Life.* Boston 1979.

———. "The 'Apollonios' of the Neoplatonic Biographies of Pythagoras." *Mnemosyne* 38 (1985): 130–144.

Gottschalk, H. B. *Heraclides of Pontus.* Oxford 1980.

Grmek, M. D. "La légende et la réalité de la nocivité des fèves." *History and Philosophy of the Life Sciences* 2 (1980): 61–121.

Guthrie, K. S. *The Pythagorean Sourcebook and Library. An Anthology of Ancient Writings which relate to Pythagoras and the Pythagorean Philosophy.* Compiled and translated by K. S. Guthrie with additional Translations by T. Taylor and A. Fairbanks, Jr. Edited by D. R. Fideler. Grand Rapids, Mich., 1987.

Guthrie, W. K. C. *A History of Greek Philosophy I.* Cambridge 1962.

Guzzo, G. *La Magna Grecia. Italici et italioti.* Turin 1996.

Haase, R. *Geschichte des harmonikalen Pythagoreismus.* Publikationen der Wiener Musikakademie 3. Vienna 1969.

Hemminger, H. *Was ist eine Sekte? Erkennen–Verstehen–Kritik.* Mainz 1995.

Heninger, S. K., Jr. *Touches of Sweet Harmony: Pythagorean Cosmology and Renaissance Poetics.* San Marino, Calif., 1974.

Hill, D. E. *Ovid,* Metamorphoses. Warminster 1985–2000.

Hölk, C. *De acusmatis sive symbolis Pythagoricis.* Ph.D. diss., Kiel 1894.

Huffman, C. A. "The Authenticity of Archytas Fr. 1." *CQ* 35 (1985): 344–348.

———. *Philolaus of Croton: Pythagorean and Presocratic.* Cambridge 1993.

———. "Pythagorisme." In J. Brunschvig, G. Lloyd, and P. Pellegrin, eds., *Le savoir grec. Dictionnaire critique,* 982–1000. Paris 1996.

———. "Archytas and the Sophists." In U. Caston and D. W. Graham, eds., *Presocratic Philosophy: Essays in Honour of Alexander Mourelatos,* 251–270. Aldershot 2002.

Humm, M. "Les Origines du pythagorisme romain: Problèmes historiques et Philosophiques: I." *Les Études classiques* 64 (1996): 339–353; "II." *Les Études classiques* 65 (1997): 25–42.

Idel, M. "Introduction to the Bison Book Edition." In Johann Reuchlin, *On the Art of the Kabbalah/De Arte Cabalistica.* Translated by M. and S. Goodman, v–xxix. Lincoln, Neb., 1993.

Isler, H. P. In P. Ciancio Rossetto and G. Pisani Sartorio, eds., *Teatri Greci e Romani. Alle origini del linguaggio rappresentato II,* 286f. Rome 1994.

Isnardi Parente, M. "Pitagorismo di Crotone e Pitagorismo accademico." *Archivio storico per la Calabria e la Lucania* 62 (1995): 5–25.

Jaeger, W. "Über Ursprung und Kreislauf des philosophischen Lebensideals." In W. Jaeger, *Scripta minora I,* 347–393. Rome 1960. (Sitzungsberichte der Preuss. Akad. d. Wiss., Phil-hist. Kl. 25, Berlin 1928, 390–421.)

Johnson, T. M. *Iamblichus,* The Exhortation to Philosophy. *Including the Letters of Iamblichus and Proclus'* Commentary on the Chaldean Oracles. Translated from the Greek by T. M. Johnson. Edited by S. Neuville. Grand Rapids, Mich., 1988.

Joly, R. *Le thème philosophique des genres de vie dans l'Antiquité classique*. Brussels 1956.

——. "Platon ou Pythagore? Héraclide Pontique, fr. 87–88 Wehrli." In R. Crahay, ed., *Hommages à M. Delcourt*, 136–148. Collection Latomus 114. Brussels 1970.

Kahn, Ch. H. "Pythagorean Philosophy before Plato." In A. P. D. Mourelatos, ed., *The Pre-Socratics*, 161–185. Garden City, N.Y., 1974.

——. *The Art and Thought of Heraclitus*. Cambridge 1979.

——. *Pythagoras and the Pythagoreans: A Brief History*. Indianapolis, Ind., 2001.

Kalogerakos, I. G. *Seele und Unsterblichkeit. Untersuchungen zur Vorsokratik bis Empedokles*. Beiträge zur Altertumskunde 52. Stuttgart 1996.

Kappel, L. "Die Paradigma-Inschrift im Tunnel des Eupalinos auf Samos." *A&A* 45 (1999): 75–100.

Kartunen, K. *India in Early Greek Literature*. Studia Orientalia 65. Helsinki 1989.

Kayser, H. *Die Harmonie der Welt*. Beiträge zur harmonikalen Grundlagenforschung 1. Vienna 1968.

——. *Akróasis. Die Lehre von der Harmonik der Welt*. Basel 1984.

Kerényi, K. *Pythagoras und Orpheus. Präludien zu einer zukünftigen Geschichte der Orphik und des Pythagoreismus*. Zurich 1950.

Kienast, H. J. *Die Wasserleitung des Eupalinos auf Samos*. Samos 19. Bonn 1995.

King, J. E. *Cicero, Tusculan disputations*. Cambridge, Mass., 1996.

Kingsley, P. "The Greek Origin of the Sixth-Century Dating of Zoroaster." *Bulletin of the School of Oriental and African Studies* 53 (1990): 245–265.

——. "From Pythagoras to the *turba philosophorum*: Egypt and Pythagorean Tradition." *Journal of the Warburg and Courtauld Institutes* 57 (1994): 1–13.

——. *Ancient Philosophy, Mystery, and Magic. Empedocles and Pythagorean Tradition*. Oxford 1995.

——. *In the Dark Places of Wisdom*. Shaftesbury, Dorset, 1999. 2d. ed. London, 2001.

Kirk, G. S., J. E. Raven, and M. Schofield *The Presocratic Philosophers. A Critical History with a Selection of Texts*. Cambridge 1983.

Koller, H. "Theoros und Theoria." *Glotta* 36 (1958): 273–286.

Kranz, W. "Vorsokratisches II." In W. Kranz, *Studien zur antiken Literatur und ihrem Fortwirken*, 103–105. Heidelberg 1967. (*Hermes* 69 [1934]: 226–228.)

Krischer, T. "Die Rolle der Magna Graecia in der Geschichte der Mechanik." *A&A* 41 (1995): 60–71.

Kucharski, P. *Étude sur la doctrine pythagoricienne de la tétrade*. Paris 1952.

Laks, A., and G. W. Most, eds. *Studies on the Derveni Papyrus*. Oxford 1997.

Leszl, W. "Pitagorici ed Eleati." In G. Pugliese Carratelli, ed., *Magna Graecia III: Vita religiosa e cultura letteraria, filosofica e scientifica*, 197–226. Milan 1988.

Leurini, A. *Ionis Chii Testimonia et Fragmenta*. Amsterdam 1992.

Lévi-Strauss, C. *La pensée sauvage*. Paris 1962.

Lévy, I. *Recherches sur les sources de la légende de Pythagore*. Paris 1926.

Lipp, W. "Charisma." In B. Schäfers et al., eds., *Grundbegriffe der Soziologie*, 33–35. Opladen 1995.

Livrea, E. "A New Pythagorean Fragment and Homer's Tears in Ennius." *CQ* 48 (1998): 559–561.

Lloyd, G. E. R. *The Revolutions of Wisdom: Studies in the Claims and Practice of Ancient Greek Science*. Berkeley 1987.

——. "Plato and Archytas in the Seventh Letter." *Phronesis* 35 (1990): 159–174.

Lloyd Jones, G. "Introduction." In Johann Reuchlin, *On the Art of the Kabbalah/De Arte Cabalistica,* translated by M. and S. Goodman, 7–32. Lincoln, Neb., 1993

Lurje, M. "Die Vita Pythagorica als Manifest der neuplatonischen Paideia." In Albrecht, Dillon, George, Lurje, and du Toit 2002, 221–253.

Macris, C., ed. Πορφύριου Πυθαγόρου βίος. Εισαγωγή—Μετάφραση—Σχόλια. Athens 2001.

——. "Jamblique et la littérature pseudo-pythagoricienne." In S. C. Mimouni, ed., *Apocryphité. Histoire d'un concept transversal aux religions du livre. En hommage à P. Geoltrain.* Turnhout 2002, 77–129.

——. "Pythagore, un maître de sagesse charismatique de la fin de la période archaïque." In G. Filoramo, ed., *Carisma profetico. Fattore di innovazione religiosa,* 243–289. Brescia 2003.

Maddalena, A. *I Pitagorici.* Bari 1954.

Mann, Chr. *Athlet und Polis im archaischen und frühklassischen Griechenland* (Hypomnemata 138). Göttingen 2001.

Manthe, U. "Beiträge zur Entwicklung des antiken Gerechtigkeitsbegriffes I: Die Mathematisierung durch Pythagoras und Aristoteles." *Zeitschrift der Savigny-Stiftung für Rechtsgeschichte.* Romanist Abt. 113: (1996) 1–31.

Marcovich, M. "Pythagorica." *Philologus* 108 (1964): 29–44.

Mathieu, B. "Archytas de Tarente, pythagoricien et ami de Platon." *Bulletin de l'Association Guillaume Budé* (1987): 239–255.

Mattéi, J. F. *Pythagore et les pythagoriciens.* Que sais-je? 2732. Paris 1993.

Mele, A. "Crotone e la sua storia." In *Crotone,* 9–97. Atti del ventitresimo convegno di studi sulla Magna Grecia, Taranto, 7–10 ottobre 1983. Tarento 1984.

——. "*Megale Hellas* e pitagorismo." In M. Tortorelli Ghidini, A. Storchi Marino, and A. Visconti, eds., *Tra Orfeo et Pitagora. Origini e incontri di culture nell'antichità,* 297–334. Atti dei seminari napoletani 1996–1998. Naples 2000.

Melero Bellido, A. *Atenas y el Pitagorismo. Investigación en las fuentes de la comedia.* Salamanca 1972.

Merlan, P. "The Pythagoreans." In A. H. Armstrong, ed., *The Cambridge History of Later Greek and Early Medieval Philosophy,* 84–106. Cambridge 1967.

Metzler, D. *Porträt und Gesellschaft. Über die Entstehung des griechischen Porträts in der Klassik.* Münster 1971.

Montepaone, C. "Teano, la pitagorica." In N. Loraux, ed., *Grecia al femminile,* 73–105. Rom-Bari 1993.

Morrison, J. S. "Pythagoras of Samos." *CQ* 50 (1955/56): 135–156.

Mühlestein, H. "Euphorbos und der Tod des Patroklos." In H. Mühlestein, *Homerische Namenstudien.* Frankfurt am Main 1987, 78–90. Also see *SMEA* 15 (1972): 79–90.

Münxelhaus, B. *Pythagoras musicus. Zur Rezeption der pythagoreischen Musiktheorie als quadrivialer Wissenschaft im lateinischen Mittelalter.* Bonn 1976.

Musti, D. "Città di Magna Grecia II: L'idea di ΜΕΓΑΛΗ ΕΛΛΑΣ." *RFIC* 114 (1986): 286–319. Reprinted, with slight modifications, in D. Musti, *Strabone e la Magna Grecia. Città e popoli dell'Italia antica,* 61–94. Padua 1994.

——. "Pitagorismo, storiografia e politica tra Magna Grecia e Sicilia." In A. C. Cassio and D. Musti, eds., *Tra Sicilia e Magna Grecia. Aspetti di interazione culturale nel IV se-*

colo a. C, 13–56. Atti del convegno, Napoli 19–20 marzo 1987. AION filol. 11. Pisa 1989.

——. "Le rivolte antipitagoriche e la concezione pitagorica del tempo." *QUCC* 65 (1990): 35–65.

Navia, L. E. *Pythagoras: An Annotated Bibliography.* New York, 1990.

Oliver, G. *The Pythagorean Triangle, or The Science of Numbers.* London 1875. Reprint. Minneapolis 1975.

O'Meara, D. J. *Pythagoras Revived: Mathematics and Philosophy in Late Antiquity.* Oxford 1989.

Ostenfeld, E. N. "Early Pythagorean Principles: *Peras* and *Apeiron.*" In K. I. Boudouris, ed., *Ionian Philosophy,* 304–311. Athens 1989.

Parise, N. F. "Le emissioni monetarie di Magna Grecia fra VI e V sec. a. C." In S. Settis, ed., *La Calabria antica,* 305–321. Storia della Calabria. Rome 1987.

Parker, R. *Miasma: Pollution and Purification in Early Greek Religion.* Oxford 1983.

——. "Early Orphism." In A. Powell, ed., *The Greek World,* 483–510. London 1995.

Patzer, A. "Die Wolken des Aristophanes als philosophiegeschichtliches Dokument." In P. Neukam, ed., *Motiv und Motivation,* 72–93. Munich 1993.

Perilli, L. "Alcmeone di Crotone tra filosofia e scienza. Per una nuova edizione delle fonti." *QUCC* 69 (2001): 55–79.

Petit, A. "Le retour éternel et l'avenir eschatologique dans le pythagorisme ancien." In *L'Avenir,* 331–335. Actes du XXIe congrès de l'association des sociétés de philosophie de langue française, Athens 1986. Paris 1987.

——. "Le pythagorisme à Rome à la fin de la république et au début de l'empire." *Annales Latini Montium Arvernorum* 15 (1988): 23–32.

——. "La tradition critique dans le Pythagorisme ancien: Une contribution au 'miracle grec.'" In A. Thivel, ed., *Le miracle grec,* 101–115. Actes du IIe colloque sur la pensée antique organisé par le Centre de recherche sur l'histoire des idées les 18, 19, et 20 mai 1989 à la Faculté de Lettres de Nice. Paris 1992.

——. "Le silence pythagoricien." In C. Lévy and L. Pernot, eds., *Dire l'évidence. Philosophie et rhétorique antiques,* 287–296. Paris 1997.

Philip, J. A. *Pythagoras and Early Pythagoreanism.* Phoenix Suppl. 7. Toronto 1966.

Pichot, A. *Die Geburt der Wissenschaft. Von den Babyloniern zu den frühen Griechen.* Frankfurt 1995. Original French ed. *La naissance de la science.* Paris 1991.

Pierris, A. L. "Origin and Nature of Early Pythagorean Cosmogony." In K. I. Boudouris, ed., *Pythagorean Philosophy,* 126–162. Athens 1992.

Prelog, J. " 'De Pictagora Phylosopho.' Die Biographie des Pythagoras in dem Walter Burley zugeschriebenen 'Liber de vita et moribus philosophorum.'" *Medioevo* 16 (1990): 191–251.

Prontera, F. "Gli 'ultimi' Pitagorici. Contributo per una revisione della tradizione." *DArch* 9/10 (1976–77): 267–332.

Pugliese Carratelli, G., ed. *I Greci in Occidente.* Milan 1996.

Radicke, J., ed. *Die Fragmente der griechischen Historiker. Continued. IV. A Biography, Fasc. 7 Imperial and undated authors.* Leiden 1999

Rathmann, W. *Quaestiones Pythagoreae Orphicae Empedocleae.* Diss. phil. Halle 1933.

Rausch, H. *Theoria. Von ihrer sakralen zur philosophischen Bedeutung.* Munich 1982.

Redlow, G. *Theoria. Theoretische und praktische Lebensauffassung im philosophischen Denken der Antike.* Berlin (Ost) 1966.

Reuchlin, Johann. *On the Art of the Kabbalah/De Arte Cabalistica.* Translated by M. and S. Goodman, Lincoln, Neb., 1993.

Riedweg, Ch. *Ps.-Justin (Markell von Ankyra?)* Ad Graecos de vera religione (*bisher* "Cohortatio ad Graecos"). Schweiz. Beiträge zur Altertumswissenschaft 25. Basel 1994.

——. "Orphisches bei Empedokles." *A&A* 41 (1995): 34–59.

——. " 'Pythagoras hinterliess keine einzige Schrift'—ein Irrtum?" *MH* 54 (1997): 65–92.

——. "Initiation—Tod—Unterwelt. Beobachtungen zur Kommunikationssituation und narrativen Technik der orphisch-bakchischen Goldblättchen." In F. Graf, ed., *Ansichten griechischer Rituale*, 359–398. Geburtstagssymposium für Walter Burkert, Castelen bei Basel 15. bis 18. März 1996. Stuttgart 1998.

——. "Poésie orphique et rituel initiatique. Éléments d'un 'Discours sacré' dans les lamelles d'or." *Revue de l'histoire des religions* 219 (2002): 459–481.

——. "Zum Ursprung des Wortes 'Philosophie' oder Pythagoras von Samos als Wortschöpfer." In A. Bierl, A. Schmitt, and A. Willi, eds., *Antike Literatur in neuer Deutung. Festschrift für J. Latacz.* München and Leipzig 2004.

——. Articles for *Der Neue Pauly* (DNP):

"Archippos [2]" and "Archytas [1. aus Tarent]." *DNP* (1996): 1002f. and 1029f.

"Damon [2]," "Diodorus [aus Aspendos]," and "Echekrates [2]." *DNP* 3 (1997): 303, 587, and 866f.

"Eurytos [2]." *DNP* 4 (1998a): 306f.

"Hippasos [5]." *DNP* 5 (1998b): 572f.

"Kleinias [6]," "Kylon [2]," and "Lamiskos." *DNP* 6 (1999a): 562, 965, and 1082.

"Lykon [5]" and "Lysis." *DNP* 7 (1999b): 567 and 611.

"Mnesarchos [1]," "Mnesarchos [2]," "Myia," and "Mylias." *DNP* 8 (2000a): 304, 569, and 592.

"Petron von Himera," "Philolaos [2]," and "Phintys" (with M. Frede). *DNP* 9 (2000b): 670, 834–836, and 904.

"Pythagoras [1 von Samos]" and "Pythagoreische Schule." *DNP* 10 (2001a): 649–653 and 656–659.

"Seelenwanderung." *DNP* 11 (2001b): 328–330.

"Timycha." *DNP* 12,1 (2002): 602f.

"Zahl III.D. Zahlenmystik." *DNP* 12,2 (2003): 679–681.

Robin, L. "La science, instrument de purification morale. Le pythagorisme et l'école italique." In L. Robin, *La pensée grecque et les origines de l'esprit scientifique*, 69–93. Paris 1923.

Robinson, Th. M. "Pythagoreans and Plato." In K. I. Boudouris, ed., *Pythagorean Philosophy*, 182–188. Athens 1992.

Ross, W. D. "Aristoteles, *Metaphysica*." In *The Basic Works of Aristotle*, ed. R. McKeon, 681–926. New York 1941.

Rudolph, K. "Wesen und Struktur der Sekte." *Kairos* 21 (1979): 241–254.

Rupprich, H. "Johannes Reuchlin und seine Bedeutung im europäischen Humanismus." In M. Krebs, ed., *Johannes Reuchlin 1455–1522. Festgabe seiner Vaterstadt*

Pforzheim zur 500. Wiederkehr seines Geburtstages, 10–34. Pforzheim 1955. Reprint H. Kling and S. Rhein, eds. Sigmaringen 1994.

Sanchis Llopis, J. L. "Los Pitagóricos en la comedia media: parodia filosófica y comediade tipos." *HABIS* 26 (1995): 67–82.

Sandbach, F. H. "Ion of Chios and Pythagoras." *PCPhS* 5 (1958–1959): 36.

Sassi, M. "Tra religione e scienza. Il pensiero pitagorico." In S. Settis, ed., *Storia della Calabria antica*, 565–587. Rome 1988.

Scarborough, J. "Beans, Pythagoras, Taboos, and Ancient Dietetics." *CW* 75 (1981): 345–358.

Schefold, K. *Die Bildnisse der antiken Dichter, Redner und Denker.* Basel 1997.

Schibli, H. S. *Pherekydes of Syros.* Oxford 1990.

———. "On 'The One' in Philolaus, Fragment 7." *CQ* 46 (1996): 114–130.

———. *Hierocles of Alexandria.* Oxford 2002.

Schmidtchen, G. *Sekten und Psychokultur. Reichweite und Attraktivität von Jugendreligionen in der Bundesrepublik Deutschland.* Freiburg 1987.

Schroeder, L. von. "Das Bohnenverbot bei Pythagoras und im Veda." *Wiener Zeitschrift für die Kunde des Morgenlandes* 15 (1901): 187–212.

Schwabacher, W. "Pythagoras auf griechischen Münzbildern." In G. Säflund, ed., *Opuscula Carolo Kerényi*, 59–63. Stockholm Studies in Classical Archaeology. Stockholm 1968.

Selincourt, A. de. *Herodotus, The Histories.* Revised by A. R. Burn. London 1972.

Sfameni Gasparo, G. "Critica del sacrificio cruento e antropologia in Grecia. Da Pitagora a Porfirio." In F. Vattioni, ed., *Sangue e antropologia. Riti e culto I*, 107–155. Centro Studi Sanguis Christi 5. Rome 1987.

Shipley, G. *A History of Samos 800–188 B.C.* Oxford 1987.

Shipton, K. M. W. "Heraclitus fr. 10: A Musical Interpretation." *Phronesis* 30 (1985): 111–130.

Skutsch, O. "Notes on Metempsychosis." *CPh* 54 (1959): 114–116.

Smith, R. R. R. "A New Portrait of Pythagoras." In R. R. R. Smith and K. T. Erim, eds., *Aphrodisias Papers 2: The Theatre, a Sculptor's Workshop, Philosophers, and Coin-Types*, 159–167. Ann Arbor 1991.

Sorg, E. *Lieblings-Geschichten. Die "Zürcher Schule" oder Innenansichten eines Psycho-Unternehmens.* Zurich 1991.

Staab, G. *Pythagoras in der Spätantike. Studien zu* De Vita Pythagorica *des Iamblichos von Chalkis.* Beiträge zur Altertumskunde 165. Munich 2002.

Städele, A. *Die Briefe des Pythagoras und der Pythagoreer.* Meisenheim am Glan 1980.

Staden, H. von "Hairesis and Heresy: The Case of the *haireseis iatrikai*." In B. F. Meyer and E. P. Sanders, eds., *Jewish and Christian Self-Definition III*, 76–100 and 199–206 (notes). London 1982.

Stephenson, B. *The Music of the Heavens: Kepler's Harmonic Astronomy.* Princeton, N.J., 1994.

Storchi Marino, A. "Il pitagorismo romano: per un bilancio di studi recenti." In M. Tortorelli Ghidini, A. Storchi Marino, and A. Visconti, eds., *Tra Orfeo e Pitagora. Origini e incontri di culture nell'antichità*, 335–368. Atti dei seminari napoletani 1996–1998. Naples 2000.

Strocka, V. M. "Orpheus und Pythagoras in Sparta." In H. Froning, T. Hölscher, and H. Mielsch, eds., *Kotinos. Festschrift für Erika Simon*, 276–283. Mainz 1992.

Szlezák, Th. A. "Zur üblichen Abneigung gegen die Agrapha Dogmata." *Méthexis* 6 (1993): 155–174.

Ternes, Ch. M., ed. *Le pythagorisme en milieu romain*. Luxembourg 1998.

Thesleff, H. *An Introduction to the Pythagorean Writings of the Hellenistic Period.* Acta Academiae Aboensis, Ser. A Humaniora 24, 3. Åbo 1961.

———. *The Pythagorean Texts of the Hellenistic Period.* Acta Academiae Aboensis. Ser. A Humaniora 30, 1. Åbo 1965.

———. "On the Problem of the Doric Pseudo-Pythagorica. An Alternative Theory of Date and Purpose." In *Pseudepigrapha I*, 59–87. Entretiens de la Fond. Hardt. 18. Geneva 1972.

Thom, J. C. " 'Don't Walk on the Highways': The Pythagorean *Akousmata* and Early Christian Literature." *JBL* 113 (1994): 93–112.

———. *The Pythagorean Golden Verses*. Leiden 1995.

Timpanaro Cardini, M. *Pitagorici: Testimonianze e frammenti* 1: Pitagora, Cercope, Petrone, Brotino, Ippaso, Callifonte e Democede, Parmenisco, Alcmeone, Icco, Parone, Aminia, Menestore, Xuto; 2: Ippocrate di Chio, Filolao, Archita e pitagorici minori; 3: Pitagorici anonimi e risonanze pitagoriche. Biblioteca di studi superiori 28; 41; 45. Florence 1958; 1962; 1964.

Toit, D. S. du *Theios Anthropos. Zur Verwendung von θεῖος ἄνθρωπος und sinnverwandten Ausdrücken in der Literatur der Kaiserzeit.* WUNT 2, 91. Tübingen 1997.

Tornau, Ch. "Die Prinzipienlehre des Moderatos von Gades. Zu Simplikios in Ph. 230,34–231,24 Diels." *RhM* 143 (2000): 197–220.

Ustinova, Y. " 'Either a Daimon, or a Hero, or Perhaps a God': Mythical Residents of Subterranean Chambers." *Kernos* 15 (2002): 267–288.

Vallet, G. "Le 'Stenopos' des Muses à Métaponte." In *Mélanges de philosophie, littérature et d'histoire ancienne offerts à P. Boyancé*, 749–759. Rome 1974.

Visa-Ondarçuhu, V. "Milon de Crotone, personnage exemplaire." In A. Billault, ed., *Héros et voyageurs grecs dans l'occident romain*, 33–62. Lyons 1997.

Visconti, A. *Aristosseno di Taranto. Biografia e formazione spirituale.* Naples 1999.

Vogel, C. J. de *Pythagoras and Early Pythagoreanism. An Interpretation of Neglected Evidence on the Philosopher Pythagoras.* Assen 1966.

Vos-Dahmen von Buchholz, T. *Der Komet von Samos. Das Leben des Pythagoras.* Stuttgart 1997. Translation of the Dutch original, published in 1995.

Waerden, B. van der. *Erwachende Wissenschaft. Ägyptische, babylonische und griechische Mathematik.* Basel 1956.

———. "Pythagoras 1 D.: Pythagoreische Wissenschaft." *RE* 24 (1963): 277–300.

———. "Pythagoras: Die Schriften und Fragmente des Pythagoras." *RE* Suppl. 10 (1965): 843–864.

———. *Die Pythagoreer. Religiöse Bruderschaft und Schule der Wissenschaft.* Zurich 1979.

Weber, M. *Wirtschaft und Gesellschaft. Grundriß der verstehenden Soziologie.* First half-volume. 1922. Reprint Tübingen 1976.

Wedekind, G. Ch. von *Der pythagoräische Orden, die Obskurantenvereine in der Christenheit und die Freimauerei in gegenseitigen Verhältnissen.* A manuscript for Freemasons. Leipzig 1820.

West, M. L. *Early Greek Philosophy and the Orient.* Oxford 1971.

———. *The East Face of Helicon: West Asiatic Elements in Greek Poetry and Myth.* Oxford 1997.

———. *Greek Epic Fragments from the Seventh to the Fifth Centuries B.C.* Edited and translated by M. L. West. Cambridge, Mass. 2003a.

———. *Homeric Hymns. Homeric Apocrypha. Lives of Homer.* Edited and translated by M. L. West. Cambridge, Mass., 2003b.

Whitehead, A. N. *Science and the Modern World.* Lowell Lectures 1925. Cambridge 1926.

Wilpert, P. "Reste verlorener Aristotelesschriften bei Alexander von Aphrodisias." *Hermes* (1940): 369–396.

Wilson, B. *Religious Sects: A Sociological Study.* London 1970.

Wilson, N. G. *From Byzantium to Italy: Greek Studies in the Italian Renaissance.* London 1992.

Wright, M. R. *Empedocles: The Extant Fragments.* New Haven 1981.

———. *Cosmology in Antiquity.* London 1995.

Zander, H. *Geschichte der Seelenwanderung in Europa. Alternative religiöse Traditionen von der Antike bis heute.* Darmstadt 1999.

Zeller, E. *Die Philosophie der Griechen in ihrer geschichtlichen Entwicklung I, 1, 1: Allgemeine Einleitung, Vorsokratische Philosophie.* Leipzig 1919. Reprint Hildesheim 1963.

Zhmud, L. *Wissenschaft, Philosophie und Religion im frühen Pythagoreismus.* Berlin 1997.

———. "Some Notes on Philolaos and the Pythagoreans." *Hyperboreus* 4 (1998): 1–17.

Zimmer, H. *Philosophies of India.* Edited by J. Campbell. Princeton 1969.

Zoepffel, R. "Sokrates und die Pythagoreer." In H. Kessler, ed., *Sokrates: Nachfolge und Gegenwege,* 167–200. Sokrates-Studien 5. Zug 2001.

Zuntz, G. *Persephone: Three Essays on Religion and Thought in Magna Graecia.* Oxford 1971.

INDEX

Abaris (Hyperborean priest), 2
Abdera, 58
Abse, Dannie, 133
abstinence, 32–33
Academy, Greek: Old, x, 94, 98, 116–19,
124; Platonic, 59–60, 93, 124, 133
"acousmatics," 106–8, 109–10, 113, 125.
See also *akoúsmata*
Acragas, conflict with Syracuse, 20
Aelian, 32
Aethalides, 5
Against Hierocles (Eusebius), 125
Against the Pythagoreans (Aristotle), 77
akoúsmata ("oral sayings"): Aristotle and,
74, 76–77; authenticity of, 42; key con-
cepts in, 79; mathematics vs., 106–8,
109–10; natural philosophical, 76–77;
obscurity of, 65–66; Orphism and,
73–76; on Pythagorean secrecy, 101; on
ritual taboos, 64, 68–69; on wisdom and
name-giving, 90. See also "acousmatics"
Alcibiades, 124
Alcmaeon of Croton: Bro(n)tinus and,
109; influence of, 85; Leon and, 94;
Pythagorean influence on, 115, 119; and
Pythagorean natural philosophy, 79
Alexander of Aphrodisias, 81–82
Alexander Polyhistor, 23, 66, 120, 121
Alexander Severus, 125
Alexander the Great, 7
Alexandria (Egypt), 124
Alexis (poet), 108
Amasis (Egytian king), 7
Ameinias, 115
Amyclas, 113
Anacreon of Teos, 47

Anaxagoras, 75, 95, 116
Anaximander of Miletus: as founder of
prose literature, 51; influence on
Pythagoras, 8, 44–45, 76, 84; on original
material, 80; and planetary measure-
ments, 84; Xenophanes and, 49
Anaximander the younger, 59, 65–66
Anaximenes of Miletus, 44, 76, 80
Androcydes, 66
Andron of Ephesus, 4, 59
Anticleides, 26
Antiope (Anaxagoras), 95
Antiphon, 7
anti-Pythagorean rebellions, 38; Cylon's
uprising and, 19–20, 104–5; effects of,
43, 105–6, 114; Lysis and, 120–21; rea-
sons for, 18
Antisthenes, 12–13, 59, 61
Antonius Diogenes, 8, 30–31, 32
Apollo (divinity): Pythagoras and, 5–6, 11,
71–73; represented as child, 15; Romans
and, 124
Apollonius (paradoxographer), 9
Apollonius of Tyana, 18, 104, 106, 125
arché, 80
Archilochus, 50
Archippus, 38, 105, 106, 110
Archytas of Tartentum: and anti-
Pythagorean rebellions, 105–6; and Cro-
ton's political influence, 61; Eurytus as
teacher of, 111; as "mathematician,"
107; Philolaus as teacher of, 110; as
Plato's pupil, 116–17; as Pythagorean,
xi, 111–12, 116
Aristippus, 59
Aristophanes, 13, 95